Architecture of the Picturesque in Canada

Janet Wright

Studies in Archaeology
Architecture and History

National Historic Parks and Sites Branch
Parks Canada
Environment Canada
1984

Available in Canada through authorized bookstore agents and other bookstores, or by mail from the Canadian Government Publishing Centre, Supply and Services Canada, Hull, Quebec, Canada K1A 0S9.

En français ce numéro s'intitule **L'architecture pittoresque au Canada** (nᵒ de catalogue R61-2/9-17F). En vente au Canada par l'entremise de nos agents libraires agréés et autres librairies, ou par la poste au Centre d'édition du gouvernement du Canada, Approvisionnements et Services Canada, Hull, Québec, Canada K1A 0S9.

Price Canada: $9.95
Price other countries: $11.95
Price subject to change without notice.

Catalogue No.: R61-2/9-17E
ISBN: 0-660-11641-3
ISSN: 0821-1027

Published under the authority
of the Minister of the Environment,
Ottawa, 1984.

Editing, layout and design: Paula Irving

The opinions expressed in this report are those of the author and not necessarily those of Environment Canada.

Parks Canada publishes the results of its research in archaeology, architecture and history. A list of publications is available from Research Publications, Parks Canada, 1600 Liverpool Court, Ottawa, Ontario, K1A 1G2.

Architecture of the Picturesque in Canada

Janet Wright

Submitted for publication in 1982 by Janet Wright, Canadian Inventory of Historic Building, Parks Canada, Ottawa.

PREFACE

This study is one of a series of studies being prepared by the Architectural Analysis section of the Canadian Inventory of Historic Building on various architectural styles and tastes that have influenced Canadian building of the eighteenth and nineteenth centuries. *Gothic Revival in Canadian Architecture* by Mathilde Brosseau and *Second Empire Style in Canadian Architecture* by Christina Cameron and Janet Wright have been completed and are now available in the Parks Canada series *Canadian Historic Sites: Occasional Papers in Archaeology and History/Lieux historiques canadiens: Cahiers d'archéologie et d'histoire,* Nos. 24 and 25. Two more studies entitled "Le style palladien dans l'architecture au Canada" by Nathalie Clerk and "Neoclassical Architecture in Canada" by Leslie Maitland will be available soon.

The purpose of these studies is to aid the Historic Sites and Monuments Board of Canada in its identification of buildings of national historic and architectural importance by providing general thematic frameworks by which to assess individual buildings submitted to the Board for possible commemoration. It is also hoped that these studies will provide useful information and analysis for anyone interested in the field of Canadian architecture and perhaps will add to the general awareness and appreciation of this important part of Canada's heritage.

The research carried out for this study has been far from exhaustive but I hope this very general survey will encourage others to pursue more diligently and in greater depth this distinctive phase of Canadian domestic building. The analysis of the origins of the Picturesque Movement in England is based primarily on a few major secondary sources and a sampling of the major aesthetic and architectural treatises and popular pattern books that defined or expressed the Picturesque point of view. Information on the architecture of the Picturesque in Canada was gathered from photographic, pictorial, cartographic and manuscript collections in archives and museums across the country. The most extensive and useful collections were located in the Public Archives Canada, Archives of Ontario, Toronto Metropolitan Library, McCord Museum, Archives nationales du Québec, Archives du séminaire de Québec, Archives civiles de Québec, ministère des Affaires culturelles, The New Brunswick Museum, Provincial Archives of New Brunswick, Nova Scotia Museum and the Public Archives of Nova Scotia.

Much of the documentation on the buildings examined in this study represents research carried out by other historians whose work has appeared in published form or who were generously willing to share their research material with me. The largest single source of documentation was located in the architectural files of the Canadian Inventory of Historic Building (CIHB) which have been increasing since their creation in 1970.

Many of the illustrations for this study are drawn from the photographic collection of the CIHB, which now includes approximately 200,000 buildings dating before 1914. The CIHB was particularly useful in identifying some of the lesser-known buildings. Because of its broad sampling it also provided a useful tool for identifying patterns of geographic distribution and concentrations of general building types such as the *cottage orné* of Ontario and Quebec.

It is not the purpose of this paper solely to examine those buildings still standing but to provide a comprehensive picture of the wide range of buildings, from the grand to the modest, that expressed to some degree the Picturesque taste. In gathering visual material it quickly became apparent that although many examples of modest vernacular villas and cottages have survived, the more sophisticated, architect-designed examples did not fare as well. Because they tended to be located on the outskirts of important urban centres, they were naturally the first to fall prey to subsequent urban development. As a result, many of the buildings illustrated no longer stand and are known to us only through old photographs and drawings located in archival collections. However, by presenting illustrations of buildings that have been lost I hope we may appreciate more the value and importance of those that have survived.

6

ACKNOWLEDGEMENTS

In preparing this study I relied on the resources of many libraries, archives and research institutions across the country and in each instance I received the full and enthusiastic co-operation of all the staff members of these organizations. I am most indebted to my fellow historians at Parks Canada, particularly Christina Cameron, Nathalie Clerk, Mary Cullen, Leslie Maitland and C. James Taylor, who read this manuscript in its various forms and whose criticisms and suggestions were most helpful. I would also like to thank Nicole Cloutier, Sandy Easterbrook and Ann Thomas who participated in the early stages of this study. I am very grateful to the many individuals and local and regional historical and architectural organizations who generously shared with me their unpublished research and their advice at every step in this project. In particular I would like to thank Margaret Angus, Kingston; City of Cobourg, Local Advisory Committee on Architectural Conservation (LACAC); Gordon Couling, Guelph; Don Cousins, St. Thomas; Pierre du Prey, Kingston; Wendy Fletcher, Toronto; Carrie Fortneath, Burnstown; Mrs. Bobi Grant and Barrie LACAC; Town of Goderich, LACAC; Mrs. Thora Harvey and the Woodstock LACAC; Harry Hinchley and the Renfrew Historical Society; Robert Lemire, Montreal; Jennifer McKendry, Kingston; Michael McMordie, Calgary; Shirley Morris, Toronto; Olive Newcombe and the Dundas Historical Society; Norfolk Historical Society; Shane O'Dea, St. John's; Robert Passfield, Parks Canada, Ottawa; Yvonne Pigott, Halifax; Lloyd B. Rochester, Ottawa; Irene Rogers, Charlottetown; J. Douglas Stewart, Kingston; I. Maxwell Sutherland, Parks Canada; Annette Viel, Quebec.

INTRODUCTION

The Picturesque does not refer to an architectural style but to an aesthetic point of view which grew out of the English love for natural scenery and around which a new approach to landscape design was formulated during the last decade of the eighteenth century. Led by a small group of English aesthetic theorists, most notably Sir Uvedale Price, Sir Richard Payne Knight and a landscape designer, Humphry Repton, the Picturesque Movement sought to bring landscape design closer to nature by restoring and preserving its inherent visual qualities defined as irregularity, variety and intricacy in form, colour and texture and their effects of light and shadow. Only by cherishing these values could the designer create pleasing and harmonious compositions in landscape.

It was generally agreed that these qualities had first been appreciated and captured by the great landscape painters of the seventeenth century such as Claude Lorrain and Salvatore Rosa. It therefore followed that landscape design should model itself after landscape painting; for, by cultivating the painter's sensitivity to nature and by mastering painterly techniques of composition, effects of light and shadow, harmony of colour, and unity of character, the landscape designer would learn to enhance but not to alter nature's inherent Picturesque beauty.

The Picturesque was primarily concerned with landscape design but it nevertheless exerted a profound impact on architecture during the nineteenth century.[1] Within the landscape of the Picturesque, architecture was viewed as an integral but subsidiary part of the overall scenic composition which should be made to blend in and be in harmony both visually and emotionally with the character of its natural surroundings. In essence the Picturesque invited an approach to design aimed at pleasing the eye and the emotions over satisfying the intellect. Principles of congruity and the creation of interesting visual effects replaced abstract standards of architectural correctness based on classical precepts. Moreover, it was a viewpoint that provided the justification for an eclectic approach to style, for any mode or type of building could be called upon if it suited the

character or mood of the landscape. Exotic modes such as Hindu and Chinese, or more familiar styles such as Gothic or classical, or even humble building types previously considered outside the realm of serious architecture, such as the traditional English cottage, the vernacular Italian villa or the Swiss chalet, were incorporated into the Picturesque landscape.

The Picturesque touched all aspects of architecture in Britain. It cultivated a taste for interesting visual effects created by effective silhouette, varied planes and textures and resulting effects of light and shadow, but it was essentially to the field of small house design in a rural or suburban environment that the Picturesque aesthetic addressed itself. Unlike urban building which existed in a completely man-made setting or large-scale building which tended to dominate its surroundings, small houses were viewed as integral parts of their landscape setting. The application of Picturesque principles to residential architecture resulted in the creation of new patterns and types of building referred to as Picturesque villas and cottages.

The Picturesque was an important architectural aesthetic throughout the nineteenth century but the manner in which architects expressed these values altered considerably as the century progressed. This study is concerned essentially with the architect's first interpretation of the Picturesque, which covers about the 1790s to the mid-1820s, that is, the late-Georgian or Regency period. (The Regency refers specifically to the reign of the Prince Regent, later George IV, from 1811 to 1820.) This generation of architects had a particular view of what constituted Picturesque effect in design. They accepted Picturesque values of irregularity, variety and light and shadow but these qualities did not necessarily have to be expressed solely in terms of architectural design. The late-Georgian architects of the Picturesque, as will be discussed, were most concerned with the general impression or atmosphere created by the overall scene composed both of landscape and architecture. The buildings themselves, whether irregular or regular in plan and outline, were characterized by a simple form, delicate detail and subtle colour which created an architecture that merged quietly into its setting. Early Picturesque architecture was eclectic in its detail but it was not a revivalist movement. By borrowing a few specific details or by the general massing the architect could suggest to the viewer the desired style but these elements were freely adapted to designs determined by nineteenth century ideas of domestic design and an eye well-atuned to Picturesque effect.

Picturesque values and approaches to design – the delight in naturalistic landscapes, the stylistic eclecticism, and the taste for qualities of irregularity and variety – remained an important influence on architecture throughout the nineteenth century. By the 1830s, however, these values became absorbed and modified by new and often conflicting attitudes to architectural design. The early architects of the Picturesque maintained a flexible view of their various stylistic models. The Victorian architect adopted a more serious-minded, academic approach to style. For example, post-1830 Gothic Revival architects, such as Augustus Welby Pugin, insisted on a greater historical fidelity to the original model and dismissed earlier experiments in the Gothic as frivolous corruptions of the vocabulary and structural integrity of medieval architecture. They also believed that the Gothic style was superior to other modes which contrasted with the egalitarian view of style of the late-Georgian Picturesque. Although by the mid- and late nineteenth century the taste for irregularity and variety in design for their own sake was revived, these effects were generally expressed in an extremely exaggerated vocabulary, characterized by a heavy ornate detailing, agitated skylines, and richly textured and polychromatic surfaces. These ostentatious, extravagantly dressed structures stood out in sharp contrast to the subtleties of design evident in early Picturesque architecture.

In Canada elements of the Picturesque taste can be identified as early as the late eighteenth century, gradually gaining a more widespread influence during the 1810s and 1820s. The most advanced expressions of the Picturesque taste belong to the 1830s and 1840s, a development due largely to the arrival of several British architects who had been indoctrinated into Picturesque ideas of landscape and design and who were able to supply their clients with residential designs based on fashionable English models. As in Britain this period saw the introduction of a whole new range of types and styles into the repertoire of our domestic building. Designs such as the low verandahed cottages of Kirk Ella in Sillery, Quebec, or Colborne Lodge in Toronto, the imposing classical villa of Summerhill in Kingston, the castellated Holland House in Toronto, or the Italianate villa of Bellevue in Kingston all express to some degree the Picturesque point of view (Figs 34, 57, 63, 65, 97). These villas and cottages, almost invariably set in landscaped gardens or parks, reflect common Picturesque concerns for the visual and emotional character of the building and its setting and how these two elements interact in the overall domestic environment.[2]

Picturesque villas and cottages were found throughout the British North American colonies of the first half of the nineteenth century but the extent to which this taste influenced patterns of domestic building varied considerably from region to region. The Picturesque was essentially a British point of view imported into this country by the middle- and upper-class immigrant from Britain, a group that formed an important but nevertheless relatively small component of the colonial population. A settler drawn from the British lower classes did not build fashionable villas and cottages for if he could afford a home at all it tended to be sturdy and functional and paid little heed to up-to-date architectural tastes. Generally the large segment of the population of French or American background was unfamiliar with Picturesque ideas and continued to build homes that reflected their own distinctive building traditions. For this reason the influence of the Picturesque in domestic architecture was very much localized to those regions that attracted these middle- and upper-class immigrants.

Upper Canada (Ontario) was by far the most popular area for settlement for this group and it was there that the influence of the Picturesque was most prevalent. In Lower Canada (Quebec) and the Atlantic provinces their presence was not as noticeable and as a result the architecture of the Picturesque was not as significant an element. The purpose of this paper is first to examine these patrons of the Picturesque and in what environments they flourished. An examination of the architectural character of their villas and cottages and how they reflected Picturesque tastes will then be broken down into the three relevant geographic areas of Ontario, Quebec and the Atlantic provinces. But before entering into the Canadian manifestations of the Picturesque we must first explore the origins of the movement in Britain.

PART I   THE PICTURESQUE IN BRITAIN

ORIGINS OF THE PICTURESQUE

The roots of the Picturesque go deep into the eighteenth century beginning with the revolution in landscape design in the early 1700s in England. As expressed in the writings of men like Joseph Addison, Alexander Pope or the Earl of Shaftesbury, a reaction set in against the prevailing classical system of landscape characterized by its structured artificial patterns in favour of a return to what Shaftesbury referred to as the genuine order of nature.[1] This sentiment was first put into practice by painter, architect and landscape designer William Kent (1685-1748), who carried out a series of landscape schemes in the 1730s which featured an irregular layout of wriggling paths and streams.

During the second half of the eighteenth century the art of landscape design in England was dominated by the figure of Lancelot "Capability" Brown (1716-83). Brown, too, believed that landscape should imitate nature but his interpretation of nature was slightly different. In contrast to the often contrived and contorted lines of the Kent style, Brown's landscapes were characterized by more fluid graceful lines defined by undulating lawns, serpentine walks, still ponds and lakes. The broad expanse of the park was then dotted by irregular groupings of trees and ornamented by garden buildings.[2]

The taste for the informal landscape style was both encouraged and shaped by the growing appreciation for the great seventeenth and eighteenth century landscape painters such as Claude Lorrain, Salvatore Rosa or the Dutch landscape school exemplified by Hobbema or Ruisdael (Fig. 1). In the eighteenth century, landscape gardening and landscape painting became closely interrelated arts for it was believed that these painters had captured the true character of nature gardeners were trying to restore to landscape. In turn, this familiarity with landscape painting sensitized the eighteenth century eye to the painterly qualities found in the natural scenery. It was in this context that the word "picturesque" was first used. Derived from the Italian word "pittoresco," meaning in the style of a painter, it was introduced into the English language in the early eighteenth century to identify those scenes in nature that provided suitable subjects for painting.[3]

After the mid-eighteenth century this adjective "picturesque" began to take on a more precise meaning. In the 1780s William Gilpin (1724-1804) produced a series of descriptive travel accounts of the English countryside in which he frequently used the term "picturesque" but applied it primarily to landscape scenes that embodied physical characteristics of roughness and irregularity - qualities Gilpin felt produced the most effective subjects for painting.[4]

This empirical definition of "picturesque" in terms of specific visual characteristics grew out of the writings of Edmund Burke (1729-97) who had divided aesthetic response into two categories, the Sublime and the Beautiful, which differed both in their physical properties and in the sensations they evoked within the viewer. In his major treatise on the subject, *A Philosophical Enquiry into the Origin of Our Ideas of the Sublime and the Beautiful* (1757), Burke defined the Sublime as vastness and obscurity which inspired sensations of fear and awe, while the Beautiful was characterized by smoothness, gradual variation and delicacy of form and colour which evoked sensations of pleasure and tenderness.[5] Gilpin accepted these categories but felt that they did not account for the pleasure gained from viewing natural scenery which was usually neither vastly Sublime nor smoothly Beautiful and to fill this gap he suggested the third aesthetic category of the Picturesque.

Both Burke and Gilpin tended to view aesthetic response in terms of natural powers within an object or scene which triggered a direct reaction on the senses or nerves of the viewer.[6] This mechanistic, physiological definition was to be superseded by a more psychological and subjective analysis of aesthetic response referred to as the "Association of Ideas." Simply stated this concept interpreted aesthetic experience in terms of the subjective responses of the viewer whereby the external world could trigger or recall past emotions or experiences through a process of association which constituted the aesthetic awareness be it of the Sublime, the Beautiful

1. Landscape with the Voyage of Jacob
Date 1677; Artist Claude Lorrain

The landscape paintings of Claude Lorrain gave visual substance to the Picturesque view of nature taking shape throughout the eighteenth century in England. His broad scenic vistas, composed of winding streams, rugged cliffs and tall feathery trees silhouetted against the sky, were bathed in a warm atmospheric light which set up contrasts of light and shadow and gave his subject a muted tonality which unified his compositions. As Uvedale Price pointed out, Lorrain's buildings — classical ruins, fortified castles, villages or farms — were treated as distant incidents in the landscape, often romantically situated on cliff tops with their irregular outlines accented by surrounding trees. Lorrain's view of nature was intricate and varied, rough and untamed but never hostile or foreboding. In his landscapes man, building and nature were unified by a mood of calm pastoral repose which was at the heart of the Picturesque point of view. (Sterling and Francine Clark Art Institute, Williamstown, Massachusetts)

or the Picturesque variety. Although the "Association of Ideas" had been recognized as a factor in our perceptions from the early eighteenth century, it was not until the end of the century that this concept, as analysed in, for example, Archibald Alison's (1757-1839) *Essays on the Nature and Principles of Taste* (1790), became regarded as the major source of all our aesthetic judgements.

While the "Association of Ideas" as a philosophical concept can be traced back to Aristotle, it had a revolutionary impact on British philosophy and lay at the heart of nineteenth century romanticism of which the Picturesque was one manifestation. In essence the acceptance of this view completely uprooted the classical idea of beauty. By interpreting aesthetic response as a subjective, internalized experience of the individual, it invalidated the classical assumption that beauty could be defined in terms of external and immutable laws.[7]

Architecture was slow to respond to this new aesthetic outlook. Throughout the first half of the eighteenth century English architecture was dominated by the academically minded classicism of the Palladian school based on the assumption that there existed set rules of proportion and classical correctness that would produce perfection and beauty in design.[8] During the second half of the century, however, this rigid view of design was beginning to break down. Archaeological examinations of the ancient monuments of Greece and Rome carried out during the post-1750 period revealed that classical architecture did not faithfully adhere to set standards but varied considerably from period to period. This awareness had a liberating effect on design. The architecture of this period, as exemplified in the work of Robert Adam (1728-92) or Sir William Chambers (1726-96), was no longer confined by a strict sense of classical decorum. While general rules of symmetry and order were maintained, architects approached the classical model with a much greater flexibility, manipulating classical form into new and more varied compositions aimed at pleasing the eye rather than strictly obeying pre-ordained laws of design.[9]

Eighteenth century architects never seriously questioned the superiority of the classical model. Although Gothic or Chinese styles were employed in garden ornaments or in a few eccentric follies built to titillate the unconventional tastes of a few gentlemen, these alternative modes were not yet regarded as serious architecture.[10] Nevertheless, the breakdown of the absolutist view of the classical model combined with the new aesthetic theories whereby beauty could be evaluated only in terms of personalized judgements or taste laid the foundations for the Picturesque Movement in landscape and architecture.

THE PICTURESQUE IN THEORY

In 1794 two major statements on the Picturesque were published: *Essays on The Picturesque* by Sir Uvedale Price (1747-1829) and *The Landscape: A Didactic Poem...* by Sir Richard Payne Knight (1750-1825).[1] The third key work on the Picturesque, *Sketches and Hints on Landscape Gardening* by Humphry Repton (1752-1818), was published the following year.[2] These treatises were not revolutionary for all three drew on aesthetic concepts or sentiments evolving throughout the eighteenth century. The importance of these works lay in their ability to synthesize the ideas of men like Addison, Pope, Burke, Gilpin and Alison. Although Price, Knight and Repton devoted a considerable amount of their energies to quibbling, often viciously, over points of aesthetics and design, their works consolidated many ideas into a fairly coherent approach to landscape design and its relationship to architecture.

The Picturesque was defined in these works as an aesthetic quality generally found in landscape characterized by irregularity, roughness, and variety of form, colour and texture and their resulting effects of light and shade.[3] This definition can be traced back to the writings of William Gilpin but, whereas Gilpin was merely observing these qualities in nature, Price, Knight and Repton believed that the Picturesque should be adopted as a basic design principle in landscape gardening.

Price, Knight and Repton rationalized the need to cultivate the Picturesque in landscape because its qualities defined the true character of nature. A respect for nature was fundamental to the Picturesque view of landscape, for, as explained by Knight, "the character of nature is more pleasing than any that can be given by art."[4] Of course, this sentiment grew directly out of the eighteenth century view of the genuine order of nature which had been given visual expression in the landscape schemes of Capability Brown. The Picturesque theorists differed from the Brown school in their intepretation of what defined that genuine order. Although Repton as a fellow landscape gardener often defended the Brown style, Price and Knight vehemently condemned the work of these "dull improvers" whom they felt had artificially manipulated the landscape into a prefigured harmony composed of smooth undulating lawns dotted by contrived clumps of trees, lifeless sheets of water, and senselessly meandering gravel paths — calm, controlled and lifeless landscapes which bore little relation to real nature. Instead the Picturesque theorists felt the role of the landscape designer was to enhance but not to alter the accidental beauties of nature in all its roughness, irregularity and variety.

The link between painting and landscape design established in the eighteenth century was also important to the theory of the Picturesque but the relationship between the two was more clearly defined. Price and Knight viewed landscape painting not as a concrete model for landscape design but as a guide for the Picturesque gardeners. They believed that a careful study of painting would cultivate in the landscape designer a painter's sensitivity to nature. It would teach him painterly techniques of "general composition, grouping of separate parts, harmony of tints, unity of character and breadth and effect of light and shade," techniques that were to be applied to the landscape to create a total Picturesque composition.[5] Although Repton disputed the relevance of the static, painted scene to the multi-viewed, transient character of landscape, his famous *Red Books*, a series of watercolour sketches of proposed landscape improvements, demonstrate that he conceived of his designs in terms of pictorial composition (Fig. 2).

Architecture was always of secondary concern to the Picturesque theorists whose first interest was landscape design. The impact of this aesthetic view, however, was to produce far more revolutionary results in architecture than in the art of landscape. The conflict between the Brown school and the Picturesque school was basically a conflict between an eighteenth century classical view of nature as being essentially rational and ordered and a nineteenth century romantic view of nature as irrational and disordered. This conflict resulted in sharp distinctions in thought but in practice the differences, although present, cannot be as clearly defined and both periods merge into the continuous tradition of the

2. Proposed Improvements to the Park at Wentworth Woodhouse, Yorkshire, England
Drawn 1790; **Landscape Gardener** Humphry Repton

When Humphry Repton was hired to improve the grounds of Wentworth Woodhouse in 1790, the estate consisted of a massive Palladian country house as well as several ornamental structures in the form of classical temples, a pyramid and an obelisk which were dotted about the park. According to Repton the defects of the landscape were not due to buildings themselves nor to the character of the landscape but to the "want of connexion and harmony in the composition." To overcome these faults he planted trees, thus varying the contours and colours of the bare hills and providing visual links between nature and the isolated pieces of architecture. Repton also introduced a large pond — a landscape feature he had advocated for its motion and reflective qualities which he felt gave a richer, more varied colour and a sense of vitality to the scene. The architectural components of Wentworth Woodhouse were far from Picturesque in their design but, as seen from the illustration, Repton was able to soften the hard contours of the architecture by his irregular plantations so that "the scattered masses of this splendid scenery" were "brought together into one vast and magnificent whole." (Humphry Repton, *Observations on the Theory and Practice of Landscape Gardening*, 1803, taken from Dorothy Stroud, *Humphry Repton,* London: Country Life, 1962, p. 31)

English landscape school. In architecture, however, the Picturesque point of view completely uprooted the traditional view of architecture based on the classical model.

Within the landscape of the Picturesque, architecture was viewed as an integral but subsidiary component of the overall scene which should blend in and conform to the character of the landscape to create a harmonious composition and mood. This fundamental principle was usually described as congruity or fitness of the architecture to the landscape. As Knight instructed,

> Mixed and blended in the scene you show
> The stately mansion rising in the view;
> But mixed and blended ever let it be,
> A mere component of what you see.[6]

The traditional architect, who conceived of design as an abstract problem of proportion and detail worked out independently of its environment, was to be replaced by the "architetto-pittore," an architect with the eye of a painter who, like Claude Lorrain, would treat architecture as a part of an overall setting – an embellishment to a composition of trees, hills, water, colour and light.[7]

The principle of congruency was not applicable to all architecture. The Picturesque, as a landscape aesthetic, branched into the field of architecture only when architecture could be viewed as an incident in the scenic composition. Although the influence of Picturesque values eventually touched all aspects and types of building in the nineteenth century, as initially formulated by Price, Knight and Repton, principles of congruency were not as relevant to urban building in a man-made, unnatural environment. Nor were they relevant to public, religious or large domestic architecture whose designs were determined by a sense of architectural decorum of what was appropriate to their function or whose large scale tended to dominate its environment rather than harmonize with it.[8] Throughout the writings on the Picturesque, discussions on architecture were generally directed to the problem of small residential buildings and their dependencies in a rural or suburban setting. Only in this type of building and environment, which in Picturesque language were most commonly referred to as the villa or the cottage, could the fusion of architecture and landscape into a Picturesque whole be achieved.

Of course, throughout the eighteenth century building had always played an important part in landscape design. Capability Brown's landscape schemes were often dotted with classical temples, Chinese pagodas and Gothic follies situated with a careful eye for effective pictorial composition.[9] During the eighteenth century, however, architecture and landscape were seen as separate problems obeying separate standards of design. In the writings of Price, Knight and Repton this relationship was redefined. They believed that architectural design should reflect and respond to the character of the landscape.

Price, Knight and Repton all believed that an architecture embodying the same visual qualities that defined the Picturesque landscape (irregularity, intricacy and variety) provided the most harmonious and effective embellishments to a setting. All agreed that these qualities were best expressed in the medieval architecture of baronial castles, ancient abbeys, or, on a more modest level, in the rustic English cottage with its irregular plan, thatched roof and casement windows. Knight also advocated the use of what he referred to as a mixed style of architecture found in the paintings of Claude Lorrain which combined several periods of building within one rambling structure.[10] Given this preference it was not surprising that both Price and Knight chose castellated designs to ornament their own estates (Fig. 3). Repton's landscape schemes often involved the building of a new residence or at least the remodelling of an older one and throughout his career he favoured the medieval styles.

The popularization of the irregular medieval forms was a key element in the architecture of the Picturesque but never was this style promoted to the exclusion of all others. The Picturesque theorists' belief that architecture should be congruent to the landscape demanded a thoroughly eclectic approach to style. The choice of an appropriate style was to be determined by the character of the landscape. Repton, a practical man who always preferred to translate the often esoteric theories of the Picturesque into concrete rules of design, attempted to define a set of criteria that would determine the most effective choice of style. He suggested that the designer should first determine the dominant shapes and lines of the landscape and then choose a style of architecture that would provide a visual counterbalance. For example, he believed that in a landscape dominated by trees with a vertical emphasis, the horizontal lines of classical forms were preferable, whereas a landscape with rounded trees invited the spikey, vertical lines of the Gothic styles.[11] This rigid, empirical approach never gained wide acceptance. Instead the character of the landscape was read more in terms of the subjective moods or emotions it aroused within the viewer. Harmony and congruency between landscape and architecture largely depended upon the sympathetic interreaction of these two emotionally charged elements.

Quiet secluded dells might bring to mind the simple rustic cottage while a mountainous setting might be associated with the Swiss chalet. Even Repton often read his landscapes in terms of the associations they evoked.

In the quiet calm, and beautiful scenery of a tame country, the elegant forms of

3. Downton Castle, Herefordshire, England
Constructed 1774-78; **Designer** Sir Richard Payne Knight; **Material** stone

Downton Castle was Sir Richard Payne Knight's own experiment in the Picturesque in which he formulated aesthetic values in architecture. He made these verbally explicit ten years later in his publication of *The Landscape: A Didactic Poem*.... This work was followed in 1805 by his more comprehensive study *An Analytical Enquiry into the Principles of Taste*. Designed in a medieval castle style inspired by Knight's foremost guide to the Picturesque, the landscape paintings of Claude Lorrain, Downton demonstrates values of irregularity set into the irregularity of nature which Knight believed was essential to the Picturesque scene. As seen today the medievalism of Downton is more pronounced. The oriel windows and stone-mullioned windows with their Gothic tracery and labels were added in the 1850s in keeping with Victorian tastes for greater antiquarian accuracy. The original design featured simpler, unadorned wall planes and very unmedieval flat-headed sash windows. This simplicity of surface and restraint in detail was typical of the Picturesque architecture regardless of its style. More interested in general mood and visual effects than in historical accuracy, Knight uses general massing and a few well-chosen details to suggest a romantic medievalism. (*Country Life*)

Grecian art are surely to be more grateful and appropriate than a ruder, severer style; but on the contrary, there are some wild romantic situations, whose rocks, and dashing mountain streams, or deep umbrageous dells, would seem to harmonize with the proud baronial tower or mitred abbey..."[12]

The fact that many of the styles and types of buildings discussed in the work of Price, Knight and Repton were not in themselves Picturesque was not in any way contradictory to their general theories. The Picturesque point of view was interested in how the building was perceived in relation to its natural environment rather than as an isolated object. Although a structure might be regular and symmetrical, if properly situated within the landscape thoroughly Picturesque effects could be created.

Price, Knight and Repton offered practical advice on how to create this union of landscape and architecture. The most important compositional technique was the management of trees around the house. By framing and overlapping these organic forms with the building and by allowing the shadows cast by the surrounding foliage to play upon the surfaces, the architect-painter could create a visual link between the two elements.[13] Subsidiary buildings (stables, coach houses, gatehouses, etc.) could also enhance the Picturesque effect, for, by exposing them to view rather than hiding them as had been the practice interesting compositions could be created.[14]

Colouring was essential to the harmony of the scene. Stone or stucco walls in grey or subdued yellow were preferred to contrast with the darker hues of the landscape. Their smooth reflective surfaces also accentuated the patterns of light and shadow across the wall planes. Repton felt white walls were harsh on the eye[15] and all were agreed that "glaring red brick," "hot and sultry in appearance" should be removed from the landscape.[16] For cottages Repton advocated the use of green trim (for porches and shutters) to blend in with the surrounding foliage.

Variety and effects of light and shadow essential to Picturesque effect in architecture were best achieved in the irregular medieval modes, but these authors also suggested a few design tricks which, in conjunction with surrounding landscape, could impart a Picturesque appearance to any type of building. Price advocated the use of tall chimneys to enliven the silhouette of even the simplest structure.[17] Repton, who was most explicit on the subject, suggested that the architect could greatly enrich the appearance of a building by breaking up the regular wall planes with recessed panels, bow windows or large projecting geometric forms created by interior room shapes.[18] These subtle manipulations of architectural form produced interesting effects in light and shadow and a sense of movement and variety in even the most regular designs.

The tie between landscape and architecture could also be expressed in concrete terms. Repton in particular was very conscious of creating a spatial bridge linking nature to a building. The wilder aspects of the parkland became more carefully groomed round the house. This area, referred to as the pleasure grounds and ornamented with climbing vines, greenhouses, garden seats, firm gravel walks and other civilized amenities for the occupants, provided a transitional space between the less cultivated park and the man-made dwelling.[19] Terraces which in the summer sometimes were used as an additional room or gallery were used to link the pleasure grounds to the building.[20] Pursuers of the Picturesque loved to commune with what they thought was wild nature and to let it into their country houses rather than shut it out. The terrace, especially when accompanied by the French window, broke down the barriers between interior and exterior space.[21] For smaller houses, without large terraces, the French window in conjunction with a verandah functioned in a similar manner; moreover, when this form was supported by treillage entwined by climbing vines the bond with the natural environment became very real. The terrace or verandah and French windows also provided an ideal spot from which to enjoy the landscape vistas.

The French window also had the advantage of allowing more light into the interior, a prominent concern of Picturesque architecture. Even when French windows were not employed, windows were generally large or placed in a projecting bow, which collected light and according to Repton enhanced the view from the interior.[22]

The plan, too, was to be responsive to the site. Principal rooms and their windows were to be turned towards the light and views so that "the architect...would be obliged to...accommodate his building to the scenery, not make that give way to his building."[23] This planning principle, of course, provided the practical justification for the use of an irregular plan initially advocated on aesthetic grounds. As will be seen, however, in practice Picturesque architecture often retained a symmetrical elevation. The importance of orienting the building to take full advantage of sun and vista did result in a much more flexible approach to interior planning which eventually undermined the rigid centre-hall plan that had dominated eighteenth century domestic architecture.

THE THEORY INTO PRACTICE

Within the writings of Price, Knight and Repton three important approaches to architectural design grew out of their theories on the Picturesque. First, architecture should conform and be congruent to the landscape. Second, architectural forms could be manipulated to enhance the visual interest of the scenic composition. Third, the varied character of the landscape required different stylistic or design solutions to visually harmonize with the setting or to enhance its mood.

The three major authors on the Picturesque did offer considerable advice on residential building, but not being architects they provided few concrete architectural models designed according to their principles. It was left to the architects of the late-Georgian period to translate these ideas into practice, but in this process they also transformed and modified these principles, often creating designs of a very different character than was advocated in the theoretical writings on the Picturesque. By examining the works of the two major Regency architects, John Nash and John Soane, and the domestic designs presented in the popular architectural pattern books, this transition and transformation from the theory to the architectural practice can be illustrated.

John Nash (1752-1835), as a master of eclecticism, has been aptly labelled the virtuoso of the Picturesque.[1] Nash was associated at a very early date with the small circle of authors on the Picturesque. In 1792 he was briefly employed by Sir Uvedale Price to design a Gothic residence, and probably through this connection he came into contact with Humphry Repton. Throughout the 1790s Nash collaborated frequently with Repton by providing suitable architectural designs to complete Repton's landscape schemes. A quarrel in 1802 ended this loose partnership. Much of Nash's work with Repton was Gothic or classical but in later years he greatly broadened his stylistic range. At Brighton in 1815 he created for the Prince Regent an exotic seaside pavilion based on a Hindu palace. In a design of 1802 for a villa at Cronkhill he introduced the irregular Italianate villa with its off-centre tower and stucco walls to the English landscape (Fig. 4). Nash was well known for his designs in the rustic or Old English cottage style as illustrated by his cottage grouping at Blaise Castle in Gloucestershire built in 1811. He also produced several designs in what was often referred to in the vocabulary of the period as the Modern Fancy or the Regular style, terms that described a villa or cottage Picturesque in character but lacking any clearly defined stylistic sources. The label "Regular" style was usually reserved for modest buildings of this astylistic type which were also symmetrical in elevation (Fig. 5). All these modes popularized by Nash became familiar architectural ornaments of the Picturesque landscape.[2]

4. Cronkhill, Salop, England
Constructed 1802; **Architect** John Nash; **Material** stucco

Cronkhill was the first and certainly one of the finest examples of the Italianate villa which was to become a popular mode of domestic building in Britain and perhaps even more so in North America in the nineteenth century. Although Nash takes as his starting point in design the vernacular architecture of the Italian countryside which had become familiar through the paintings of the Italian landscapists such as Claude Lorrain, Cronkhill could not be described as an accurate recreation of this type. Nash was never noted for his fidelity to his sources. Like Knight in his design of Downton, Nash borrowed a few characteristic details, such as the off-centre tower, round-headed windows and arcade with a balustrade, to suggest this villa type and at the same time evoke a sense of the calm pastoral mood of the Claudian landscape. As was essential to a villa Cronkhill was situated on an elevated, well-wooded site. The surrounding foliage contrasted with the sharp clean lines of the stucco walls whose surfaces were enlivened by the flowing plane of the circular tower and the shadows cast by the arcade and wide bracketed eaves. (National Monuments Record, London)

5. Double Cottage, Park Village East, Regent's Park, London, England
Constructed 1824; Architect John Nash; Material stucco

In 1811 John Nash produced a massive scheme to convert the Crown's Marylebone Estates in London into a smart residential area providing plenty of open space, fresh air and the scenery of nature. Nash's "rus in urbe" was one of the first examples of a planned garden city and it represents the most comprehensive expression of Picturesque principles transported into the urban setting. Instead of working with a single estate, Nash devised a plan for an entire community composed of terraces, shops, markets, model villages and fifty-six elegant villas, all to be situated amid an irregular landscape setting complete with a serpentine lake, canals and extensive plantations. The double cottage was situated in one of Nash's model village groupings called Park Village East. A double residence, it was designed in the simple Regular style featuring smooth stucco walls, large venetian windows on the ground floor, smaller windows on the second floor, large chimneys and treillaged porches. The scalloped trim under the eaves, perhaps intended to suggest the transient character of a canvas awning, was a popular decorative device for enlivening the roofline of these plain structures and it appeared on several villa and cottage designs in Canada. On the rear two treillaged balconies overlooked the canal and the parklands behind. (National Monuments Record, London)

Sir John Soane (1753-1837) was a very different type of architect who cannot be slotted comfortably into the Picturesque Movement.[3] Whereas Nash epitomized the architect of the Picturesque, Soane stands as an isolated figure whose highly individualistic and unconventional style places him on the fringes of the popular architectural trends of the late-Georgian period. Although Soane did dabble in alternative Picturesque modes, his works always remained classical in spirit and contrasted with the light-hearted, fanciful eclecticism of Nash. In the early years of his career, before 1790, his designs were still very much influenced by the formal classicism of the eighteenth century (Fig. 6). As his style matured, however, he became less tied to classical precedent and a strong element of the Picturesque entered his work. The need for congruency between landscape and architecture became an important theme in his domestic architecture. But it was in his handling of architectural forms that Picturesque values were expressed most clearly. Although Soane's style always retained a strong sense of rational order, simplicity of form and structural clarity of design, this underlying classicism was tempered by Soane's eye for Picturesque effects of dramatic lighting, shifting wall planes, varied massing and striking skyline (Fig. 7).[4]

6. Plan for Chilton Lodge, Berkshire, England; Published 1793; **Architect** Sir John Soane

Sir John Soane's early work, as illustrated by his design for Chilton Lodge in Berkshire, was marked by a strong sense of classical order and balance characteristic of eighteenth century architecture in England. The use of a Palladian plan with a central block flanked by two low wings was typical of his work of this period. But even at this early stage in his stylistic development, his designs were characterized by a purity and simplicity of form. Visual effect was achieved, not by enriching the facade with applied classical detail, but by the massing of simple geometric forms (the cube and the semicircle) to create, what Soane would later describe, as a pleasing balance between simplicity of design and variety in mass and light and shadow. This modest type adapted well to Upper Canada. Summerhill in Kingston (Fig. 57) and Rideau Hall in Ottawa (Fig. 58) are closely related to this building. (Sir John Soane, *Sketches in Architecture*, etc., 1793; reprint ed., Farnborough: Gregg International Publishers, 1971, p. xvii)

7. Butterton Farmhouse, Staffordshire, England
Constructed 1815-16; **Architect** Sir John Soane; **Material** brick

As Soane's style matured it became less classical, in the strict sense of the word. Although his designs always maintained a sense of rational order, simplicity and structural honesty which could be called classical in spirit, his architectural vocabulary became more abstract and astylistic and less dependent on historical precedent. The period between 1810 and 1820 is often referred to as Soane's Picturesque phase in which he experimented with Picturesque effects of dramatic lighting, varied wall planes and broken skylines. The Butterton Farmhouse of 1815-16 was a modest but striking product of this late period of his career. This design with its wide eaves, splayed or chamfered corners, slightly projecting piers and deeply recessed doorway illustrates Soane's delight in manipulating bold simple masses to create a visually dynamic and varied design. Soane was too individualistic and unconventional an architect to attract a school of followers but it is noteworthy how closely the Dublin-born Canadian architect, George Browne, has imitated the Soanian quality of astylistic simplicity in his design for Saint Andrew's Manse in Kingston (Fig. 72). (National Monuments Record, London)

The architecture of Nash and Soane represents the more advanced and original manifestations of Picturesque values in building and for this reason their work could not be considered typical. On a more popular level there existed a substratum of domestic design produced by younger, less prominent architects, influenced both by the literature of the Picturesque and by Nash and Soane but whose buildings were generally more modest to appeal to popular tastes and economy. The most important vehicle for the dissemination of this popularized Picturesque taste was the architectural pattern book.[5]

Between 1790 and 1835 more than sixty of these books were published in England.[6] Aimed at the rapidly expanding middle-class market they provided designs for small suburban or country residences which were moderately priced yet which offered some pretensions to style and fashion. Unwieldy titles such as Robert Lugar's publication of 1807, *Architectural Sketches for Cottages, Rural Dwellings and Villas in Grecian, Gothic and Fancy Styles Suitable to Persons of Genteel Life and Moderate Fortune. Preceeded by Some Observations on Scenery and Character Proper for Picturesque Buildings*, explicitly identify the clientele to which the author was catering as well as the aesthetic point of view he was adopting.

In the earliest of these domestic pattern books of the 1780s and 1790s, such as John Soane's first publications of 1788 and 1793 or John Plaw's *Ferme Ornée* of 1795, eighteenth century classicism was still very strong but by the turn of the century the influence of Picturesque aesthetics became more prevalent. The first thing one notices about the pattern books of this late-Georgian or Regency period is the manner in which the architects present their designs. Unlike the hard, linear elevations isolated from their setting which had characterized architectural drawing of the previous century, buildings were invariably illustrated in a painterly manner surrounded by a landscape and usually viewed from a natural-looking oblique angle. The plates were accompanied by a brief description, which pointed out the aesthetic merits of the design and its suitability to its function and location. Often a short introductory chapter laid out the author's purpose and aesthetic philosophy which consisted of reworked ideas drawn from the major writers and architects working within the Picturesque point of view. The stylistic eclecticism that Picturesque invited becomes more evident and the architects introduced designs ranging from classical to Gothic and rustic cottage modes. But despite this stylistic diversity these early houses of the Picturesque shared a common quality of restraint and simplicity in design. A few details or characteristics were applied to suggest rather than to recreate a past style.

By the late 1820s and 1830s the character of the domestic pattern books begins to change. The best-known villa and cottage book of this period was John Claudius Loudon's *An Encyclopedia of Cottage, Farm, and Villa Architecture...* (1833). This massive work in a sense culminates the Picturesque Movement but it also marks a shift in direction into the Victorian era. In contrast to the generalized, descriptive prose of the earlier pattern books, Loudon's lengthy text tended to take on an instructional, often pedantic tone in which he offered explicit advice on every aspect of residential design down to the furnishings. The most obvious difference in appearance was the absence of landscape setting for Loudon's designs. Although very concerned with landscape, its once intimate connection with architecture has begun to break down. The designs remain eclectic but they tend towards the Victorian view of the Picturesque in their often agitated skyline, and a richer and more abundant decorative detail.[7]

It is the pattern books of this late-Georgian period exemplified by the works of architects like Robert Lugar (1773-1855), Joseph Gandy (1771-1843), Edward Gyfford (1773-1856), John B. Papworth (1775-1847) or William Fuller Pocock (1779-1849) that are most relevant to this study of the early architecture of the Picturesque. These architects of the Picturesque were concerned with all buildings in the residential environment — stables, gate lodges, gardener's cottages and garden ornaments — but the focus of this taste was directed to the villa and the cottage. As stated previously "villa" and "cottage" are terms applied to small residential buildings set in a natural or garden setting. The difference between these two types is much more difficult to define for they are distinguished from each other more by the ideas or emotions with which they were associated than by their physical appearance.

Originally, a cottage referred to the traditional medieval house occupied by the English rural peasantry and characterized by an irregular plan, thatched roof and half-timbered and roughcast walls. First recognized as an object of Picturesque interest by landscape painters such as Thomas Gainsborough, it became a symbol of romanticized rural values. Its primitive rustic character seemed closer to the true character of nature than did the polished forms of the Grecian temple. To the eighteenth and nineteenth century mind the cottage as an idea evoked a sense of retired rural tranquility – unaffected, unpretentious and free from the pressure of modern urban life.[8]

At first rustic cottages were built as ornaments to a gentleman's estate to be occupied by his employees or tenants as exemplified by Nash's cottage complex at Blaise Castle. By the early 1800s, however, the pattern books were offering illustrations for the "Cottage or Câbane Ornée." These were cottages built for gentlemen who wanted to surround themselves with this atmosphere of rural ease. As explained by one author, William Fuller Pocock, "the câbane ornée... though humble in appearance affords the necessary conveniences for persons of refined manners and habits, and is, perhaps, more calculated than any other description of building for the enjoyment of the true pleasures of domestic life, unencumbered with the forms of state and troublesome appendages."[9]

Cottage design remained largely dependent on the traditional medieval model, sometimes adding modern inventions such as rough, untrimmed logs for porch supports as a means of accentuating its rustic character (Fig. 8).[10] But the term cottage did not necessarily refer to a specific stylistic type. John Plaw's plan for an "American cottage" or John Papworth's design for a *cottage orné* both symmetrical in elevation ornamented with verandahs, bore no resemblance to the medieval cottage (Figs 9, 10). Nevertheless, they were labelled as such because the architects who designed them viewed them as suggestive or conducive to an air of relaxed informality which defined the cottage.

The villa was also charged with associations of the peaceful country life but of a less rustic and more refined, civilized character. Generally larger in scale than the cottage and more sophisticated and polished in its design, the villa was suited to "Inhabitants... of some Rank in Life" who were "entitled to more Show as well as conveniences."[11] Although this category of building had undergone a revival in the mid-1700s in England, these early villas remained tied to classical forms.[12] The Picturesque villas were thoroughly eclectic in style. Gothic (Fig. 11), Italianate, classical (Fig. 12), or the so-called Modern Fancy or Regular styles (Figs 13, 14) were all popular modes for villa building.

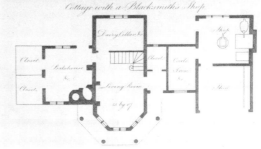

Cottage with a Blacksmiths Shop

8. Cottage with a Blacksmith's Shop
Published 1807; **Architect** Robert Lugar
Robert Lugar (1773-1855), who practised in London from 1799, was a skillful and popular practitioner of the Picturesque. Between 1805 and 1828 he published four architectural pattern books for villas and cottages executed in a wide range of styles. This illustration is a good example of the English cottage mode with its varied and picturesque outline, thatched roof, tall chimneys, and porch supported by rough untrimmed logs. Similar designs could have been found in most of the popular early nineteenth century cottage pattern books. Some were designed as a gentleman's country retreat, or, as in this example, a picturesque embellishment to the gentleman's park landscape to be occupied by an employee or tenant. Although this English cottage type did not initially play an important role in Canada's Picturesque architecture, elements of its plan – the projecting octagonal living room encircled by a verandah, raised second storey and side entrance – resemble the outline of Toronto's Colborne Lodge of 1836 (Fig. 33). (Robert Lugar, *The Country Gentleman's Architect*, 1807; reprint ed., Farnborough: Gregg International Publishers, 1971, pl. 4)

9. American Cottages, Feversham, Kent, England
Published 1795; **Architect** John Plaw (1746-1820)
In style these American cottages with their steeply pitched roof, dormers and three-sided "piazza" (the American term for a verandah) most closely resemble a modified version of the Dutch Colonial house found in regions of the northeastern United States. Although this American cottage style never became a popular mode in England, it nevertheless demonstrates the process of architectural discovery characteristic of this period whereby unfamiliar or exotic building types, whether an Italian villa, a Hindu palace, or a Swiss chalet, could in the mind of an architect become a suitable object to ornament the landscape. There is no firm documentation that Plaw had visited New England, but in 1790 he displayed in London a plan drawn for a house in Philadelphia and in 1807 he immigrated to Prince Edward Island, suggesting that he had been to North America and was familiar with this indigenous Dutch style house. (John Plaw, *Ferme Ornée; or, Rural Improvements*, etc., 1795; reprint ed., Farnborough: Gregg International Publishers, 1972, pl. 17)

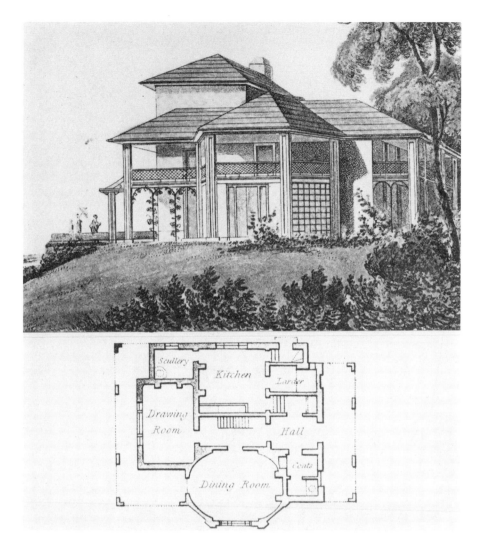

10. *Cottage orné*; **Published** 1818; **Architect** John B. Papworth

John B. Papworth (1775-1847), one of the most successful designers of Picturesque villas and cottages, believed that the *cottage orné* should "combine utility with picturesque beauty at a moderate price" while avoiding the architectural embellishments that "should only belong to buildings of greater pretensions." To achieve this balance between simplicity and variety Papworth created a thoroughly astylistic design composed of simple, unadorned masses arranged in an irregular plan surmounted by a series of broken roof forms which extended well beyond the walls to incorporate verandahs and galleries. The elimination of all historic references to style and the treatment of design as an abstract composition of simple volumes, explains the very modern, twentieth century appearance of this cottage. In accordance with the Picturesque principle of orienting the interior layout to the site, Papworth has placed the service areas along the north and east walls, thereby leaving the southern and western exposures, which offered the best views and maximum sunlight, for the principal living rooms. (John B. Papworth, *Rural Residences*, etc., 1818; reprint ed., Farnborough: Gregg International Publishers, 1971, p. 13)

11. Villa in the Gothic Style (Garden Facade)
Published 1806; **Architect** Edward Gyfford; **Material** wood and stucco

The indiscriminate blending and modifying of various styles to achieve Picturesque effects and to meet functional requirements of a residential building is evident in this design. A crenellated tower of a medieval castle and a gabled, possibly thatched, roof of the English cottage have been applied to a symmetrical composition of classical leanings. Large French windows and a verandah provide modern domestic amenities appropriate to a villa. Unfortunately, the flimsy verandah looks out of place against the bolder, heavier forms of the underlying structure. A more satisfying solution to this basic design appeared thirty years later in Toronto in the design for Holland House (Fig. 63). Not surprisingly, Edward Gyfford (1773-1856) was never very successful in private practice and was employed throughout most of his career as a draughtsman. (Edward Gyfford, *Designs for elegant cottages and small villas*, etc., 1806; reprint ed., Farnborough: Gregg International Publishers, 1972, pl. 7)

12. Grecian Villa; Architect Francis Goodwin; **Published** 1833

Francis Goodwin described this villa as semi-Grecian because the design does not accurately conform to Greek models of architecture. Its design is thoroughly nineteenth century but a few Greek details, in the form of Grecian Ionic columns, have been applied. The smooth stucco walls are defined by a simple, chaste pattern of void and solid relieved by typical Picturesque devices such as the projecting bow front on one facade and a recessed portico on another. In many respects Francis Goodwin was a transitional architect caught between the Picturesque Movement as defined in the late Georgian period and the architecture of the Victorian era. This illustration was not typical of Goodwin's work but its simplicity and restraint in design was characteristic of early Picturesque architecture. Although Goodwin's pattern book, *Domestic Architecture,* first published in 1833, reflects the strong influence of the Picturesque point of view, new, distinctly Victorian characteristics and approaches to design are introduced. The most notable difference is Goodwin's Gothic architecture. Medieval designs had played an important part in the earlier pattern books but generally the architects retained an eclectic and egalitarian view of style. In Goodwin's publication Gothic designs, either rustic cottages or castellated country houses, dominate his work, and his writings demonstrate a strong medieval bias which had originated in the Gothic Revival of the 1830s. (Francis Goodwin, *Domestic Architecture*, etc., 3rd ed. rev., London: Henry G. Bohn, 1850, Vol. 2, pl. 24)

13. Design for a Villa; Published 1807; **Architect** William Fuller Pocock; **Material** stucco

William Fuller Pocock (1779-1849) belonged to that group of architects who believed that in villa design every part must be uniform and symmetrical. It should be Regular but not classical for Pocock adhered to the belief that ancient Greek and Roman architecture, developed for another purpose and climate, was "unsuitable to the domestic buildings of this climate without essential and radical variations." His solution to villa design was a simple, plain structure devoid of any stylistic references except for a small columned porch over the main door. Popular design devices such as the octagonal bay, recessed panels, and deep eaves impart some sense of "novelty, variety and effect" which the architect sought to capture. But in keeping with the Picturesque point of view, the architect believed that these qualities could be "accurately ascertained" only by "embodying it in the mind's eye ... and then judging its appearance in different points of view, as it regards the character of the design itself, and the situation for which it was intended." (William Fuller Pocock, *Architectural Designs for Rustic Cottages*, etc., 1807; reprint ed., Farnborough: Gregg International Publishers, 1972, pl. 20, 21)

The Rev.ᵈ Dᵣ Johnson Yaxham Parsonage . Norfolk.

London Pub.ᵈ by J. Taylor 59 High Holborn.

14. Yaxham Parsonage, Norfolk, England; Published 1828; **Architect** Robert Lugar

In cottage design Lugar believed that the broken, irregular outline "must be considered particularly in character for a picturesque cottage." In the design of villas, however, different rules were applied. To quote Lugar "...here the style should at once declare the residence of a gentleman. Exact proportion and regularity of parts must here be obvious, and all deviation from uniformity must be carefully avoided...." Architectural detailing should be handled with restraint; "a small portico as a shelter to the door, with two or four columns of the ancient Greek doric may be considered the best." All these characteristics as well as other typical villa features, such as the bracketed eaves, heavy chimneys, broken wall planes and of course the irregular landscape setting, are well illustrated in this design. (Robert Lugar, *Villa Architecture*, etc., London, 1828, pl. 13)

To be accurate, however, one cannot impose too rigid a definition on either of these two terms. The use of phrases such as "a villa in the cottage style" – a label applied to a design based on the rustic cottage type but executed on a larger scale – or a "cottage villa" referring to a Regular or classical design on a cottage-like scale, often renders the distinction between these two types hazy and imprecise.

Whether a villa or a cottage the same principles of design based on Picturesque values were to be applied. The fundamental consideration in determining the character of the villa or cottage was congruency with the setting. According to William Fuller Pocock "the design ... in a great measure will depend on the situation, and the manner of laying out the grounds..."[13] so that, as John Papworth explains, the building "should combine properly with the surrounding objects, and appear native to the spot."[14] Even John Soane recognized that in villa design congruency with setting must always be considered.[15] This integration of landscape and architecture was made visually explicit in the illustrations of the pattern books. Not only were the buildings depicted as part of a landscape setting but often parts of the structure were obscured by surrounding vegetation and by shadows cast by the architectural forms and landscape. These atmospheric effects were worked out on paper as an integral part of the design.

The architects of the Picturesque diverge from the theorists in their interpretation of what visual qualities constituted Picturesque effect in design. Although Price, Knight and Repton felt that all architecture could be blended into the Picturesque landscape by arranging landscape features around the structure into interesting compositions, they firmly adhered to the belief that qualities of irregularity, intricacy, variety and effects of light and shade were the most effective causes of the Picturesque in architecture. While many of the domestic building types that emerged during the early 1800s, such as the rustic cottage, the Italianate villa or the castellated or Gothic villa, did conform faithfully to these characteristics, a large percentage of designs were both symmetrical in elevation and intentionally plain and simple in their ornamentation.

Picturesque architecture was permeated by an undercurrent of rationalism and utilitarianism expressed by the concept of "fitness." In other words, the design of a villa or cottage must reflect its residential function. Grand and elaborate architectural embellishments might be appropriate to large public or religious buildings or even to the large country mansions of the nobility but they were not in keeping with the small scale and relaxed domestic comforts of a villa or cottage.[16] A call for simplicity in design echoed throughout the pattern books. Soane insisted that "whatever style... the most simple forms will always be best fitted and most proper."[17] According to Robert Lugar "simple ornaments may very properly be applied, but such great architectural ornaments such as colonnades and porticos, are misapplied and take off that lightness which should ever distinguish a villa."[18]

A simple character did not make the buildings any less picturesque in appearance but was, in fact, very conducive to these effects. As explained by David Laing, "when Grandeur and Magnificence are less thought of, the most painter-like effects may be produced, even by the Mixture of the simplest things, when properly placed and combined with others."[19] The smooth, frequently stuccoed walls coloured in muted tones, which characterized so many small villa and cottage designs of the period, blended easily into the surrounding landscape. By adopting a more neutral appearance the walls functioned as a reflective foil which "under the influence of every varying light and shadow assume those pictorial effects which delight the imagination."[20]

Nor was a simplicity in design incompatible with Picturesque values for pleasing and interesting visual effects in architecture. John Soane argued for simplicity but he also believed that architecture must have "variety in Mass, and Light and Shadow in the whole, so as to produce varied sensations of gaiety and melancholy, of wildness, and even of surprise and wonder."[21] To achieve these effects Soane suggested, as did Humphry Repton, that simple geometric forms – the ellipse, circle or any of the polygons – which reflected interior room shapes be extended beyond the exterior walls to enliven the exterior elevation and silhouette.[22] Slight projections in the wall planes or decorative recessed panels, usually placed around windows, were frequently used to produce similar effects.

Tall chimneys, advocated by Price to enliven the roof silhouette, were often applied to the rustic cottage but were considered inappropriate to compact horizontal lines of a villa or cottage in a Regular style. Although treated as a prominent feature chimneys on this type assumed a lower profile often elaborated by decorative panels.

A cantilevered eave was a recurring feature of villa design. Perhaps intended to suggest the roofline of an Italian vernacular villa, it was felt that this feature produced a Picturesque effect.[23] Its wide overhang, often decorated by a simple scalloped trim or, more commonly, by slender paired brackets, cast deep and varied shadows over the wall surface and offered protection from water damage.

The verandah was regarded as one of the most efficient methods of lending a touch of the Picturesque to a design. Identified as being of "eastern and very ancient origin"[24] this feature appealed to romantic tastes for the exotic; moreover, when combined with Repton's French windows it created a spatial bridge to link the garden with the interior and provided "a convenient ambulatory from which the garden could be enjoyed."[25] Usually conceived as a light flimsy structure with a flared roof supported by treillage, preferably entwined with climbing vines, the verandah offered a simple and inexpensive device for enlivening the appearance of the facade. "No decorations have so successfully varied the dull sameness of modern structures as the 'verandah', the lengthened window and the balcony" which "afford a degree of embellishment ... by the variety of light and shadow which they project."[26]

The combination of the tent-like verandah and the French window became so popular in Britain that it was applied to all types of domestic building regardless of its suitability to setting. James Malton, an avid promoter of the rustic charms of the English thatched-roof cottage, was critical of the indiscrimate use of this form which he regarded a pretentious affectation of retired colonials from India.

The returned Nabob, heated in the pursuit of wealth, imagines he imports the "chaleur" of the East with his riches; and

we behold the stretched awning to form the cool shade, in the moist clime of Britain; the new fashioned windows of Italy, opening to the floor, originally intended to survey the lawns, the vistas, and the groves of Claude, in their summer attire, or the canals of Venice; are now seen in every confined street of London...[27]

Despite these unkind criticisms verandahs and French windows continued to be prominent features of the rural and urban landscape throughout the first third of the nineteenth century.

In terms of future directions in nineteenth century architecture the most significant legacy of the Picturesque was the legitimization of an eclectic approach to style, particularly the revival of the Gothic vocabulary, and the cultivation of a taste for qualities of irregularity and variety in design. Out of these principles developed the two major themes of Victorian architecture — the archaeologically minded Gothic Revival style as defined by Augustus Welby Pugin in the 1830s and the extravagant High Victorian styles, be it Renaissance, Gothic or Jacobethan, with their characteristic irregularity of form, agitated silhouette, richly varied colours and textures and profusion of intricate decorative detail.

The immediate influence of the Picturesque taste on popular domestic building produced far less flamboyant results. We have seen how the theorists' view of what constituted Picturesque effect in architecture was altered considerably by the practicing architects as illustrated by the Picturesque pattern books. But even an examination of these publications alone can be misleading. The purpose of producing a pattern book was to demonstrate the architect's versatility in the whole spectrum of the Picturesque styles. In practice the preferences of his client, usually from moderately well-off gentry, tended more to the conservative Regular or Modern Fancy styles or to modestly Gothicized cottages than to exotic Hindu palaces or rambling medieval abbeys. Two modest stuccoed and verandahed villas, Fairfield House in Hampshire and Oakfield in Dulwich built in the early nineteenth century, more accurately illustrate the typical Picturesque villa of Regency England (Figs 15, 16).

15. **Fairfield, Hampshire, England; Material** stucco

16. **Oakfield, Dulwich Village, England; Material** stucco

Both these residences represent a common type of villa design being built by moderately well-off gentry in England during the Regency period of the early nineteenth century. As in Canada this type of residence was generally located in modest picturesque gardens situated in the suburbs of the major cities or county towns. Both these buildings were designed in the Modern Fancy or Regular style, popular because it blended economy and simplicity of design with a suitable degree of fashion and taste. The smooth surfaces of the stucco walls, punctuated by French or floor-length sash windows and accented by flared metal verandahs, treillage and climbing vines, were standard ingredients of this house type. Fairfield with its sweeping bow windows and formal columned porch may represent the work of a minor architect schooled in the popularized Picturesque taste, while Oakfield, with its awkward massing of wings and window distribution, suggests the work of a local builder. This type of modest villa dwelling provides the closest equivalent to the Picturesque villas of British North America. (Fig. 15, *Country Life*; Fig. 16, Stanley C. Ramsey, *Small Houses of the Late Georgian Period, 1750-1820,* London: Technical Journals, 1919, pl. 95)

This level of architectural taste represents the final distillation of the pure theory into popular practice. The typical Regency villa or cottage demonstrated the Picturesque taste for informal park settings, but not the wild, uncultivated landscape Price and Knight had so admired. A more refined and genteel environment with firm gravel walks, ornamental gardens, clusters of trees amid rolling lawns, and preferably a wide pleasing vista, was more to the liking of the average country gentleman. The Picturesque concept of congruency, whereby architectural design and style must reflect the character of the setting, was probably never a serious consideration for the popular architect. It is more likely that the choice of style would have reflected the preferences of the client rather than a careful analysis of the landscape features. Instead congruency was expressed in more general terms of co-ordinating architectural design to the landscape, first by organizing interior layout to take advantage of aspects of sunlight and vista, second by creating transitional spaces between exterior and interior with French windows, verandahs or terraces, and third by visually overlapping the architecture with natural elements of the landscape in the form of trees, vines or shrubbery. Picturesque qualities of irregularity and variety were evident in popular design but usually they were expressed in the overall composition of landscape and architecture.

In design Picturesque effects were translated as a taste for simplicity accented and visually enriched by subtle variations in surface, outline and contrasting effects of light and shadow. Details, although they often tended to fanciful and delicate forms, were usually applied with a tasteful restraint. This popularized version of the Picturesque, while not as significant in terms of future trends in architecture, provided the important models for villa and cottage building in Canada.

PART II   THE PICTURESQUE IN CANADA

INTRODUCTION

The influence of the Picturesque taste on Canadian domestic architecture can be traced back to the end of the eighteenth century. The villas and cottages of this early phase dating before 1830 represented only a rough translation of Picturesque values in architecture as formulated in England. Although buildings of this period often employed verandahs and French windows — features associated with Picturesque architecture — these elements were usually applied to designs derived from either eighteenth century British classical modes, or from a North American vernacular tradition, or often from functional building types developed by the British military for use in the colonies. These early domestic buildings relied mainly on an effective choice of setting — preferably a site that was of a dramatically romantic character but, if not, always secluded and well-wooded - to create the desired Picturesque effect.

Post-1830 villas and cottages were distinguished from those of the previous three decades, not so much by a change in taste, but by the greater degree of sophistication by which Picturesque ideas were expressed. This transition was due largely to two interrelated factors. During the 1830s emigration from Britain rose sharply and these new residents demanded homes designed according to contemporary English tastes. More important, however, was the arrival of British-trained architects who had been indoctrinated into Picturesque principles of design and who were able to supply fashionable residential designs based on popular English models.

PATRONS OF THE PICTURESQUE

The Picturesque remained an important influence on villa and cottage design in Canada throughout the first half of the nineteenth century; however, these buildings represent only a small portion of what was constructed during this period. Canadian architecture in the early years of the British North American colonies does not present itself as a cohesive study given the diverse cultural backgrounds of the original settlers. In Lower Canada the British conquest of New France in 1759 resulted in the introduction of British styles of architecture in buildings constructed for the new English colonial elite, but generally French building traditions survived this political upheaval unscathed. A second cultural group was drawn from the United States. Waves of American immigrants arrived in Canada before and after the American Revolution and settled in the Maritime colonies, the Eastern Townships of Quebec and along the shores of Lake Ontario and Lake Erie. Naturally they built homes similar to those they left behind rather than ones that reflected up-to-date British tastes. Even emigration from Britain can be divided roughly into two groups. The majority of new arrivals from England, Scotland and Ireland were drawn from the British working classes who fled their homes to escape poverty and starvation. If they could afford a home at all, they built a square, sturdy, functional one which paid little heed to architectural fashion.

The group that concerns this study was also of British, usually English origin, but from the more genteel, wealthier middle classes and occasionally from the British aristocracy. It is not the purpose of this study to draw rigid parallels between a particular social and cultural group and Picturesque architecture in Canada. The buildings examined were selected purely for their design characteristics, but in identifying the original owners of these buildings, a fairly consistent cultural and social profile of the typical villa and cottage dweller emerges.

The most prominent patrons of the Picturesque were those envoys of the Crown – the high colonial officials, such as John Graves Simcoe (governor of Upper Canada, 1791-96), the Duke of Kent (resident in both Quebec and Halifax, 1791-1801), Lord Aylmer (governor of Lower Canada, 1831-35) and Sir Peregrine Maitland (lieutenant-governor of Upper Canada, 1818-28) – who were sent from England to oversee the local administration. While their stay was usually brief their superior social position easily established them as leaders of fashion and taste. This upper echelon of colonial society often led the way in introducing Picturesque tastes in Canadian architecture.

Their lead was followed by the middle-class English immigrant who set up permanent residency in Canada. The largest single portion of this social group were ex-military officers who had retired on their half-pay pensions and who were encouraged to emigrate by generous grants of land which amounted to as much as twelve hundred acres for an ex-lieutenant-colonel. Many others were drawn from civilian ranks – either professional men (doctors, lawyers or clergy), private gentlemen of moderate income who belonged to good "respectable" families, or businessmen with money to invest in the expanding colonies. The presence of these gentlemen settlers in British North America became particularly evident in the fifteen and twenty years following the Napoleonic Wars (1803-15). High taxes and an economic depression in England rendered it increasingly difficult for persons of moderate income to maintain their accustomed genteel lifestyle. They hoped immigration to the colonies was a solution to this financial pinch and a means of bettering their economic and social standing.[1]

Not all these patrons of the Picturesque were direct British imports. It is noteworthy that some of the most avid pursuers of the Picturesque, such as John Beverley Robinson of Toronto, John Solomon Cartwright of Kingston, Sir Alan Napier NcNab of Hamilton, or John Molson Junior of Montreal, were native-born British North Americans. These men were drawn from old and prominent families, generally of Loyalist origins who had established themselves early as leaders of colonial society. Although born here they turned towards England for their cultural direction. Often they had been sent to England to finish their education where they learned, among other things, English ideas of a gentleman's residential estate. Some of the most ambitious experiments in Picturesque architecture were carried out under their patronage. Perhaps as native British North Americans they felt a much deeper commitment to their colony and wanted to build homes that would vie with those found in Britain rather than just pale colonial imitations.

Whether recent immigrants or born to this country the colonial experience of these people was usually quite different from that of the impoverished working classes. They were equipped with three important tools which set them apart from the typical immigrant – an education, social position and the influential connections it implied, and most importantly, money. It was this group that came to Canada well-versed in attitudes of the Picturesque and who had the financial resources to indulge these tastes in the building of fashionable villas and cottages set amid well-treed, landscaped parks, ornamented with flower gardens, winding walks and roadways. To echo the works of Robert Lugar they built homes "Suitable for Persons of Genteel Life and Moderate Fortune."

Their response to the Canadian landscape was very much coloured by their Picturesque point of view. As a literate people they frequently wrote about their experiences and impressions of Canada either as settlers or as visitors and their accounts are permeated with this romanticized sensibility to nature. The following description of the landscape along the St. Lawrence River north of Quebec which appeared in the travel accounts of Sir Richard Bonnycastle, an officer in the Royal Engineers who travelled throughout British North America in the 1830s and 1840s, was typical of the English gentleman's view of the countryside.

> Here, at nightfall, I observed a scene worthy of Claude Lorraine's pencil. The sun went down rather hazy, but exhibited till near nine a beautiful picture, backed by the bold mountains of the north shore, set in a frame of a rich subdued red sky, mingled with yellow, whilst all other

shores and the river were shaded by a cold gloomy tint, showing the continuous line of farms, churches and villages, ...[2]

A similar poetic tone is struck in the journals of Catharine Parr Traill, the wife of an emigrant officer who settled in the Peterborough area in the 1830s. She describes the surrounding countryside as

> ...a beautiful natural park, finely diversified with hill and dale, covered with lovely green sward, enamelled with a variety of the most exquisite flowers, and planted as if by Nature's own hand, with groups of feathery pine, oaks, balsam, poplar and silver birch. The views from these plains are delightful; which ever way you turn they are gratified by diversity of hill and dale, wood and water....[3]

In both passages, the writers show themselves to be well atuned to the Picturesque point of view. Like Sir Uvedale Price or Sir Richard Payne Knight they respond to the landscape as they would a painting by Lorrain or Poussin — a rich composition of diverse forms and colours created, as Mrs. Traill expressed it, "by Nature's own hand."

These genteel immigrants regarded the natural environment with the respect instilled in them by Picturesque values. Anna Jameson, writing in the 1830s, was appalled by the typical settler's treatment of Canada's native beauty and the ruthless destruction of its primeval forests.

> A Canadian settler *hates* a tree, regards it as his natural enemy, as something to be destroyed, eradicated, annihilated by all and any means. The idea of useful or ornamental is seldom associated here even with the most magnificent timber trees, such as among the Druids had been consecrated, and among the Greeks would have sheltered oracles and votive temples.[4]

She of course could afford to hold such idealized views of the wilds for as wife of the attorney-general to Upper Canada she could retire to the more domestic and civilized comforts offered by Toronto. Nor could she accurately be called an immigrant as she lived in Canada only a few years before returning to England. Her sentiments were nevertheless shared by those of her educated background who did settle here. Mary O'Brien, wife of a half-pay officer who settled near Shanty Bay on Lake Simcoe in the early 1830s, named her log farmhouse "Cedargrove Hall" in reference to the stand of cedars they had carefully preserved around the house.[5] The application of Picturesque principles to the Canadian backwoods was more explicitly stated by Catharine Parr Traill.

> Another plan which we mean to adopt on our land is, to leave several acres of forest in a convenient situation, and chop down and draw out old timbers for firewood, leaving the younger growth for ornament.[6]

Mrs. Jameson would no doubt have nodded with approval at this careful blend of the useful and the ornamental in landscape.

Although an appreciation for the Picturesque can be observed in the writings of these colonists of gentle birth, this taste was not always expressed in the buildings they erected for themselves. In the Canadian backwoods one does not find many Picturesque villa and cottage estates. Although many half-pay officers and their families, like the Traills or the O'Briens, took up farming in the bush, the task of clearing the land and planting a crop had to take priority over building a residence suitable for a gentleman. Many like Mrs. Traill did their best to tastefully embellish their backwoods homes by planting flower gardens and adding a verandah overgrown with climbing vines, but the primitive conditions generally only permitted the construction of a simple log structure whose form was shaped by the need for immediate shelter and bore little evidence of English concepts of the Picturesque in architectural design.[7]

While many of these middle-class settlers adapted well to this rugged life it was not suprising that many found the harsh realities of the Canadian wilderness in conflict with their original romantic vision.[8] The journal of Susanna Moodie, entitled *Roughing It in The Bush; or Life in Canada*, provides the best known account of the rude awakening to pioneer life experienced by many English gentlewomen.[9] Many such people were forced to return to England, or to immigrate to the United States, or, like the Moodies, to use their good connections to earn government appointments in one of the colonial towns.[10]

Many of these well-bred colonists opted for

the greater comforts of the more civilized parts of the country or, to use Susanna Moodie's phrase, to *Life in the Clearings.*[11] Some took up farming but not as backwoodsmen. Often they came with substantial financial resources and bought up more expensive land in areas already penetrated by an earlier generation of pioneers. In this more comfortable environment they were able to devote more of their efforts in surrounding themselves with the civilized amenities of tasteful cottages or villas with park and pleasure grounds after the English taste.

The towns of Woodstock and Cobourg and their surrounding areas of Oxford County and Northumberland-Durham counties in Ontario both provide good examples of a gentleman's farming community. In both cases the first settlers were of American origin but in the 1820s and 1830s in Cobourg and in the 1830s in Woodstock these areas attracted several "respectable" families — half-pay officers, remittance men, businessmen and professionals. In Woodstock the wave of English emigrants was inaugurated by the arrival of retired Admiral Henry Vansittart and his partner and agent ex-Captain Andrew Drew.[12] The Cobourg area, colonized by this English gentry at a slightly earlier date, was described as having a much greater concentration of wealth and fashion and gentility than any other district in Ontario in the early nineteenth century.[13] While neither of these two areas was the product of any organized settlement programme, gentlemen of rank were naturally drawn to those areas that offered social interaction with persons of their background and class. The imprint of British gentility borne by both these communities was often noted by visitors to the area. In the 1849 travel journal of Sir Richard Bonnycastle, Woodstock was described as "a thriving place, and their cottages and country houses are chiefly built and their grounds laid out in the English style."[14] The genteel quality of life in Woodstock and Cobourg was well appreciated by Upper Canadians. John Beverley Robinson, a staunch defender of conservative and aristocratic values in Upper Canada, lamented the lack of cultured society in most parts of the colony. In contrast, he saw Woodstock and Cobourg as model communities, composed of educated and respectable persons and characterized by a sense of refinement and a "proper tone" that he hoped to see established throughout Upper Canada.[15]

But the most sophisticated examples of villas and cottages of the Picturesque were concentrated in the outskirts of the major colonial towns such as Toronto and Quebec and to a lesser extent in the environs of Kingston, Montreal and Halifax. They were built for wealthy merchants, professionals and members of what was generally known as the "official set," those well-placed, influential persons who held the reins of colonial power. In Toronto in the early 1800s gentlemen of rank were sold large "park lots" which encircled the more densely populated town, first taking prime sites along the lakefront and later in the area between what is now Queen and Bloor streets.[16] Visitors to Toronto often remarked on the Picturesque and decidedly English quality of these dwellings and their park estates. According to British traveller, Frederick Marryat:

> The minute you put your foot on the shore, you feel that you are no longer in the United States; you are at once struck with the difference between English and American population, systems, and ideas.... The private houses of Toronto are built, according to the English taste and the desire of exclusiveness, away from the road, and are embowered in trees; the American, let his house be ever so large, or his plot of ground however extensive, builds within a few feet of the road, that he may see and know what is going on.[17]

Marryat's description of the fashionable residences of Toronto was equally applicable to many of the major colonial towns. In Kingston, for example, several villa and cottage estates were developed in the late 1830s and 1840s just to the west of the city, along the lakefront on King Street West. A detail taken from an 1865 plan of the city clearly depicts the general character and layout of these properties (Fig. 17). Residences such as Bellevue (Fig. 65) and its attached Hales's Cottages (Fig. 50), Saint Helen's (Mortonwood) (Fig. 71) and Sunnyside (Fig. 70) were all set away from the road and embowered by trees to create that sense of exclusiveness that Marryat had observed in Toronto.

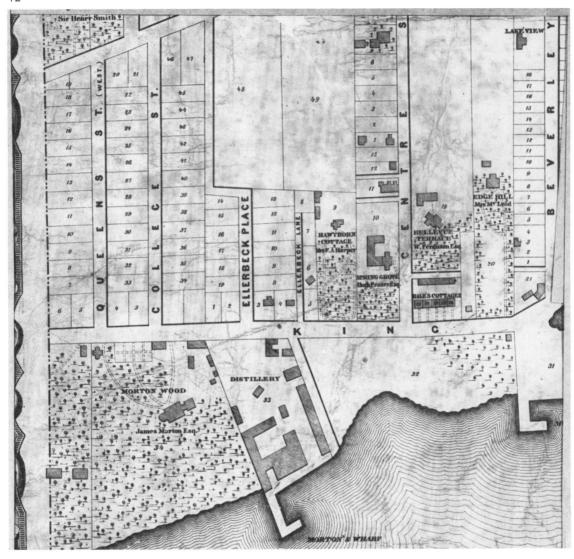

17. Detail from a Plan of Kingston, Ontario

Surveyed by John Innes in 1865. This compact grouping of villas and cottages dating primarily from the late 1830s and 1840s was located in the area referred to as the "Western Liberties," Kingston's most fashionable residential district of the mid-nineteenth century. In the early decades of the century men of wealth had lived in the city, either above their offices or in separate residences nearby. By the late 1830s it had become the fashion for members of the Kingston elite to set themselves up in the healthy, pastoral environment offered by spacious suburban estates. In this era of cholera epidemics it was considered desirable to escape the more crowded urban areas where the risk of disease was greater; moreover, by separating the place of work from the place of residence, they were able to cultivate a more aristocratic image as gentlemen of leisure and of independent means. (Public Archives Canada, National Map Collection, V1/440-Kingston-1865)

In Quebec, the major governmental centre for Lower Canada, there was also a large concentration of elegant villa and cottage estates which dated from the late eighteenth and the first half of the nineteenth centuries.[18] As in Toronto these dwellings were built mostly by the English colonial elite although some did belong to native "canadiens," whose education and social standing gained them entrance into the upper levels of the colonial hierarchy. The geographic distribution of these Picturesque dwellings was more concentrated than in Toronto, a result of being forced to build around an already well-developed city. Many villas and cottages could be found in the suburban communities of Ste-Foy, Sillery (Fig. 18) and Beauport. The most prestigious estates were located along Saint-Louis Road between the Plains of Abraham and Cap-Rouge. The

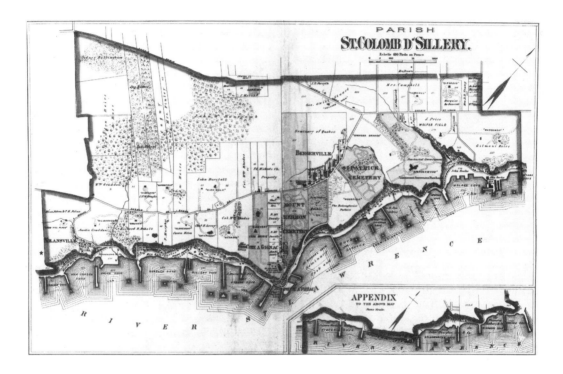

18. Plan of Sillery, Quebec

Surveyed by H.W. Hopkins in 1879. From the end of the eighteenth century the community of Sillery was one of the most popular and exclusive residential areas for the wealthy gentlefolk of Quebec. It was within easy commuting distance from the city yet it offered a retired rural environment enhanced by its magnificent setting on top of the high cliffs overlooking the St. Lawrence River. Its main road, Saint-Louis Road, was lined with some of Canada's most elegant suburban estates such as Spencer Wood (Fig. 79), Spencer Grange (Fig. 93), Benmore (Fig. 90), and Kirk Ella (Fig. 97). Although this map dates from 1879 little would have changed from pre-1850, and it provides an explicit illustration of the extent and layout of the Picturesque estates occupied by the Quebec élite. The residences, always set well back from the road, were partially obscured from view to the casual passerby by the screen of trees in front. Often a lodge marked the entrance to the long curving roadway which led up to the house at an oblique angle to create the shifting, picturesque viewpoints of the house rather than a static image created by a formal central avenue. (Public Archives Canada, National Map Collection)

desirability of this location was determined by its spectacular setting on top of the cliffs overlooking the St. Lawrence River. Again this characteristic distribution is well illustrated by an 1872 plan of Sillery.

The villa and cottage dweller's delight in wooded, elevated sites, which provided broad vistas with a degree of privacy, was a recurring theme of villa and cottage building. In Montreal the south slope of Mount Royal naturally formed the most exclusive residential area. In 1843 James Silk Buckingham described this area as "well wooded over the greatest part of its extent, and its side toward the Saint Lawrence is dotted with many beautiful villas and gardens, which add much to the charm of the landscape, while the view from its summit is extensive and picturesque in the extreme."[19]

In Halifax, the major military and colonial centre for the Maritime colonies, the pattern of suburban development echoed that of its western neighbours. During the first half of the nineteenth century clusters of gentlemen's residences situated within a comfortable distance of the city sprung up either along the Bedford Basin or in the area known as the North West Arm.

These suburban environments offered the ideal compromise between the peaceful pastoral repose of the countryside and the civilized amenities of the city. While close enough to the comforts and safety of the urban environment these patrons of the Picturesque were free to dabble in their voyeuristic delight in nature as seen from the cool comfort of their verandahs or front lawns. Their Picturesque gardens provided a buffer against the harsh realities of the bush and the noisy bustle of the towns.

REGIONAL STUDIES IN THE PICTURESQUE

Picturesque architecture flourished in a suburban or at least in a cultivated rural environment, but more importantly, being a taste identified with the educated, middle-and upper-class colonial from Britain, it flourished in areas that attracted significant concentrations of immigrants drawn from this social group. Ontario was the most popular area of settlement for this group and it was here the Picturesque influence was most prevalent. In other parts of the country architectural expressions of the Picturesque can be found but the influence of other building traditions, namely French in Quebec and American in the Maritimes, both limited and modified the impact of this taste on the character of domestic architecture. For this reason Picturesque villas and cottages will be examined within the context of their particular regions, beginning with Ontario where the Picturesque taste manifested itself in its purest and most sophisticated form and then turning to regional variations found in Quebec and the Atlantic provinces.

Ontario: 1790 to 1830

In terms of architectural tastes Upper Canada was the most British of all the North American colonies, an inevitable result of a substantial British element in the population. Of course the first waves of immigrants to Upper Canada originated from the United States, being either United Empire Loyalists or simply Americans drawn north by the promise of cheap land, bringing their own native building styles based on a colonial classical tradition. While the American element was to remain an important factor in Upper Canada building, contemporary British tastes in architecture became more and more prevalent in the early 1800s as the flow of population from the south diminished and British immigration picked up.

The changing tide became particularly evident after the Napoleonic Wars (1803-15). The British Colonial Office, fearing the colony was being overrun by an unsavoury "democratic" element which would eventually undermine British social order, tried to discourage immigration from the American Republic.[1] Instead the much needed settlers would be drawn from the surplus British population created by the economic depression of the post-war years — a population they felt would be loyal to British rule.[2] These immigrants settled in all parts of British North America but the majority preferred the vast unsettled areas of Upper Canada which, according to the numerous emigrant guides of the period, offered the most comfortable climate, whose political stability was not threatened by the French presence and where the recent emigrant would, as one author explains, "meet thousands of our countrymen ... with all the feelings, habits, tastes, etc. of British subjects, living under the protection of British Laws, and having all the privileges of Commerce which are possessed by us."[3]

Although the most sophisticated expressions of the Picturesque point of view in Ontario domestic architecture belong to the 1830s and 1840s, elements of this taste can be identified as early as the 1790s. In 1796 the lieutenant-governor of Upper Canada, John Graves Simcoe, built a small log cottage called Castle Frank in the form of a classical temple featuring four unpeeled logs which functioned as columns to support the pedimented gable roof (Fig. 19). Although this strict classicism cannot be interpreted in terms of Picturesque values in architectural design, it does illustrate sentiments fundamental to the Picturesque, namely the delight in romantic setting and the idea of the rural retreat. Its elevated site on the brow of a steep bank on the edge of the Don Valley provided a broad vista over the landscape and beyond to Lake Ontario.[4] While the property was not extensively landscaped, the Simcoes took advantage of the native beauty of the wooded setting to visually enframe the little structure thereby creating a picturesque composition of landscape and architecture. Not only was this setting pleasing to the eye but its rugged natural environment evoked a sense of a rustic retreat into the wilderness. Out of sight and sound of the town, the Simcoe family and friends could make weekend escapes from the small community of York (Toronto) and immerse themselves in the splendours of Canada's primeval forests.

Castle Frank did not appear to have any immediate descendants in Upper Canada, but by the 1810s and 1820s and the first influx of gentlemen colonists from Britain new domestic building forms appeared. Their residences related to Castle Frank in terms of their taste for quiet retreats in romantic landscapes but the designs were quite unlike the formal classical temple plan of Castle Frank. In this early period the educated British gentleman built plain, functional structures almost devoid of any identifiable stylistic reference.

One of the most common design types of this period can be identified as the cottage or more accurately the *cottage orné* type, the term being used, as it was in England, to refer to rural residences of small and humble appearance occupied by persons of refined manners and habits. The Wilderness, a small cottage built for Colonel Daniel Claus, provides a very simple example of this common mode typified by its simple rectangular form, one or one and a half storeys high (Fig. 20). Roofs were generally hipped although straight gable roofs did appear as in Samuel Ridout's cottage of Roselands in Toronto (Fig. 21). In either case the roof pitch was gentle, accentuating the low profile of the building. The facade tended towards a symmetrical arrangement although residences such as The Wilderness or Major Hillier's Cottage in Toronto did not bow to this convention (Fig. 22).

Verandahs, placed either along the main facade or partially or fully encircling the building as illustrated by William Cayley's cottage of Drumsnab in Toronto or Colonel By's residence in Ottawa, were common features of the period (Figs 23, 25). Their roofs were supported by plain posts or, as in the case of Major Hillier's cottage or Roselands, supported by rough patterns of treillage. An umbrage, a shelter created by a recess in the wall, featured on the cottage called Charles Place in Kingston, offered an unusual variation of the verandah form (Fig. 26).

Contrary to Picturesque values for light and vista, windows tended to be small in these early cottages. Charles Place with its large sash windows, the French windows on Drumsnab, and the bay windows seen on both Drumsnab and the cottage Inverarden at Cornwall (Fig. 27) were atypical of the period. The widespread popularity of these window forms belongs to the 1830s.

19. Castle Frank in 1796, Toronto, Ontario; Constructed 1796; Demolished; Material log
Drawn by Mrs. John Graves Simcoe. Castle Frank, named after John Graves Simcoe's youngest
son, Francis, was a square log structure overlooking the Don Valley just south of present-day Bloor
Street. Its classical temple design with a front pediment supported by four unpeeled logs was
perhaps intended as a literal translation of the Vitruvian and Neoclassical theory of the primitive
hut stating that the elements of classical architecture, such as the column, had originated in
natural forms, such as the tree trunk. Primitive man had simply borrowed these elements from
nature in constructing his crude shelter. The Picturesque qualities of Castle Frank were well
appreciated by Mrs. Simcoe who sketched this scene on several occasions. (Archives of Ontario)

20. The Wilderness, 407 King Street, Niagara-on-the-Lake, Ontario
Constructed 1816-17; Material stucco
The Wilderness, a long, low rectangular structure (the right wing being a later addition), differed
little in design from small British military buildings found throughout the early nineteenth century
Empire. Unlike military buildings, however, its light stucco walls, large windows along the front
facade, canopied French window on the side elevation and its garden setting in an open glade with
an informal arrangement of shrubs, flowers and overhanging trees create a cheerful, relaxed
atmosphere which defined the Picturesque cottage. (Canadian Inventory of Historic Building)

21. Roselands in the Nineteenth Century, Queen Street East, Toronto, Ontario
Constructed 1808; **Demolished** ca. 1880; **Material** log sheathed in clapboard
Roselands, set well back from Queen Street and bounded by Seaton and Sherbourne streets, was one of those 200-acre park estates sold to gentlemen of rank in Toronto. In this case the owner was Samuel Ridout, a member of a prominent Loyalist family, who served as sheriff of the Home District from 1815 to 1827 and later as registrar of York County. A log structure finished by an outer sheathing of clapboard, its rough, unpolished appearance indicated the still primitive, pioneer conditions of life in Toronto in the early 1800s. Its low-lying profile, verandah, and crude patterns of treillage, however, suggest an embryonic version of the *cottage orné*. (Metropolitan Toronto Library Board)

22. Major Hillier's Cottage, Front Street West, Toronto, Ontario
Constructed pre-1808; **Demolished** ca. 1840; **Material** wood
Situated on the northeast corner of Front and Bay streets, this one-storey wooden building was, according to Toronto historian John Ross Robertson, built for the Honourable Peter Russell sometime before 1808 but was generally known as Major Hillier's Cottage in reference to a later occupant, Major Hillier, who served as aide-de-camp to Lieutenant-Governor Sir Peregrine Maitland from 1818 to 1828. Although a plain, undistinguished residence, elements such as its treillaged verandah, pretty retired setting with a picket fence, flower beds and overshadowing trees, and its gentlemanly occupants justified its 1808 description as an ornamental cottage. (Metropolitan Toronto Library Board)

23. Drumsnab ca. 1845, 5 Castle Frank Crescent, Toronto, Ontario
Constructed 1830; **Material** stone and stucco

24. Drumsnab after alterations

Now engulfed by the wealthy residential neighbourhood of Rosedale, Drumsnab was situated on a 118-acre estate overlooking the Don Valley not far from the site of Castle Frank. At one time the cottage was approached via a long private road marked at the entrance by a small lodge which the owner, William Cayley, a gentleman artist, used as his studio. A one-storey cottage, it featured verandahs on three sides and an off-centre bay window on the south facade which, according to an 1849 description by James Alexander, offered a long vista of Lake Ontario which had been "cut judiciously through the forest." The French windows with their slender, off-centre mullions or glazing bars were a common motif in Picturesque architecture. Although one of Toronto's oldest surviving residences, Drumsnab has been much altered by the addition of a second storey in 1850 and the rebuilding of the verandah and construction of a kitchen wing in 1874. (Fig. 23, Metropolitan Toronto Library Board; Fig. 24, Canadian Inventory of Historic Building)

25. Colonel By's Cottage in 1827, Nepean Point, Ottawa, Ontario
Constructed 1826-27; **Material** stone

Detail from drawing by Lt.-Col. By, 20 November 1827. In the fall of 1826 Lieutenant-Colonel John By of the Royal Engineers arrived at the mouth of the Rideau River to supervise the construction of the Rideau Canal which would eventually link Lake Ontario with the Ottawa River. The one-and-a-half-storey stone residence he built for himself at his own expense adopted a design similar to that of the Commissioner's Residence at the Point Frederick Naval Dockyards in Kingston. But despite this physical likeness the overall impression and atmosphere imparted by these two structures were not at all alike. As is evident from two descriptions of Colonel By Cottage in the 1830s, one by Captain J.E. Alexander and the other by Captain Joseph Bouchette, the addition of "a rustic verandah and trellis work" to the residence and its romantic setting on top of a "bold eminence" which provided splendid views over the "broken and wild shores opposite" and of the "tumultuous streams" of the Ottawa River below was able to transform this structure from a functional military barrack into a "handsome *cottage orné*." (Royal Ontario Museum)

26. Charles Place, 75 Lower Union Street, Kingston, Ontario
Constructed 1820-32; **Material** stone

This snug low-lying cottage with its large sash windows is notable for its sensitive handling of the masonry in which the smooth dressed limestone of the trim contrasts with the rough stone of the walls creating an interesting and varied surface texture. Charles Place also provides a rare example of a recessed porch or umbrage in cottage building. This feature was never very popular in Canada, perhaps because it demanded a more complex and therefore less economical plan or perhaps because, being sheltered on three sides, it cut off the cool breezes which must have been a major attraction of the more popular projecting verandah. The Gothic dormer was added in the 1840s. (Canadian Inventory of Historic Building)

27. Inverarden, Cornwall, Ontario; Constructed 1816; **Material** stone and stucco

John McDonald was one of several wealthy fur traders of the Northwest Company who retired to the predominantly Scottish areas of eastern Ontario. McDonald's cottage, known generally by its late nineteenth century name, Inverarden, but referred to by McDonald himself as "Gart," overlooks the St. Lawrence River just east of the town of Cornwall. Originally the cottage consisted only of the central one-and-a-half-storey block. The two octagonal wings were added around 1821. Both periods of construction feature the small windows characteristic of pre-1830 *cottage orné* design. In 1972 Inverarden was purchased and restored by Parks Canada and later turned over to the municipality of Cornwall who operates it as a public museum. (Parks Canada)

A second category of building introduced by the British colonist is illustrated by buildings such as Stamford Park near Niagara Falls, Government House and Davenport in Toronto, and The Poplars in Cobourg (Figs 28-31). Although similar to the *cottage orné*, this type was composed of two or two and a half storeys with a low hipped roof, stucco sheathing and usually a verandah. They were built generally by the upper echelons of colonial society as their more imposing appearance would suggest. Because of their larger scale and more polished character these buildings could be described as villas as opposed to the more informal character implied by the term "cottage."

28. Stamford Park in the Nineteenth Century, Niagara Falls, Ontario
Constructed 1822-26; **Demolished; Material** brick with wood sheathing

In 1822 Sir Peregrine Maitland, lieutenant-governor of Upper Canada from 1818 to 1828, purchased this fifty-one-acre property in Stamford Township approximately four miles from Niagara Falls. Here he built this summer retreat. At one time a great social centre, Stamford Park was much admired for its fine views and landscaped parklands. This early drawing of the estate, depicting ladies and their gentlemen escorts out for a leisurely stroll over the wooded grounds or along the shaded verandah, captures the atmosphere of gracious gentility amid cultivated wilderness that characterized an English gentleman's estate. Although discussed in this study as an early example of villa building, there was some discrepancy over the appropriate label applied to this building. While in 1833 Anna Jameson saw it as an "elegant, well-furnished English villa" both Maitland himself and an earlier visitor, Lieutenant de Roos, referred to it as a cottage. This inconsistency in terminology was not unusual in Picturesque jargon for the distinction between a cottage and a villa was as much determined by the impression created on the viewer as by its architectural attributes. (Metropolitan Toronto Library Board)

29. Government House in 1854, King Street West, Toronto, Ontario
Constructed pre-1815; **Demolished** 1862; **Material** wood and stucco

Watercolour by Owen Staples based on a lithograph of 1854. Although originally constructed for John Elmsley this building was taken over in 1815 by the colonial government for use as the lieutenant-governor's residence. At this time £2000 worth of renovations and repairs were carried out which must have amounted to an almost complete rebuilding of the structure. According to an 1827 description and plan, Government House, located on a five-acre lot at the corner of King and Simcoe streets, was a large, wooden, two-storey structure with a low kitchen wing to the west and a verandah on the south and east elevations. In 1836 an outer sheathing of stucco was applied. In 1838 a large addition thirty by fifty feet containing a ballroom was added and numerous other alterations were carried out according to the designs of Toronto architect John Howard. From this drawing, which dates after the 1838 addition, it is not clear which wing was the original, for Howard's design adhered closely to the simple character of the earlier sections. Despite repeated attempts to build a more commanding gubernatorial residence, this building served as Government House until 1862. (Metropolitan Toronto Library Board)

30. Davenport in the Nineteenth Century, Toronto, Ontario
Constructed ca. 1821; **Demolished** ca. 1913

Lieutenant-Colonel Joseph Wells, first resident of Davenport, provides a good example of a wealthy, well-connected, ex-military gentleman who immigrated to Canada in the post-Napoleonic period. After serving in the Peninsular Wars, Wells was posted to Upper Canada as inspecting field officer of the militia. Recognizing the potential of the new colony he petitioned the colonial government as early as 1817 for the 1200 acres of undeveloped land to which a retired officer of his rank was entitled. Wells, being a man of some personal wealth, did not settle on a backwoods farm but instead sought out the more amenable surroundings of Toronto where in 1821 he purchased his estate of Davenport on the northwestern outskirts of the city. Possessing suitable credentials — position, money and connections — he easily gained entry into Upper Canada's official set, being appointed to both the legislative and executive councils. (Metropolitan Toronto Library Board)

31. The Poplars, 18 Spencer Street East, Cobourg, Ontario
Constructed 1827; **Material** wood and stucco

Supposedly a house had existed on this site before 1820, but this particular building was built in 1827 for John Spencer, a Loyalist and the first sheriff of Northumberland County. In many respects its design marks a transitional period between the simpler, more functional villas of the 1810s and 1820s and the more sophisticated expressions of the 1830s. The compact rectangularity of form characteristic of the early villa has been avoided by the addition of two one-storey bow windows, a feature advocated in the literature of the Picturesque both for its light-collecting properties and as a means of adding variety to the wall planes. Unlike the later bow-windowed villas, in which the curved or broken planes flowed easily into the flat surfaces, the bow windows on The Poplars seem too squat and heavy for the facade and appear to be an afterthought rather than an integral part of the design. (Canadian Inventory of Historic Building)

The division of these buildings into two separate categories — the *cottage orné* and the villa — is to some extent artificial. Although these terms were not synonomous there was always a certain degree of ambiguity in their usage. For example, Stamford Park was described by one author in 1826 as being in the cottage style[5] while in 1833 it was described by another visitor as an elegant English villa.[6]

As in Britain the distinction between these two types was defined more by the impression created in the viewer's mind rather than by any specific design characteristics. But, because Picturesque architecture in Canada seems to fall generally into two main design types — the small one-storey building, suggestive of the modest character of the *cottage orné*, and the larger, two-storey residence with its greater air of elegance and refinement associated with the villa – these general categories will be maintained.

The design of these early villas and cottages only slightly resembles the domestic architecture of the Picturesque found in Britain. In the villa type one can identify a vague stylistic affiliation with the English villa in a Regular style with its verandah and stucco walls, although at this point they were still fairly austere, conservative structures very much tied to an eighteenth century British classical tradition.

The *cottage orné*, on the other hand, seems less dependant on cottage types as they developed in England. The traditional medieval house with its irregular plan and thatched roof, which provided the most important model for cottage design in England, was not immediately absorbed into Canadian domestic architecture. Perhaps the colonies lacked the skilled craftsmen able to build in these traditional techniques or perhaps the middle-class colonial rejected a design type that evoked such strong associations with the labouring classes.

Instead the low, hipped roof *cottage orné* of the Canadian landscape seems to have been borrowed from the type of British military building found throughout the British colonies. The drawing of the Naval Dockyards in Kingston of 1815 (Fig. 32) dpicts a low, one-storey structure with a hipped roof and full encircling verandah similar to many of the cottages examined. Many similar wood, stone or brick structures used as guardhouses, barracks or hospitals were erected in the early nineteenth century. Military establishments in Quebec, Ottawa, Toronto, Fort Malden in Amherstburg and Fort George in Niagara-on-the-Lake all included examples of this building type. While these plain functional buildings were not Picturesque in themselves, this basic design was adopted by British colonials as a suitable architectural ornament for their Picturesque garden estates. As many of these cottage owners were active or retired military or colonial officers it is not surprising they should imitate this type. They would have been familiar with its design and construction; moreover, its association with the British military institutions rendered it a suitable model for those who considered themselves leaders of the colonial establishment.

It is perhaps difficult for us to appreciate these villas and cottages as products of the Picturesque because these simple designs seem far removed from the fanciful eclecticism of the British pattern books of the Regency period in England. But the fact that an early visitor to Ottawa referred to Colonel By's residence as a *cottage orné*[7] and Major Hillier's house was advertised for sale in 1808 as an "ornamental cottage,"[8] terms familiar to the Picturesque Movement, indicates that these unpretentious buildings created a different impression on contemporary observers than they do on us.

Elements such as the stucco sheathing or the occasional use of a French or bay window all belonged to the architectural paraphernalia of the Picturesque. But the most important building element that contributed to the perception of these modest dwellings as expressive of the Picturesque was the verandah, a form that to the early nineteenth century mind held great visual appeal and strong associational values.

There has been much speculation about the origins of this form.[9] Did it originate from India, as suggested by the British pattern books, or was it introduced to North America from Portugal via its colonies in the West Indies?[10] To further complicate the question of origin travellers to Upper Canada in the 1790s noted sheltered galleries on many dwellings which they referred to by the Dutch word "stoop."[11] While the British colonial network was no doubt largely responsible for the dissemination of this form throughout its colonies, an answer to the question of its source requires further research. The problem of derivation does not hinder this study for what is more relevant to our understanding of the popularity of the verandah is how it was interpreted by the people who built them.

To the patrons of the Picturesque the verandah was a basic ingredient in the "picturesquizing" of their villas and cottages. The idea of creating a spatial bridge between interior and exterior advocated by Humphry Repton was well appreciated by Upper Canadian colonials. Basil Hall, a Royal Naval officer stationed in Upper Canada, describes the delightful aspects of the verandah.

From this apartment (living-room) a single step placed one on a verandah, as

32. **Commissioner's Residence in 1815, Naval Dockyard, Point Frederick, Kingston, Ontario**
Constructed pre-1815; **Demolished; Material** wood; watercolour by Emeric Essex Vidal
Point Frederick, now the site of the Royal Military College at Kingston, was occupied by the
Royal Naval Dockyards from 1789 to 1837. As seen from this drawing there was nothing
picturesque about the dockyard setting of the commissioner's residence nor was there anything
self-consciously picturesque in its design. This building type could have been found on British
military bases throughout the early nineteenth century Empire. The verandah was, at least in
Canada, an added amenity usually, although not exclusively, reserved for the officers' residences
or barracks. But when this design was lifted from an unflattering construction yard environment
and set down amid a romantic park setting, ornamented with flower gardens, climbing vines and
perhaps dressed with a bit of treillage, this functional military structure was easily transformed
into a pretty *cottage orné*. (Reproduced with permission of the Commandant of Royal Military
College of Canada)

wide as the room bound in front and both
ends by trellis work so thickly twined
with hop vines, that the sun, and that
still more troublesome intruder, the
blazing glare of the red sky, had no
chance for admission, while the breeze
from the garden easily made its way
through.[12]

Visually the verandah added variety to the
exterior of these otherwise plain structures.
As Catharine Parr Traill explained, it not only
provided a "sort of outer room" but concealed
"the rough logs" and broke up "the barn-like
form of the building" while giving "a pretty
rural look to the poorest log house."[13] While
pre-1830 villas and cottages were almost

always composed of flat wall planes, the projecting verandah with its thin post supports cast interesting patterns of light and shadow across the surface, an effect accentuated by the reflective qualities of a roughcast or stucco wall. Ideally climbing vines grew up the post or treillage supports, establishing a concrete link between landscape and architecture and adding a touch of rustic charm to the building.

Equally important to the appreciation of the verandah was its associational value. Our present confusion over the origin of this form stems largely from the rather confused associations held by people who built them. To Anna Jameson a rambling log house near Woodstock which featured wide open galleries reminded her of "an African village — a sort of Timbuctoo set down in the woods."[14] To Captain Basil Hall the verandah brought forth associations with "the sultry winds of the Hindustan."[15] Mary O'Brien, although rather dubious about the addition of a verandah to her house, clearly expressed the colonial's exotic associations with this form:

> Our verandah is covered in and we are in the most picturesque gloom .... Edward says it is delightful; I am not quite sure. He says it is like a West Indian House, I say that is not English.[16]

Whether read as an African, Indian or West Indian feature clearly the verandah conjured up visions of places remote and lent a touch of the romantic to a dwelling.

The most important factor in these colonials' perception of the Picturesque qualities of their villas and cottages was the character of the landscape setting. To appreciate the Picturesque frame of mind one must first learn to view these buildings not as isolated objects, but as integral parts of a landscape. While the buildings themselves may have been plain when seen in the context of their natural environment, or as in Sir Richard Payne Knight's words "Mixed and blended — a mere component of what you see," a visual composition of varied and irregular forms, textures and lights and shadows, true to Picturesque principles, is created. Although it is impossible to recreate accurately these landscape settings as they originally appeared because most of these estates have either been altered or have disappeared entirely, we can determine general characteristics of their landscape settings from the few that have survived intact and from contemporary descriptions and drawings.

As noted in Castle Frank, these colonial gentlemen delighted in wild and romantic settings which could imbue even the plainest building with a sense of the Picturesque. Especially popular were those well-wooded, elevated spots, preferably on the edge of steep embankments providing broad vistas of the countryside. It was certainly not convenience that led Colonel Wells to build Davenport on the edge of a steep slope with a spectacular view over Lake Ontario. Similarly, William Cayley built Drumsnab on the eastern side of Toronto overlooking the Don Valley, a setting described in 1849 as "the most picturesque spot near Toronto".[17] At the other end of the province Colonel By chose the rugged grandeur of the high cliffs at Nepean Point for the site of his *cottage orné*. Even today, the views from this spot of the Chaudière Falls and the Ottawa Valley are unparalleled.

The most frequently described and highly praised setting of the 1820s was Stamford Park, the summer residence of Sir Peregrine Maitland, lieutenant-governor of Upper Canada. Although far from Lake Ontario, its elevated site was said to offer a panorama of the Niagara River, Lake Ontario and the distant high grounds of Upper Canada. The romance of this spot was further enhanced by its proximity (approximately four miles) to nature's masterpiece of the Sublime, Niagara Falls. To add a civilized touch to his estate Maitland laid out gravel walks, ornamental gardens and a long driveway while reverently preserving a "magnificent grove of venerable oaks" said to provide the principal feature of the foreground.[18] When Anna Jameson visited the property in 1836 she wrote that she was "altogether enchanted" with the estate which she praised for "combining our ideas of an elegant, well furnished English villa and ornamented grounds, with some of the grandest and wildest features of the forest scene."[19] The introduction of artificial landscape features while preserving the native beauties of the settings expresses a fundamental sentiment of the Picturesque.

Stamford Park was a sophisticated example of a villa estate with few counterparts in Upper Canada before 1830 with the possible exceptions of Government House and a few other large villas in the Toronto area. Although the majority of the early Picturesque cottages and villas did not possess such elaborate landscape schemes nor had the advantage of such romantic settings, almost all were set in spacious park lots. While part of the estate may have been under agricultural cultivation, the area immediately surrounding the residence was usually conceived according to English landscape tastes with trees and shrubs preserved or planted in an informal pattern about the dwelling.

Perhaps the best surviving example of an early cottage in a landscape is The Wilderness. Set back from the road the cottage is seen nestled amid a growth of trees and shrubs. Its low horizontal emphasis, a common characteristic of these Picturesque cottages, visually meshes the building into its environment rather than rising above it, thereby accentuating the integration of architecture and landscape.

This early period represented an embryonic phase in the development of the Picturesque taste in Upper Canadian domestic architecture. Generally the product of local builders or of the owners themselves, these early villas and cottages were characterized by simple functional designs rooted in vernacular colonial traditions. To mask the rough, unrefined appearance of their homes, pre-1830 villa and cottage dwellers relied primarily on the romantic character of the setting and on a few easily applied details, such as the verandah, to imbue their dwellings with a sense of the Picturesque.

Ontario: Post-1830

By the 1830s the rough pioneer character of Upper Canada was being transformed into a more permanent, more highly developed community. Emigration from Britain rose sharply during this period resulting in the expansion of the frontier and the transformation of small colonial settlements into bustling towns and cities.[20] More construction was being carried out and the availability of better materials and the presence of skilled craftsmen meant that a better quality of building was being constructed. But the most important factor contributing to the growing sophistication of colonial architecture was the arrival of the British-trained architect. Men like John George Howard, George Browne and Daniel Charles Wetherell who had grown up and been trained amid the writings and works of Sir Richard Payne Knight, Sir Uvedale Price, Humphry Repton, John Nash and John Soane all immigrated to Canada during the 1830s. As their architecture will attest, they were capable of providing their colonial patrons with fashionable designs according to popular English tastes.

In terms of the *cottage orné* the transition between the early period and the more advanced expressions of the 1830s is most markedly illustrated by Colborne Lodge in Toronto (Fig. 33). Designed in 1836 by John George Howard as his own residence, Colborne Lodge in its design, plan and setting and the integration and interaction of these elements epitomized Picturesque values in the architecture of the *cottage orné*.[21]

A suburban residence on the western outskirts of Toronto, Colborne Lodge, like many of its *cottage orné* predecessors in Canada, was situated on elevated ground overlooking Lake Ontario. The large estate, known as High Park, was devoted mainly to agricultural development but the area immediately surrounding the cottage featured a well-wooded landscaped park. Unfortunately, twentieth century improvers have removed much of the vegetation around the building, no doubt out of respect for Howard's design; however, its present denuded appearance is not in keeping with Howard's original intentions. A late nineteenth century photograph depicts the building in a more sympathetic and picturesque environment - embowered by overhanging trees with lush vines thickly entwined around the verandah so that landscape and architecture become inseparable elements (Fig. 34).

Typical of cottage architecture, Colborne Lodge maintains a low-lying profile and features a wide verandah and French windows, standard elements in the Upper Canadian *cottage orné* of the 1830s and later. The desire for a balance between simplicity and variety expressed in literature of the Picturesque was well appreciated by Howard. The wall received little architectural embellishment beyond a simple band of moulding around the doors and windows. A sense of variety in form and outline is achieved by the manipulation of these simple planes and forms created by the projecting octagonal front and raised second storey with its overhanging eaves and exposed rafters. The liveliness of the silhouette is further enhanced by the tall decorative chimneys.

The most revolutionary aspect of Colborne Lodge is the co-ordination of the interior plan to the character of the site (Fig. 35). While the facade is symmetrical, the typical centre-hall plan, so entrenched in the Georgian sense of architectural decorum, was abandoned in favour of an inconspicuous side entrance. By adopting such an arrangement, the long centre hall was eliminated. It was replaced by a large front living room on the southern facade which led directly onto the verandah via large French windows and which benefited from all the advantages of both sun and vista.

John Howard also attempted to import the traditional medieval cottage which had so charmed English tastes for the Picturesque. Around 1836 he produced a design for a rustic cottage which featured pointed-arch windows, half-timbering, tall decorative chimneys and a multiplicity of gables (Fig. 36). Only the thatched roof is lacking. For Canada, Ridout Cottage was in advance of its time and probably for this reason never built. Designs of such a strong medieval character generally did not become popular in Canada until the late 1840s and 1850s and the advent of the Gothic Revival style. In 1836 only the mildest Gothic flavour was palatable to Upper Canadian tastes. Howard's design for a pair of gate lodges in Toronto which featured pointed-arch windows applied to the symmetrical one-storey cottage type was more acceptable to his conservative clientele (Fig. 37).

Both Colborne Lodge and Ridout Cottage represent the work of an architect capable of working comfortably in any of the popular modes found in England. But neither of these buildings were typical of Upper Canadian cottage architecture. As will be seen repeatedly the immigrant architect was versatile in a wide range of Picturesque styles but he was continually restricted by the conservative tastes of his colonial patrons.

The typical post-1830 *cottage orné* adopted a much less ambitious design based on its cottage predecessors of the 1810s and 1820s.

Similar to the earlier cottage this type was defined by a low, one-storey block, but by the 1830s features such as the low hipped roof, verandah and French window, which had previously appeared only sporadically, became mandatory ingredients of the *cottage orné*. Woodale in Dundas, the Andrew Drew Cottage in Woodstock and Ridgewood Park near Goderich are classic examples (Figs 38–41).

Like Colborne Lodge these cottages were characterized by a general restraint in architectural detailing. The walls, whether stucco or stone, or less frequently wood or brick, were treated as smooth unbroken surfaces almost devoid of any extraneous architectural embellishment as was appropriate to the simple unpretentious character of the cottage. Unlike Colborne Lodge, however, these buildings rarely deviated from the conservative symmetrical three-bay facade with a centre-door/centre-hall plan. Occasionally, elongated chimneys were employed to enliven the skyline, as at Ridgewood Park near Goderich, but these functional forms lacked the fanciful sculptural quality of the Colborne Lodge chimneys.

As in the earlier cottage, the verandah provided the essential Picturesque touch to these otherwise plain buildings. The most common type of verandah, illustrated by Woodale in Dundas, consisted of a gently flared roof supported by thin posts linked by suspended arch motifs. A unique example is Riverest at l'Orignal which employed a suspended trefoil motif to echo the profile of its Venetian windows (Fig. 42). Treillage supports, as seen on Oswald House in Niagara Falls, characterized by light crisscrossing members in a geometric pattern offered a popular alternative to the plainer post supports (Fig. 43). Because of the flimsy construction of this element, few treillaged verandahs survive into this century. The only example of a design employing tree-trunk supports, a feature popular in England, appeared in an 1835 plan by John Howard for a cottage in West Oxford near Woodstock — an avant-garde solution which, typically, was never carried out (Fig. 44).

Usually the flared-roof verandah was treated as a separate element from the straight pitch of the low, hipped roof. This, however, was not true of John Howard's cottage designs, which generally opted for a

(cont. p. 68)

33. Colborne Lodge, High Park, Toronto, Ontario; Constructed 1836
Architect John George Howard; **Material** stucco

John Howard (1803-90) was trained in London in the office of John Grayson, architect, and in 1824 he entered the office of William Ford, later becoming a partner. By 1832, however, business was falling off and Howard, armed with a portfolio of drawings and London credentials, decided to try his luck in Upper Canada. There he met with immediate success. Within a year of his arrival he had been appointed drawing master of Upper Canada College and was able to write back to England that he could not possibly leave York as business was too good and that there was "upwards of one hundred houses for me to build next summer." During Howard's early years in Toronto he was occupied almost entirely with meeting the housing demands of Toronto's wealthy establishment. In his later years (from approximately 1850), he became increasingly involved with his duties as city surveyor and with major public and commercial commissions. Little of Howard's residential work remains but fortunately Colborne Lodge, Howard's own country residence and one of his most distinctive designs, has survived with both building and grounds intact. The original Colborne Lodge consisted of only the present ground storey. Around 1843 Howard raised the tall decorative chimney and inserted a second storey creating a design similar in its lively silhouette to John B. Papworth's design for a *cottage orné* published in 1818 (Fig. 10). The rear two-storey addition was built in 1855. On Howard's death in 1890 the entire estate was bequeathed to the city of Toronto who converted the grounds into a public park and the house into a museum. Although the setting has lost some of its picturesque wildness and atmosphere of rustic seclusion, Colborne Lodge still provides a rare opportunity to appreciate Canada's early Picturesque architecture in its original landscape. (Fig. 33, Canadian Inventory of Historic Building; Figs 34, 35, Archives of Ontario)

34. Colborne Lodge in the Late Nineteenth Century

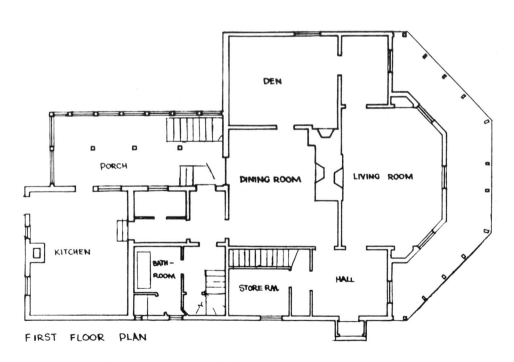

FIRST FLOOR PLAN

35. Ground Plan of Colborne Lodge After Additions

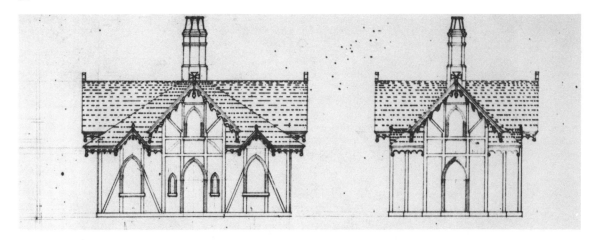

36. Plan for a Rustic Cottage; Drawn 1830s; **Architect** John George Howard

37. Sketch of a Gate Lodge to Upper Canada College in 1885, Queen Street West, Toronto, Ontario; Constructed 1834; **Demolished; Architect** John George Howard

This design for a half-timbered rustic cottage (Fig. 36) was reworked by Howard on several occasions throughout his early career, yet none was ever built. Although this plan is unidentified it probably dates from the mid-1830s as in 1836 he produced a similar but much enlarged version for a cottage for Joseph Ridout of Toronto. This design also appeared in a rough pencil sketch by Howard accompanied by two alternative designs — one a typical one-storey *cottage orné* with a three-sided verandah and flat-headed windows, and the other of the same design but with pointed-arch windows. These three drawings were probably preliminary proposals for a set of four gate lodges which were to mark the entrances to Upper Canada College. The third alternative as illustrated here (Fig. 37) was chosen. Apparently Howard's conservative Upper Canadian patrons found only the mildest Gothic flavour acceptable to their tastes. (Fig. 36, Metropolitan Toronto Library Board, Howard Collection; Fig. 37, Metropolitan Toronto Library Board)

38. Woodale, 35 Cross Street, Dundas, Ontario; Constructed 1841; **Material** stone

39. Drawing of Woodale in 1859

A well-preserved example of the common Ontario variety of the *cottage orné*, Woodale is distinguished for its finely dressed stonework for which the Scottish masons of the Hamilton area were well noted. Typically, Woodale was built for a retired colonel, Thomas H. MacKenzie, who later became mayor of Dundas. As so often happened, the original verandah with its flimsy post supports did not survive, leaving a more austere-looking structure than was intended. (Fig. 38, Canadian Inventory of Historic Building; Fig. 39, detail from County of Wentworth map, *Canada West*, compiled by Robert Surtees, Hamilton: Hardy Gregory, 1859, copy, Archives of Ontario)

40. Drew Cottage, 735 Rathbourne Street, Woodstock, Ontario
Constructed 1833; **Material** stucco

Andrew Drew epitomizes a certain type of English gentleman that settled in Upper Canada in the 1830s. A retired captain from the Royal Navy, Drew had been living in England on his half-pay pension for eight years, and although far from destitute, he was finding it increasingly difficult to maintain his gentlemanly habits within the economically strained conditions of England. Like so many in his position he decided to immigrate to Upper Canada rather than compromise his accustomed lifestyle. Backed by the resources of Vice-Admiral Henry Vansittart, under whom Drew had served and for whom he was to act as agent for Vansittart's land investments and eventual settlement in Upper Canada, Drew could afford to buy land that had already been partially cultivated rather than being forced into the inhospitable life of a backwoods farmer. Much of Drew's story — his background and origins — are revealed in his stuccoed, hipped-roof cottage which he built for himself on his arrival in 1833 and which was so typical of a genteel immigrant's small country retreat. In Canada, the large sash windows which opened to the floor were never as popular as the casement, French window type, but were common to villa and cottage design in England. (Canadian Inventory of Historic Building)

41. Ridgewood Park, Colborne Township, Huron County, Ontario
Constructed ca. 1834; **Material** stucco

The history of Ridgewood Park has never been accurately documented but it is believed to have been built in the mid-1830s for a Baron de Tuyl, a wealthy landowner in the Huron Tract. (The area consisted of over one million acres purchased in 1824 by the Canada Company, a land development and colonization company established in England by John Galt.) Typically, the baron selected a spacious wooded site for his cottage on top of the bluff along the Maitland River that provided the expansive vistas over the town of Goderich and Lake Huron. The design of Ridgewood Park is distinguished by its exceptionally tall and elaborate chimneys composed of three separate stacks banded together at the top and decorated with three stone crosses. These chimneys along with the wooden railing lend a lively accent to the roofline as was advocated by the English writers on the Picturesque. The present, rather austere facade would probably have originally been masked by a verandah. The massive three-storey building attached to the rear was built by Henry Yarwood Atrill who purchased the property in 1873. (Canadian Inventory of Historic Building)

42. Riverest, L'Orignal, Ontario; Constructed 1833; **Material** stone

Riverest is a rarity within the context of the architecture of the lower Ottawa Valley. Generally the early building of this area was dominated by the simple, sturdy, stone farmhouses of the Scottish Highlander and French settlers who pioneered the Ottawa Valley. Riverest with its verandah and hipped roof is one of the few examples of a typical *cottage orné* built in this area. The use of the Palladian window across the front and river facades is a feature unique to this building. (Canadian Inventory of Historic Building)

43. Oswald House, 1078 Saint Paul Avenue, Niagara Falls, Ontario
Constructed 1832; **Material** stucco

Because of their delicate construction, treillaged verandahs, an essential ingredient in the visual impact of a cottage, rarely survived into this century. This example, despite its unusually intricate geometric forms, has endured. A drawing of this building, which appeared on an 1862 map of Welland and Lincoln counties, shows it is unchanged except for a new shed dormer. Even the ornate cast-iron fence which the original owner, James Oswald, had imported from England still outlines the small cottage lot. Although now situated within the municipal boundaries of Niagara Falls, Oswald House was originally considered part of the town of Stamford near Queenston Heights not far from Sir Peregrine Maitland's country retreat of Stamford Park (Fig. 28). (Canadian Inventory of Historic Building)

44. Plan of a Cottage for Mr. Place, West Oxford, Oxford County, Ontario
Designed 1835; **Architect** John George Howard
Howard produced several similar designs for one-storey, five-bay cottages with French windows and verandahs, although this building is the only example incorporating rustic tree trunk supports for the verandah instead of Howard's usual thin post supports. (Howard never employed treillage in his designs.) In Howard's autobiography of 1885 he describes having drawn up a plan for R. H. Place but unless the client purchased the plans and had them executed without Howard's knowledge, it is doubtful that the building was ever constructed. (Drawing based on plan held by Metropolitan Toronto Library Board, Howard Collection)

single roofline extending beyond the eaves to incorporate the verandah. A unified roofline was also characteristic of eastern Ontario cottages as illustrated by Riverest in L'Orignal, or The Cottage Property near Renfrew (Fig. 45). This regional characteristic probably indicates an influence of the so-called Anglo-Norman cottage, the Quebec version of the *cottage orné* which adopted this roof treatment. The link with Quebec is most apparent in Crawford Cottage in Brockville (Fig. 46) which featured treillage supports, a full encircling verandah and a bellcast roof, all basic ingredients of the Quebec *cottage orné*.

Another variation of the straight hipped roof, which appeared on several southern Ontario designs of the 1840s, is illustrated by the cottage at Normandale near Simcoe (Fig. 47). The roofline has been raised in the middle and infilled with a row of clerestory windows. This feature provided additional light to the

interior, yet its long profile maintained the low-lying silhouette characteristic of the cottage. In Cobourg several cottages, including the William's cottage of 1834, were designed without a verandah but with wide overhanging eaves (Fig. 48). This design, advocated in the Picturesque pattern books as a means of visually enriching the eaves while casting interesting patterns of light and shadow, was more commonly found in villa design of the 1830s in Upper Canada.

Otterburn in Kingston provides an interesting variation of the standard theme (Fig. 49). Although French windows were used, there was clearly no intention to build a verandah. Its recessed walls and projecting frontispiece accented by a small decorative gable lend sufficient vitality to the facade that it requires no further enrichment. The French windows led onto an open terrace with steps down to the garden. No architect has

(cont. p. 73)

45. The Cottage Property, Burnstown, Renfrew County, Ontario
Constructed ca. 1850; **Material** wood

46. Crawford Cottage in 1853, Brockville, Ontario; Constructed pre-1853; **Demolished**

Rochester Cottage at Burnstown in the Upper Ottawa Valley and Crawford Cottage at Brockville on the St. Lawrence River are both situated relatively near the Quebec border. This geographical proximity is reflected in the design of both these buildings in their use of the bellcast roof and a treillaged verandah on three sides, features echoing the standard pattern of the typical Quebec *cottage orné*. The low railing between the upright supports is also a feature more common to the cottage architecture of Quebec than of Ontario. Both buildings employ a light scalloped fringe, a popular decorative device in Picturesque architecture. Rochester Cottage was the residence of George Rochester, a Scotsman of American birth who immigrated with his family to Ottawa in the late 1820s. In the late 1840s Rochester moved to Burnstown where he established a grist mill on the Madawaska River. The house was probably built soon after his arrival in Burnstown. Crawford Cottage was built before 1853 for John Crawford who served as mayor of Brockville from 1849 to 1855. No trace of Crawford Cottage could be found. (Fig. 45, Canadian Inventory of Historic Building; Fig. 46, detail from Brockville map, *Canada West*, New York: Wall and Forest, 1853, copy in Public Archives Canada, National Map Collection)

47. Cottage, 6 Main Street East, Normandale, Ontario; Constructed ca. 1842; **Material** brick

Several cottages that employed these low monitors or lanterns on the roof were constructed in southern Ontario in the 1840s and 1850s. The origin of this unusual form is unknown but it provided an effective alternative to the dormer window as a means of providing light to the attic storey. This desire for a well-lit interior also seemed to have determined the design of the ground floor which featured large French windows on all three sides. The present verandah which looks like a later addition probably replaced a lighter, more fanciful-looking structure which extended along three sides of the building. (Canadian Inventory of Historic Building)

48. Cottage, 250 Mathew Street, Cobourg, Ontario; Constructed 1834; **Material** stucco

The exaggerated eave extension on this cottage built for Mathew William in 1834 is an unusual feature in cottage design but it is not unique to Ontario. Several cottages in Cobourg employed this motif but none has as wide an overhang as the William cottage. A similar building was, however, erected on Spadina Avenue in Toronto in the 1830s and occupied by Sir Francis Hincks. Although this now-demolished building was larger in scale, featuring five French windows across the main facade, it incorporated the same distinctive roofline. Considering the proximity of Toronto to Cobourg, the Hincks cottage may have provided the model for the more modest Cobourg building. (Canadian Inventory of Historic Building)

49. Otterburn, 124 Centre Street, Kingston, Ontario
Constructed 1840-44; **Architect** George Browne; **Material** stone and stucco

In 1818 Smith Bartlett of Kingston purchased a 100-acre farm lot west of the city fronting onto Lake Ontario. He first tried to sell some of this property in 1830 but was unsucessful. By 1840 rumors of the impending arrival of the government of the United Canadas to Kingston resulted in a sharp increase of land values in and around the city and in 1840 Smith Bartlett again subdivided his property into park and villa lots. Within a few years this large tract of farmland was transformed into an exclusive residential suburb dotted with new villas and cottages including Hales's Cottages, Bellevue and Sunnyside as well as many others (Figs 50, 65, 70). Otterburn is situated at the corner of Union and Centre streets on a one-acre cottage lot within the original Bartlett farm. Bartlett retained the property until April 1844 when he sold it to James Hutton for £20. Hutton in turn sold the lot to John Counter for £725 in 1846. At that time Counter was residing at nearby Sunnyside and apparently he purchased the property for his son-in-law Charles Jenkins. At what point in this succession of deed transfers was Otterburn constructed? The initial purchase price of £620 would have been exorbitant for a small vacant lot particularily when one considers that it was purchased after land values had fallen following the departure of the capital from Kingston late in 1843. For this reason Otterburn was probably built by Bartlett himself between 1840 when he first subdivided his property and 1844 when he sold the lot. Perhaps Otterburn was built for his own use or perhaps, like Hales's Cottages, it was built as a rental property but sold when the real estate market collapsed in 1843. The 1840 date is supported by similarities in design between Otterburn and the nearby Hales's Cottages designed in 1841 by George Browne. Although Otterburn is a detached building, considerably larger in scale and lacking the fanciful wooden eave fringe, the articulation of the two facades is almost identical. Both are three bays wide with a central entrance flanked by two large windows with sidelights which at Otterburn have been extended to floor level. The elliptical fanlight is slightly flatter on Hales's Cottages but both doorways are deeply recessed while the surrounding wall areas project forward and are accentuated in the eave line by small gables. The shifting quality of the planes and the resulting effects of light and shade are further enhanced by the slight projections of the wall at the corners. Unless the design was a blatant plagarism by another architect, Otterburn must have been designed by George Browne. (Canadian Inventory of Historic Building)

been identified for Otterburn; however, this same design was adapted for a row format at Hales's Cottages in Kingston in 1841 designed by the Dublin architect George Browne (Fig. 50).

Except for these individual variations, this familiar hipped-roof *cottage orné* of the 1830s with its symmetrical facade, large (usually French) windows, verandah, and unornamented stucco or stone walls was not only remarkably consistent but also remarkably enduring. As late as 1851 Colonel Vanstittart built Bysham Park in Woodstock which showed little deviation from the established pattern (Fig. 51). This basic cottage form became absorbed into the vernacular repertoire of Ontario domestic building, its long-standing popularity derived from the fact that its small scale made it a practical economical design yet with some pretentions to architectural fashion. The low-lying hipped roof cottage profile was found dotted throughout the towns and countryside of southern Ontario throughout the nineteenth century (Figs 52, 53). These modest residences were not conscious expressions of Picturesque values. Instead they represent a generic building which had grown out of this aesthetic movement but which had become incorporated into the vernacular patterns of Ontario domestic building.

The post-1830 *cottage orné* with a few notable exceptions, adhered to a fairly conservative pattern. By Upper Canadian standards the most daring and sophisticated examples of Picturesque architecture are found in the villa designs of the same period. Of course, as noted in cottage design, the majority of the villas constructed in Upper Canada were derived from established vernacular traditions which incorporated only a few characteristics or details associated with the Picturesque, but during the 1830s and 1840s a small but very prominent group of villas was constructed which reflected a knowledgeable grasp of Picturesque principles as expounded in England.

The reason these outstanding architectural statements of the Picturesque are found in villa designs rather than in the cottage lay in the nature of their clientele. Names such as John Solomon Cartwright, John Henry Boulton, William Augustus Baldwin, Sir Alan Napier MacNab and John Simcoe MacCaulay emerge in connection with the villas to be examined

and all represent wealthy and socially prominent families of the colony. Like the English villa dweller described in the pattern books, these men were gentlemen "of some rank" in life who felt "entitled to a little more show as well as convenience" in their country residences. Often these villa dwellers had been born in England or had visited there, either to complete their education or just to get back in touch with their cultural roots. As a result they were aware of popular English tastes in residential building and on returning to Canada they could afford to hire the likes of John Howard or George Browne to provide them with a design similar to what they had observed in England. By English standards these prominent Upper Canadians had conservative architectural tastes (although probably no more so than a provincial country gentleman in Britain). They nevertheless showed a greater willingness to give their architects freer vent to their imaginations. In contrast to the repetitious quality observed in the modest cottage, villas of the period were designed in many styles ranging from classical, Gothic and Italianate to the most popular Regular style. These gentlemen demanded that their residences stand apart from the ordinary as proof of their cultivated and refined tastes.

Dundurn in Hamilton, begun in 1834, had all the ingredients necessary for an elegant Picturesque villa (Figs 54-56). First, Sir Alan Napier MacNab was its wealthy gentleman patron who was determined to build a house of great distinction to reflect his noble Scottish ancestry and his perceived position in society.[22] Although Canadian-born MacNab had never visited England before constructing his "castle," he was fortunate to have at his service an architect like Robert Charles Wetherell, who was able to give stylish form to MacNab's vision. Unfortunately, little is known of Wetherell's origins, training or his architectural activities in Canada with the exception of Dundurn and an Anglican cathedral in Hamilton. In 1840 Wetherell advertised himself as a designer of "cottages, farmhouses, villas and public edifices," a claim echoing the offerings of the English pattern books.[23] But it is the design of Dundurn that provides the strongest evidence of the architect's training in the aesthetics of the Picturesque.

50. Hales's Cottages, 311-317 King Street West, Kingston, Ontario
Constructed 1841; **Architect** George Browne; **Material** stone and stucco

A rare Canadian example of a Picturesque cottage in a row format, Hales's Cottages were constructed for Charles Hales as a speculative investment which capitalized on the demand for housing created by the arrival of the government of the United Canadas to Kingston in 1840. Situated near the governor's residence these fashionable cottages, set back from the street behind small walled gardens with stone stables to the rear, provided small but prestigious accommodation for newly arrived government officials. Elements of the design, such as the scalloped eaved trim and roughcast sheathing were borrowed from Hales's own residence, Bellevue (Fig. 65), which overlooked the cottages giving the buildings of the Hales's estate a visual coherence considered essential for a harmonious, picturesque scene. Of the original five units, one has disappeared and three have received an additional storey. The fourth, Number 317, remains relatively unchanged except for two dormer windows added later. (Canadian Inventory of Historic Building)

51. Bysham Park, 1193 Dundas Street, Woodstock, Ontario; Constructed 1851; **Material** stucco

Although built eighteen years after Andrew Drew's residence nearby, little has changed in the basic design format of the *cottage orné*. The link between these two buildings was more than architectural for Bysham Park was built for John George Vansittart, a son of Drew's partner and patron Vice-Admiral Vansittart. As was so often the case, the verandah has disappeared and supposedly the present front dormer replaced a small lantern similar to the lantern at the roof peak. (Canadian Inventory of Historic Building)

52. House, 1 Sainte Anne Place, St. Thomas, Ontario
Constructed post-1850; **Material** brick

There is a wide stylistic gulf between a *cottage orné* like Colborne Lodge and this modest one-storey residence probably built in the 1850s. The standard paraphernalia of the Picturesque *cottage orné* of the 1830s and 1840s — the verandah, the French windows and the tall chimneys — have disappeared. The vista and the landscaped gardens so important to the visual effect and pastoral mood of the *cottage orné* are gone. All that is left to link this building with its more elegant ancestors is its general scale and silhouette. (Canadian Inventory of Historic Building)

53. House, 191 Sydenham Street, London, Ontario
Constructed 1886; **Material** brick

This modest buff-brick residence could not be described as being consciously Picturesque in its design. Although its square, one-storey, hipped-roof form can be traced back to the Picturesque *cottage orné*, by 1886 this basic form had become part of the standard repertoire of vernacular domestic building in Ontario. Houses of this type were mass-produced by builders for modest residential developments throughout Ontario. On this example a verandah originally extended across the full facade but apparently it was removed in the 1920s and replaced by the present porch. (Canadian Inventory of Historic Building)

54. Dundurn (York Street Elevation), York Street, Hamilton, Ontario
Constructed 1834-35; **Architect** Robert Charles Wetherell; **Material** brick and stucco

In terms of exterior design, plan, and landscape setting, Dundurn represents the most comprehensive statement of the Picturesque values of Canadian architecture. The Dundurn estate, originally the property of Richard Beasley who had built a two-storey brick residence on the site in 1800, was purchased by John Solomon Cartwright of Kingston in 1832. The following year Cartwright sold the property to Allan Napier MacNab, who began construction of his "castle" in 1834. When completed by 1835 it surpassed in scale and in lavishness and sophistication of design anything previously known to the young colony. Dundurn has changed little over the years. Only the addition of a monumental portico on the York Street facade, designed by the Hamilton architect Frederick Rastrick in 1855, has altered its original appearance. After MacNab's death in 1862 Dundurn had several private owners. In 1964 it was purchased and fully restored by the city of Hamilton. (Figs 54, 55, Canadian Inventory of Historic Building; Fig. 56, Archives of Ontario)

55. Dundurn, Garden Elevation

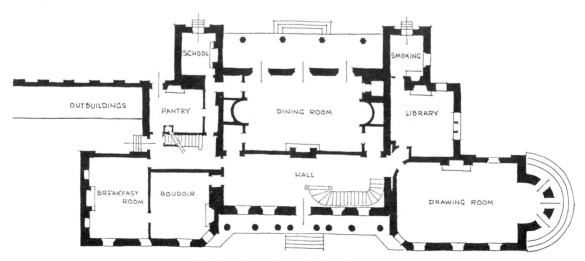

56. Dundurn, Ground Floor Plan

As a starting point for his design Wetherell was handed one of the most romantic settings in Upper Canada. The lot was situated on a high bluff known as Burlington Heights which rose 250 feet above the waters of Burlington Bay on Lake Ontario. The land, purchased by MacNab in 1833, had been partially developed by an earlier resident but fortunately the estate still possessed many fully grown oak trees, gardens and orchards. It also contained the remnants of military fortifications from the War of 1812, the closest thing Upper Canada had to offer in the way of romantic ruins. Over the years MacNab, with the help of his Scottish gardener William Reid, improved the estate, dotting the landscape with several buildings designed in a style sympathetic to the main residence.[24]

Such a grand setting demanded an eye-catching architectural embellishment and Wetherell's solution was unique to Canadian building. The eclectic approach to style inherent in the Picturesque point of view was used to full advantage by Wetherell. Instead of drawing on one particular stylistic idiom he combined classical, Italianate and Gothic details as well as the usual Picturesque paraphernalia — verandahs and French windows, stucco walls — into a single composition which gave clear expression to the Picturesque taste for simplicity joined to variety in mass and light and shadow.

The main facade facing York Street was composed in a fairly straightforward classical manner defined by a low row of Doric columns and a balustraded roofline masking the low pitch of the roof behind. Dundurn, however, does not represent an academic classicism, for many of the details, such as the stylized eave brackets with their smooth, curved profile, do not strictly adhere to correct classical vocabulary and are applied solely to enhance the visual appeal of the design. A sense of movement is achieved by the subtle manipulations of the wall planes constantly advancing into light and receding into shadow in the form of simple recessed panels and slight projections in the wall surface. The tall massive chimneys pierced by arches accent this varied play of simple forms. The window distribution defined by the short sash windows over tall ground-storey windows serves to de-emphasize the upper storey. This proportioning was common on villa design in Upper Canada.

On the garden facade these qualities are even more evident. In contrast to the formality of the York Street elevation, the east facade overlooking the bay is composed of exotic architectural elements in the form of tall Italianate towers topped by slender finials and a light verandah featuring a row of delicate medieval ornamentation.

Dundurn presents two distinct architectural personalities — its public face is formal, monumental and overlooks the city while its private face turned towards the garden is more individualistic and fanciful and hence to be enjoyed only by the occupants of the house. This split architectural personality is not an eccentric feature of Dundurn but will be observed on several villas of the period.

The flexible approach to the interior plan and the arrangement of space to take best advantage of the site, noted in John Howard's design for Colborne Lodge, became a more significant factor in villa design. The rigid interior organization of the earlier Georgian period with a central-hall plan balanced by rooms on either side is not evident in the plan of Dundurn. Although a certain degree of symmetry in both the elevation and plan is retained, the architect was never strictly bound to this convention. Wetherell placed a bow window in the main parlour to collect the light of the southern exposure with little concern that its intrusion upset the regularity of the layout. The rooms on either side of the two large central rooms are arranged in an irregular pattern to satisfy demands of convenience rather than any abstract sense of architectural order.

A few villas in a more correct classical vein were constructed around the same time as Dundurn, the most notable examples being Summerhill (the villa of George O'Kill Stuart), Thomas MacKay's Rideau Hall, and the slightly later Rockwood villa built for John Solomon Cartwright (Figs 57-61). Although these buildings show none of the eclectic blend of styles evident at Dundurn, they do share similar qualities of landscape, design and planning which place these Neoclassical buildings within the Picturesque's sphere of influence.

Like Dundurn these buildings were situated on large landscaped estates improved according to Picturesque principles. Their elevated sites provided the mandatory vista of Lake Ontario, in the case of Rockwood and

(cont. p. 86)

57. Summerhill, Stuart Street, Kingston, Ontario; Constructed 1836-39; **Material** stone

Like so many of Upper Canada's grandest villa residences, Summerhill was not built for a recent British immigrant but for a well-established, long-term resident of Upper Canada, the Reverend George O'Kill Stuart. Born in 1776 in New York State, he came to Canada with his Loyalist parents in 1781. He was carefully groomed by his father, a prominent Anglican minister, for a position of importance in the Church of England, and in 1827 he became archdeacon of Kingston. Stuart's suburban residence of Summerhill displayed none of the fanciful exoticisms often found in Picturesque architecture, but instead employed a grandly dignified classical design perhaps considered more appropriate to the head of the established church in Kingston. Features such as the projecting cylindrical forms of the facade, the varied planes, colonnaded terraces facing the lake, and its naturalistic park setting were characteristic of Picturesque villa design in the 1830s in Upper Canada. Unfortunately, Mrs. Stuart was not entirely happy with their new home and in 1840, when Kingston became the capital, the Stuarts returned to the city. Summerhill was used as a boardinghouse for newly arrived government officials and later as office space. In 1854 Summerhill was purchased by Queen's University and today it serves as the residence for the principal of the university. Unfortunately, Summerhill has undergone numerous alterations. The roof parapet and the colonnades have disappeared and the one-storey wings which flanked the central block have been raised to meet the roofline of the two end pavilions thereby leveling out the once varied silhouette. (Queen's University Archives)

58. Reconstructed Elevation of Rideau Hall
13 Sussex Drive, Ottawa, Ontario
Constructed 1838; **Material** stone

Rideau Hall was built for Scottish-born Thomas MacKay, a master mason, who had earned his fortune in Canada as the contractor for the Lachine Canal in Montreal and later for the lower locks of the Rideau Canal in Bytown (Ottawa). With the profits of these two major contracts he opened several mills at the Rideau Falls around which developed the town of New Edinburgh (now part of Ottawa). He built Rideau Hall amid a large estate which overlooked his mills, the river and the town and by 1864 boasted 100 acres of gardens and ornamental woods. Although his property is still standing Rideau Hall has not fared well in the hands of its subsequent owner, the Government of Canada. In 1864 the government rented the house as a temporary residence for the governor-general and it retained this "temporary" status until the 1910s when it was reluctantly accepted as the official Government House. In this intervening period, however, Rideau Hall had been haphazardly expanded with makeshift additions which now almost complete- ly engulf the original building. Only the elegant oval drawing room on the second floor, detailed in a delicate Adamesque style, has remained intact. Fortunately, the landscaped park or the "pleasure grounds" immediately around Rideau Hall have survived and preserve the original pastoral environment. (Figs 58, 59 from Marion MacRae, *The Ancestral Roof: Domestic Architecture of Upper Canada*, Toronto: Clarke, Irwin, 1963)

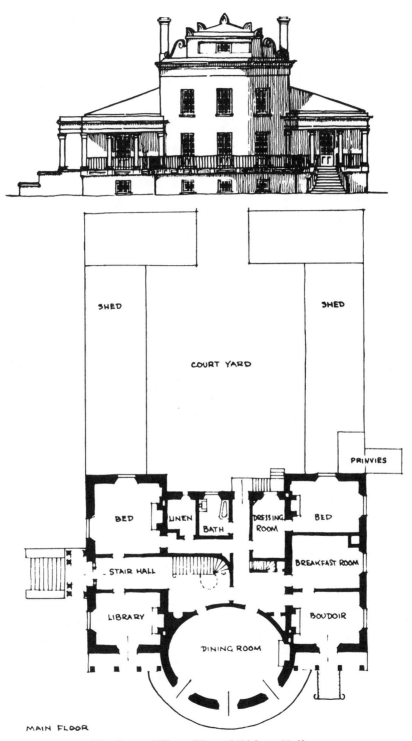

59. Ground Floor Plan of Rideau Hall

60. Rockwood, 740 King Street West, Kingston, Ontario
Constructed 1841-42; Architect George Browne; Material stone and stucco

The balance between the peaceful rural and the civilized urban environments that defined the Picturesque villa was well expressed in an 1845 "Notice of Sale" for Rockwood which described the 116-acre estate as a "quiet retired spot...near enough town for convenience but sufficiently far to escape from many of the harassing interruptions impossible to avoid in town." The design of Rockwood, with its deeply recessed entrance, subtle shifts in wall planes along the front facade, and the tall chimneys, illustrates George Browne's eye for Picturesque effects of movement and variety, and light and shadow. The grand front portico with its Tuscan columns and piers, a favorite Browne motif, demonstrates the architect's preference for the more monumental forms which distinguishes his work from the lighter, more whimsical character of a villa by John Howard. The addition of the exotic oriental balcony on the south elevation, which provides an amusing counterpoint to all this imposing classicism, characterizes the Picturesque flexibility towards stylistic correctness. (Canadian Inventory of Historic Building)

61. Rockwood, Rear Balcony

Summerhill, and of the Ottawa and Rideau rivers for Rideau Hall. Although much of the original land surrounding these villas was swallowed up by subsequent development, all still retain some of their original landscape features. A fairly complete description of Rideau Hall in 1864, while the property was still in the MacKay family, describes the setting very much as it appears today — as an "Elysian retreat" covered with "ornamental woods" and a "serpentine road...lined with elegant cedar hedges" leading up to the house.[25]

Rockwood villa offers a slightly more elaborate landscape scheme laid out by George Browne, who, in the manner of the true *architetto-pittore* of the Picturesque, also designed the villa and adjacent outbuildings. Supposedly the original character of the land was flat and uninteresting. Browne improved this by creating a series of rises and falls in the landscape which gave tantalizing glimpses of the villa as approached from the winding driveway. Behind the house Browne built a series of terraces leading down to the lake, a favorite landscape technique of Humphry Repton for establishing a visual transition between landscape and architecture. This Repton influence is not surprising because John Solomon Cartwright had purchased a copy of Repton's *Sketches and Hints on Landscape Gardening* during his years of schooling in England and it certainly would have been available to Browne for consultation.[26]

The designs of Summerhill and Rideau Hall have much in common. Both demonstrate the lingering influence of the Palladian manner with their large central sections flanked by low colonnades which in the case of Summerhill were completed by two end pavilions. But the regular, formal visual rhythm of a typical Palladian facade created by breaking up the elevation into a balanced series of separate cubic forms is not evident in either of these two buildings. Instead the introduction of cylindrical forms denies the rigid cubism of the Palladian style and establishes a fluid transition between one plane and another — a treatment that brings to mind the visually oriented classicism of John Soane based on the Soanian principles of variety in mass, and light and shadow.

At Rockwood the sprawling Palladian layout is abandoned for a compact rectangular plan. The stucco sheathing, painted a subdued ochre scored to resemble ashlar, and the proportioning of the bays with small windows over tall casement windows echo design characteristics observed at Dundurn. Like Dundurn the main street facade facing north imparts an air of grandeur in its massive pedimented portico articulated by the austere Tuscan order. Similarly, the southern garden elevation is less imposing, featuring French windows leading out to the terraced garden and a whimsical, pseudo-oriental balcony with a flared canopied roof. Although not as radical a transition as at Dundurn, Rockwood expresses that same architectural duality between the formal public facade and the private garden facade which faced toward the south and the vista.

The plans of these villas are varied, but all respond to the same principle of orienting the main living rooms towards the sunlight and vista. At Rockwood villa a formal centre-hall plan was acceptable because the front elevation faced north and away from the sun, the garden and the vista over the lake, and therefore did not interfere with arrangement of rooms to the south. At Rideau Hall the main entrance was shifted to the west side with the ground-floor dining room and second-storey drawing room located in the southern-facing bowed front. Summerhill was located on the north side of King Street which, unlike Rockwood, meant that the southern elevation was also the street facade. The side entrance of Rideau Hall was not feasible in this case because the long flanking service wings did not provide a suitable location for a main entrance. To solve this problem the entry hall was shifted slightly off-centre of the main block thereby leaving the projecting southern front free for use as the main drawing room.

The rambling, irregular castles promoted by Sir Richard Payne Knight and Sir Uvedale Price as the most Picturesque of all architectural idioms had little impact on Upper Canadian building. The few examples of medieval castle building known in Canada, namely Castlefield built for James Hervey Price in 1832 (Fig. 62) and John Henry Boulton's Holland House of 1831 (Fig. 63), leaned towards the more conservative, regularized Gothicisms illustrated in the popular Regency pattern books such as Edward Gyfford's *Designs for Elegant Cottages and Small Villas* (Fig. 11). In both these now

62. Castlefield in the Nineteenth Century, Toronto, Ontario
Constructed 1832; **Demolished** 1918; **Material** brick and stucco

Although the design was supposedly intended to duplicate James Hervey Price's Welsh ancestral home, this neatly stuccoed, symmetrical villa with its few applied Gothic details resembled only slightly an authentic medieval baronial castle. It is more likely that the inspiration for this castellated structure with its projecting frontispiece, turrets and crenelations was the similar design for Holland House which had begun construction the previous year (Fig. 63). (Metropolitan Toronto Library Board)

88

63. Holland House, 61 Wellington Street West, Toronto, Ontario
Constructed 1831; **Demolished** 1904; **Material** brick and stucco

Although it is unusual to find such an unabashed expression of the Gothic vocabulary at this early stage in Upper Canada, the basic elements of Holland House — the bow front, deeply shaded arcaded terrace, French windows, stucco walls scored to resemble ashlar, and the tall chimneys (disguised as turrets) — could have been found in different stylistic guises on several Picturesque villas in Upper Canada in the 1830s. Like many of the most outspoken and extravagant expressions of the Picturesque, Holland House was built, not for a newly arrived emigrant from England, but for a long-term resident of Upper Canada, John Henry Boulton. Born in England, Boulton came to Canada at seven and, following common practice for the sons of wealthy colonial families, was sent to England in 1815 to complete his education. Along with his legal training Boulton obviously schooled himself in the latest Regency fashions — lessons he was known to flamboyantly display both in dress and, of course, in architecture. (Metropolitan Toronto Library Board)

demolished buildings a few borrowed details, turrets, crenelations, pointed-arch windows and label mouldings, were deemed sufficient to suggest a Gothic character but the basic form diverged little from the classical villa type. These buildings, with their symmetrical elevations, central projections, Gothic terraces and French windows of Holland House, more closely resemble a classical villa like Rideau Hall than a true medieval castle.

The Italianate or Tuscan villa style, first created by John Nash in his design for Cronkhill of 1802, had two immediate descendants in Upper Canada: one was designed by John Howard in 1844 and the other, known as Bellevue, was built for Kingston grocer Charles Hales in the early 1840s (Figs 64-66).[27] In both these buildings the conservative restraint which seemed to prevail in many of the villa designs of the period has been lifted.

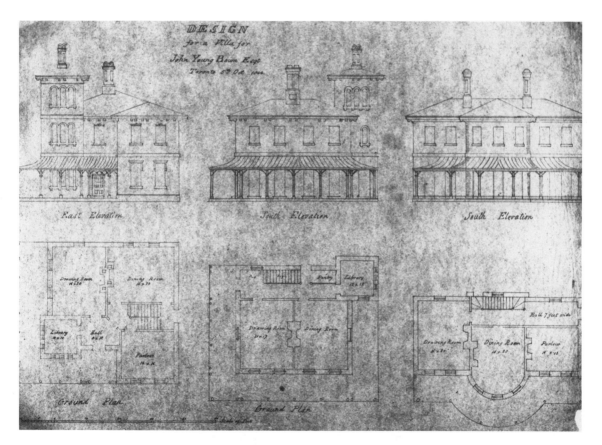

64. Three Proposals for a Villa for John Young Bown
Date 1844; Architect John G. Howard

On several occasions Howard employed this sales technique of providing his client with a series of designs, one fairly conservative and probably more what the client would have originally had in mind, and the others more innovative and likely more expensive. While Upper Canadians were not generally known for their architectural boldness, this particular client, a twenty-three-year-old medical student from Dorchester, England, by the name of John Young Bown, who is said to have had a liking for lavish and stylish living, might have preferred the irregular Italianate villa. Unfortunately, Bown's ambitions far exceeded his funds and none of the proposals was ever executed. (Metropolitan Toronto Library Board, Howard Collection)

65. Bellevue, 35 Centre Street, Kingston, Ontario
Constructed post-1841; **Material** stone and stucco

Bellevue was built for Charles Hales, a prosperous Kingston grocer, during the height of the building boom created by the arrival of the colonial government in 1841. During this period many elegant villas were erected on the outskirts of the city but even by Kingston's fashionable standards this exotic looking structure must have created quite a startling impression amid the grey stone and more discreetly stuccoed Regular villas which lined popular King Street West. Several years later its novelty still had not worn off. When Sir John A. Macdonald rented the house in 1848 he mockingly referred to his new "Eyetalian Willar" as "the most fantastic concern imaginable." To increase the value of the property and perhaps to help finance the construction of his new house, Charles Hales built a row of five cottages along his King Street frontage which he then leased to government employees (Fig. 50). Hales's Cottages were built in 1841 according to designs prepared by George Browne. Bellevue was probably begun at the same time or soon after the completion of the cottages. Both structures share common elements including stucco walls and an identical eave fringe but whether these similarities indicate a common architect or simply the intent of a second architect to establish a visual harmony between the two designs is now a popular subject of debate. Bellevue was the first true Italianate villa built in Canada, but by the late 1840s and 1850s this mode gained wide popularity in Upper Canada. These later examples, however, demonstrated High Victorian tastes for ornately worked detail in the form of heavy scroll brackets along the eaves and elaborate door and window surrounds. By contrast, the design of Bellevue was characterized by crisp lines defined by the light decorative eave fringe, columned verandah and ornamental balcony, which are brought into sparkling relief against the smooth, pale stucco walls. (Parks Canada)

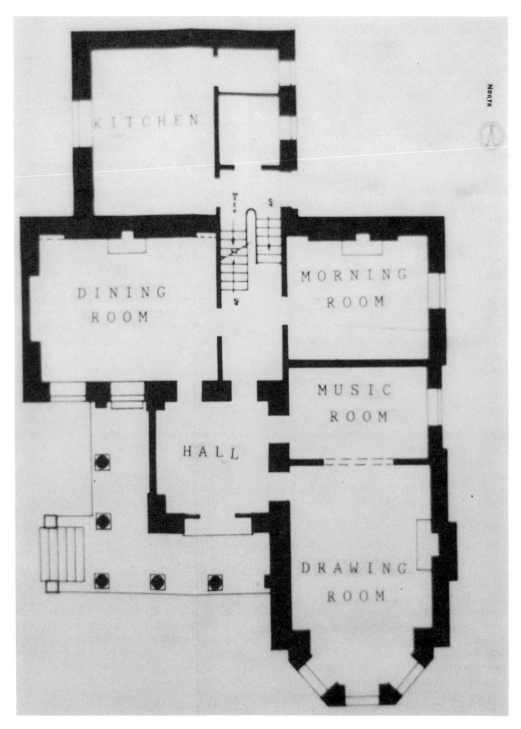

66. Bellevue, Ground Floor Plan

For the first time the Picturesque quality of irregularity was expressed not only in terms of the interior plan and setting but in elevation as well. The irregular masses pivot around the off-centre Tuscan towers or campaniles. This Picturesque variety is accented in the roofline by finialed towers and tall chimney pots. Howard's design, which was never built, was not as visually effective as that of Bellevue. Howard has applied a broad-roofed verandah across the full length of the facade which masks its intricate play of wall planes. The verandah at Bellevue, composed of heavy Tuscan columns, does not dominate the facade in the same way and allows the eye to appreciate the sense of variety and movement of the shifting wall planes. The smooth stucco walls provide a neutral surface which accents and sets off the exotic, decorative flourishes in the scalloped eave trim (almost identical in form to Nash's cottage at Regent's Park, Fig. 5) and decorative balconies painted an appropriate dark green as advised by Repton. Both these buildings represent a radical departure from usual design standards of Upper Canada – a fact Howard must have been well aware of as he hedged his bets by offering his client two alternative designs, each progressively more regularized and less daring.

The interior organization and room usage based on the simple logic of the best utilization of light and vista is again apparent in both these Italianate buildings. As always the main drawing rooms, the centre of family activities, faced south which at Bellevue included a light-collecting bay window. The Morning Room at Bellevue was oriented towards the morning eastern light. From this, one can also assume that the parlour as opposed to the drawing room at Howard's villa was to be used primarily for morning gatherings and perhaps informal breakfasts. Continuing this logic the dining room, used primarily in the evening, faced west at the Howard villa for evening light and south at Bellevue for light throughout the day.

The most popular villa type for Upper Canada was designed in Regular style, that is, villas symmetrical in elevation but of no specific stylistic source. The architect might borrow a few elements from an established architectural vocabulary, perhaps no more than a columned porch over the front door, but the overall effect was one of astylistic simplicity. Any added decorative touches, usually applied to either the eaves or the verandah, were contemporary inventions devised by the architects of the Picturesque to enhance the visual appeal of their buildings.

The best examples of this villa type were built for suburban estates on the outskirts of Toronto and Kingston. John Howard of Toronto was the most proficient master of this Regular style but he was not alone. The Thomas Mercer Jones Villa and the William Augustus Baldwin Villa of Mashquoteh, both in Toronto, typify Howard's work in this idiom (Figs 67, 68). Equally fine Regular villas include Elmsley Villa of 1839 built in Toronto for John Simcoe MacCaulay, Sunnyside of 1840-42 and Saint Helen's of 1838-39, both in Kingston (Figs 69-71).

All these buildings were two-storeys surmounted by a low hipped roof and equipped with all the standard villa accoutrements — the French window and the verandah usually defined by a slightly flared roof supported by thin posts. The characteristic disposition of windows, with French windows or floor-length sash windows below and shorter windows above, are found on these buildings. The wide cantilevered eave, a feature advocated in the English pattern books for its Picturesque effect, gave these villas their distinctive profile. As seen on the villas of Mashquoteh, Saint Helen's or Sunnyside, the paired modillions or brackets which appeared on Nash's design for Cronkhill provided the most popular means of decorating the extended eave. The scalloped edging of the Jones villa or the exposed rafters of Elmsley Villa, similar to those on Colborne Lodge, offered alternative decorative embellishments to the eave line.

With the exception of a few decorative flourishes these Regular villas were characterized by that same simplicity of design so prevalent in Picturesque architecture. Effects of light and shade were exploited by subtle variations and the constant movement of the stuccoed wall planes. Slight projections and recessions in the form of bay windows, chamfered corners or simply by small recessed panels, usually around the doors or windows, as seen on Sunnyside and Saint Helen's, break up the regularity of the design and cast varied patterns of light and shade over the surface. These environmental effects and their interaction with the architectural forms were

(cont. p. 98)

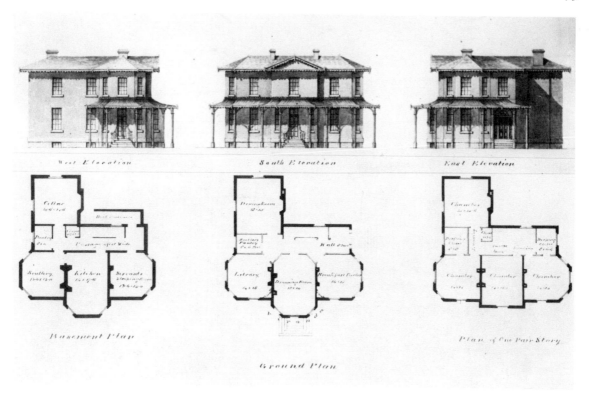

West Elevation   South Elevation   East Elevation

Basement Plan   Ground Plan   Plan of One Pair Story

67. Design for Thomas Mercer Jones Villa
Northwest Corner of Front and York Streets, Toronto, Ontario
Constructed 1833; **Demolished** 1893; **Architect** John George Howard; **Material** brick

Built in 1833 the Thomas Mercer Jones "cottage villa" (to use Howard's terminology) was the first in a long series of Regular villas designed by John Howard. Other related drawings found in the collection of Howard drawings held by the Toronto Public Library include a "cottage villa" for W.H. Draper (1834), a "cottage" for J.J. Arnold (1835), a "villa" for J.G. Spragge (1840), a villa for William Proudfoot (1844) and, what was perhaps the last in the series, William Augustus Baldwin's villa of Mashquoteh (Fig. 68). The Thomas Mercer Jones Villa was built on a lot located at the corner of Front and York streets which was secluded from the dust and noise of Front street by a high brick wall. It was later purchased by James McGill Strachan, Jones's brother-in-law, who in 1854 commissioned Howard to design a new wing on the northeast elevation. (Metropolitan Toronto Library Board, Howard Collection)

68. Mashquoteh in the 1870s, Toronto, Ontario
Constructed 1850; **Demolished** 1889; **Architect** John George Howard; **Material** wood and stucco

Although a late example of a Howard villa, Mashquoteh was more conservative in design than those of the 1830s and 1840s. With the exception of a later addition to the left, the building features a square, centre-hall plan without any of the projecting forms or irregularities of interior layout that distinguished much of Howard's earlier work. To compensate for its plainess Howard has added an exceptionally fanciful verandah and balcony decorated with an intricate lace-like trim. Mashquoteh was said to have been constructed of "hewn timber ... filled in with brick and roughcast." This once vast 300-acre estate, remembered in 1927 for its beautiful landscaped gardens, was located between present-day Saint Clair and Eglinton avenues, west of Yonge Street. It was owned by a member of one of Toronto and Upper Canada's leading families, William Augustus Baldwin. (Metropolitan Toronto Library Board)

69. Elmsley Villa in the 1840s, Toronto, Ontario
Constructed 1839; **Demolished** 1921; **Architect** James Smith; **Material** stone and stucco

Elmsley Villa, built for Colonel John Simcoe Macaulay, an ex-Royal Engineer and a leading figure in Upper Canadian politics and society, was noted for its particularly fine grounds described in 1851 as "delightfully laid out with winding way and shady groves and love-provoking bowers interspaced with smoothly mown lawns." The orientation of its verandahs to the north and east breaks with the established preference for the southern exposure but can perhaps be explained by John Ross Robertson's observation that the best views faced in those directions. In 1849, when the capital of the United Canadas was moved from Montreal to Toronto, Elmsley Villa became Government House, as it was considered the only residence in Toronto suitable for the purpose. In 1854 it was acquired by the trustees of Knox College who built a large addition to provide dormitories for the students. Elmsley Villa was demolished in 1921. (Metropolitan Toronto Library Board)

70. Sunnyside, 239 Union Street, Kingston, Ontario
Constructed ca. 1841-42; **Material** brick and stucco

In 1840 John Counter, a local businessman and entrepreneur, purchased a twenty-two-acre lot on the north side of Union Street. Although not a prime waterfront property its situation in the "Western Liberties" near Government House and several other fashionable estates made it a very desirable address. The house was habitable by May 1842, as the *Kingston Chronicle and Gazette* of 11 May 1842 announced the birth of a child to John Counter at "South Rude Cottage." (South Roode — as it is usually spelled — was the original name of Sunnyside.) Since 1842 Sunnyside has undergone a few alterations. At one time a bellcast verandah enclosed three sides of the building and the low sweeping arcade to the right of the main block was added before 1869. The local builder and architect, William Coverdale (1801? - 65), was hired to supervise the construction of Sunnyside but it is questionable whether he was also responsible for the design. Trained as a builder, Coverdale had emerged as a fairly active architect in Kingston by the early 1840s. His work of this period, however, tended to be very conservative. He designed several stone town houses, executed in a plain functional manner and one more sophisticated design for the villa of Roselawn (1840) designed in a late Palladian style. None of these works bore any stylistic resemblance to Sunnyside and for this reason his authorship is doubted. Not until later in the decade does Coverdale begin to use Picturesque motifs (Fig. 73). A strong stylistic parallel can be established between Sunnyside and two other Kingston villas of the late 1830s. Many of its typically Picturesque elements — roughcast walls, verandah, French windows, blocky chimneys, wide bracketed eaves and chamfered corners — had previously appeared in the design of Saint Helen's (Fig. 71) and Edgehill House. Neither of these buildings has been connected to Coverdale but their similarities suggest a common, unidentified architect. (Canadian Inventory of Historic Building)

71. Saint Helen's, 440 King Street West, Kingston, Ontario
Constructed 1838-39; **Material** stone and stucco

Built for Thomas Kirkpatrick, a prominent Upper Canadian lawyer and one-time mayor of Kingston, Saint Helen's was one of the finest products of the retreat into the suburbs which became the fashionable practice for wealthy Kingstonians during the 1830s. Like many of the villa properties in the area the ample, well-treed grounds situated on a gentle rise of land overlooking the lake, which according to an 1857 description had been "tastefully laid out" by Kirkpatrick, have been well preserved and capture the mood of genteel, rural tranquility appropriate to a Picturesque villa. The building itself has undergone numerous alterations. In the 1850s a monumental, two-storey portico was added to the south garden facade probably replacing a typical, flared roof. The *porte cochère* dates from 1866 and in 1910 the west wing (*right side*) received an additional storey after the plans by Kingston architect William Newlands. (Canadian Inventory of Historic Building)

regarded as a very real part of the architect's design. When John Howard prepared his plans for the Thomas Mercer Jones Villa (Fig. 67), the patterns of shadow cast by the decorative elements and the varied planes of the structure were worked out first on paper so that the full visual effect of the building could be assessed.

By definition these Regular villas were symmetrical in elevation but not necessarily symmetrical in plan. The layout of rooms was determined by the building's orientation on the site. Verandahs and French windows line the south facade which lead directly into the principal living rooms. At the Jones villa and Sunnyside, the main entrance is located on a side elevation with the main hall running parallel to the front facade behind the southern-facing rooms. Saint Helen's, on the other hand, responds to a site similar to that of Rockwood which inevitably results in a similar plan. Like Rockwood, the Saint Helen's property was sandwiched between the lake to the south and King Street to the north, thereby separating the street facade from the southern garden facade and permitting the use of a centre-door/centre-hall plan. As at Rockwood or Dundurn the two elevations had their own distinctive character. The smaller casement windows on the public, street facade contrast with the more relaxed and open-to-nature appearance of the garden facade with its verandah (since removed) and large French windows.

This Regular villa spawned a related building type illustrated by George Browne's Saint Andrew's Manse and William Coverdale's Kerr House, both in Kingston, and by John Howard's unidentified plan of 1833 (Figs 72-74). These two-storey buildings with their low hipped roof and wide cantilevered eaves resemble a Regular villa but they could not be included accurately within this category. To the Picturesque frame of mind the landscape and vista were more important to the villa idea than were qualities of design. When these natural attributes were not present a building could no longer be defined as a villa. Both Saint Andrew's Manse and Kerr House, although accompanied by gardens, were situated in smaller, more confined lots offering no vista beyond buildings across the street. The Howard design, although originally intended as a residence, was eventually built to house the

Canada Company Offices in Toronto (Fig. 75). It was set in a most unpicturesque environment directly fronting onto a busy urban street.

This sense of spatial confinement is well expressed in the facades of both Saint Andrew's and the Howard plan which feature shorter sash windows. These windows set up a barrier between interior and exterior which the French window and verandah eliminate. Moreover, as the interaction of architecture and landscape was not as important in these more urban settings, the manipulation of plan to aspects of sun and vista is no longer evident and all feature a centre-hall/centre-door plan regardless of the orientation of the building. The distinction between the villa type and its urbanized descendant was recognized by Howard who often identified this later type by the label "house" as opposed to his usual term "villa" or "cottage villa."

The villas examined so far reflect in terms of the Upper Canadian experience the most sophisticated expressions of Picturesque villa design. All were designed, if not by skilled architects, at least by persons who were well atuned to Picturesque concepts of residential design. Underlying this group there exists a secondary level of villa building which borrowed a few features characteristic of Picturesque architecture but applied them to structures that reflected building patterns rooted in a conservative vernacular tradition.

The typical villa of this vernacular level was a symmetrical, two-storey structure, three or five bays wide (Figs 76-78). The plan rarely deviated from a simple square or rectangle and lacked that varied play of wall planes that distinguished more sophisticated villa designs. These buildings maintained the characteristic simplicity of design imparted by the smooth unadorned walls but they had none of those fanciful decorative touches, such as the wide overhanging eaves ornamented with brackets or a decorative fringe, which had enlivened the villa facade. The roof was usually hipped although some employed a straight gable roof. The most popular and enduring feature borrowed from architectural vocabulary of the Picturesque was the French window and the verandah. Unfortunately, this latter feature often did not survive to the present day imparting a much more austere appearance to these buildings than originally

(cont. p. 105)

72. Saint Andrew's Manse, 146 Clergy Street, Kingston, Ontario
Constructed 1841-42; **Architect** George Browne; **Material** stone

Although George Browne resided in Kingston only four years from 1851 to 1855 he left behind some of Kingston's most outstanding architectural monuments. Saint Andrew's Manse, while not as imposing as Browne's other commissions in the city such as the Kingston City Hall, demonstrates Browne's sensitive handling of texture, mass and the play of light and shadow, characteristic of all his work. The contrasting textures of the rough limestone and the smooth dressed stone of the bold simple stringcourse and door and window surrounds, the sense of movement created by the slight projections in the wall surfaces (a device used to similar effect in Hales's Cottages and Otterburn), and the deep shadows cast by the broad eaves bring a sense of vitality to this simple cubic form. The small wrought-iron balconies under the second-storey windows were common features on urban and suburban residences in England but never widely used in Canada. (Canadian Inventory of Historic Building)

73. Kerr House, 155 Earl Street, Kingston, Ontario
Constructed 1848-49; **Architect** William Coverdale; **Material** stone
In the late 1840s William Coverdale, Kingston's leading architect of the period, designed three, almost identical dwellings on Earl Street of which the Kerr House is the best preserved example. Situated on a relatively small suburban lot approximately one-sixth of an acre, this residence falls into the category of the suburban house as opposed to the villa type which implied more spacious grounds. Features such as the wide bracketed eaves and recessed arch around the main doorway were common design devices of this type and characteristic of Coverdale's work. The use of the heavier and more formal balustraded terrace and columned portico indicates the declining fashion for the lighter, more delicate forms associated with Picturesque architecture or perhaps it represents a later addition. (Canadian Inventory of Historic Building)

Figure 75 illustrates how Howard modified his Regular villa type, exemplified by the Thomas Mercer Jones Villa (Fig. 67), to suit a more confined urban environment. Because this building fronted directly onto a busy street, the free flow of space between exterior and interior created by the verandah and French windows was no longer appropriate. The windows become smaller and the porch a more formal entrance. An early work by Howard, it was originally designed as a private residence for W.H. Lee but never constructed. In 1834 Howard used the same design, modified only by the addition of a projecting columned porch, for the Canada Company office. (Fig. 74, Metropolitan Toronto Library Board, Howard Collection; Fig. 75, Metropolitan Toronto Library Board)

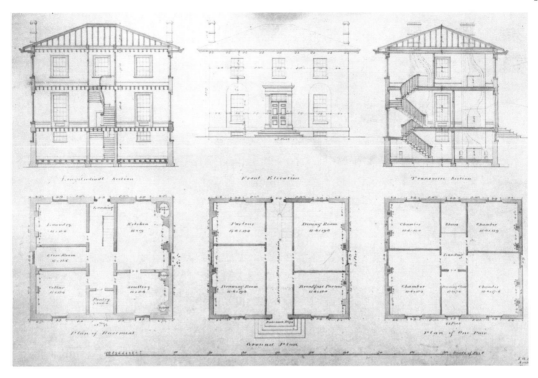

74. House for W.H. Lee; Drawn 1833; **Architect** John George Howard

75. Canada Company Office in the 1830s, Frederick Street East, Toronto, Ontario
Constructed 1834; **Architect** John George Howard; watercolour by John Howard, 1830s

76. Chalmer's Presbyterian Manse, 59 Green Street, Guelph, Ontario
Constructed ca. 1867; **Material** stone

By 1867 high fashion in domestic architecture had succumbed to the High Victorian taste for richly carved and abundant decorative detail usually in a Gothic or Italianate style. This fine stone residence, built as the manse for Chalmer's Presbyterian Church, has remained oblivious to this prevailing extravagance and has retained the basic form as well as the general simplicity and restraint in design that characterized the early villa architecture of the Picturesque in Ontario. The French windows, noted for their extremely delicate glazing bars, suggest the manse may have originally featured a verandah although there is no documentation to support this supposition. (Canadian Inventory of Historic Building)

77. Richardson House, 419 Vincent Street, Woodstock, Ontario
Constructed 1848; **Material** brick

Richardson House retains the French windows and the three-sided verandah (since disappeared) of the typical Picturesque villa but it also introduces new influences and tastes more characteristic of post-1850 architecture in Canada. Although eave brackets were frequently employed in the design of early Picturesque villas they were usually conceived as simple, very stylized forms. The richly carved scroll brackets of Richardson House were more in keeping with the mid-Victorian tastes for heavy ornate detail. The central focus created by the projecting frontispiece and pediment was also uncharacteristic of a typical Picturesque villa which tended to avoid placing a strong emphasis on the main doorway. Richardson House was built for Hugh Richardson who was a prominent Woodstock lawyer, judge and politician but who is best known as the judge who presided over the trial of Louis Riel in 1885. (Canadian Inventory of Historic Building)

78. House, 9 Bradford Street, Barrie, Ontario; Constructed 1855; **Material** stucco

The design of this house in Barrie is not a conscious expression of Picturesque values in architecture but a composite of various building traditions and types common to Ontario architecture. The use of the French window and treillaged verandah is clearly derived from architecture of the Picturesque. But if these elements were stripped away and the stucco removed one would be left with a two-storey, gable-roofed structure that differed little from the early colonial houses built in Upper Canada during the late eighteenth and early nineteenth centuries, houses that reflected the eighteenth century British classical tradition. (Canadian Inventory of Historic Building)

intended. Again, the use of the French window creates the impression that the second storey was lower than the first.

This vernacular villa type lacked the sophistication and variety found in the architect-designed villas but it represents the most enduring legacy of the Picturesque taste in Ontario domestic architecture. When architects had long abandoned these forms in favour of more up-to-date Victorian fashions, villas based on this popular pattern continued to be constructed by local builders as late as the 1860s.

Quebec: 1780 to 1830

In Quebec, or Lower Canada, the taste for the Picturesque was, as in Upper Canada, imported by the middle- and upper-class immigrant from England, but unlike Upper Canada the influence of this taste was both contained and modified by the French presence. The conquest of New France in 1759 had little initial effect on existing patterns of domestic building, and although by the early years of the nineteenth century English architectural influences became more evident, they were generally absorbed into vernacular building forms. As a result, the traditional Quebec house retained its distinctive character throughout much of the nineteenth century.[28] For the most part, the villas and cottages that will be examined were built for those English colonials connected with or part of the "official set" in Quebec and to a lesser extent for the commercial elite of Montreal.

As in Upper Canada the earliest manifestations of the Picturesque point of view were expressed in eighteenth century terms of classical architecture set in a pictorially composed landscape. In Lower Canada, however, these early buildings were more extravagant than, for example, Mrs. Simcoe's little classical temple, Castle Frank, in Toronto. Whereas the Upper Canadian colonial in the late eighteenth century was faced with a rugged wilderness, his counterpart in Lower Canada was greeted by a well-developed community which could supply skilled local craftsmen capable of carrying out more ambitious architectural schemes. Spencer Wood,

built in the 1780s for General H.W. Powell, is a good example of the elegant country seats being built by the upper echelons of Quebec colonial society in the post-conquest years (Fig. 79). Originally a square symmetrical structure with a central pediment over the main entrance, it was later transformed into a Palladian "house of parade" by the addition of two flanking colonnades and end pavilions.[29] The Picturesque aesthetic was expressed primarily in terms of its spectacular cliff-top setting on Saint-Louis Road which by the 1830s consisted of 200 acres of parklands said to have been "clothed in dense primeval forests,"[30] gardens, cliff-side walks, and "a noble avenue leading to the house which reminded one of England."[31] Finally, in 1852 George Browne gave Spencer Wood a Picturesque face-lift by adding a flared-roof verandah, an ornamental balcony, French windows and projection bays to the older building (Fig. 80).

There were several such country estates established on the outskirts of Quebec in Ste-Foy, Sillery and Beauport in the late eighteenth century. Known by such pastoral sounding names as "Woodfield," "Belmont," "Sans Bruit," most of these buildings have disappeared but many are known to us through the drawings and descriptions of James Pattison Cockburn in his 1831 publication of *Quebec and its Environs; a Picturesque Guide to the Stranger*. His detailed accounts of the country villas and "their improved grounds" with "shaded walks" and avenues, and endless variety of picturesque vistas "worthy of a painter's study," recapture the original romantic atmosphere of these early country seats.

Several large country estates also appeared on the outskirts of Montreal although all have been demolished. The villa of Louis Foucher, picturesquely situated high on the slopes of Mount Royal, is a typical example (Fig. 81). Like the Quebec examples discussed, this two-and-a-half-storey residence built of dressed grey stone and featuring a central pediment and a close-eaved, hipped roof adopts a very conservative design drawn from the eighteenth century Palladian tradition. The addition of a treillaged verandah which looked out over the city lent a fanciful touch to its otherwise sombre appearance.

At the same time that these late-Palladian

(cont. p. 109)

79. Spencer Wood in 1849 (Bois-de-Coulonge)
Saint-Louis Road, Quebec City
Constructed ca. 1780; **Burned** 1860; **Material** wood
Lithograph by Lemercier

The evolution of Spencer Wood outlines the changing tastes in villa design from the end of the eighteenth century to the mid-nineteenth century. As built in the 1780s for General Henry Watson Powell, Spencer Wood (then known as Powell Place) was a square, two-storey building with a slightly projecting, pedimented frontispiece, small windows and corner quoins — a design that reflected the ordered formality of the Palladian style which dominated architectural tastes throughout much of the eighteenth century. (The original building formed the central portion visible in both the lithograph and the plan.) Sympathy with Picturesque values is expressed only in the informally laid out, wooded grounds, which overlooked the St. Lawrence River. In the 1830s its new owner, Henry Atkinson, who had purchased the property in 1825, added two flanking wings. Although this arrangement still falls within the Palladian tradition, its Ionic colonnade and large

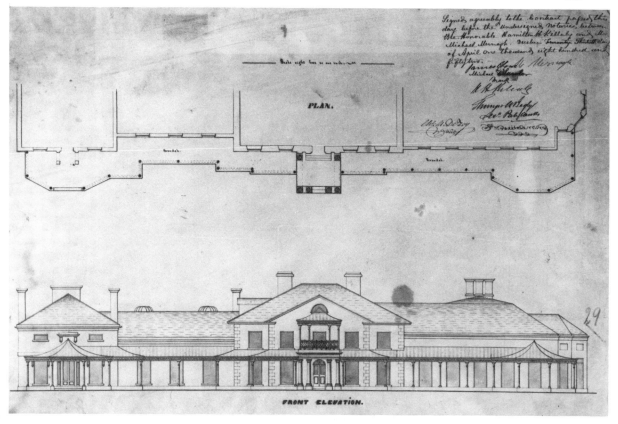

PLAN.

FRONT ELEVATION.

80. Plan of Proposed Alterations to Spencer Wood; Drawn 1852; **Architect** George Browne

windows which appear to open to the floor enliven the facade and provide immediate access to the gardens. Its design demonstrates the same blend of Palladian planning modified by forms associated with Picturesque architecture found on the villa of Summerhill in Kingston in 1836 (Fig. 57). In 1850 Spencer Wood was taken over by the government of the United Canadas for use as the governor's residence and in 1852 the ubiquitous George Browne was hired to enlarge and renovate the old structure. He rebuilt the east wing (*right*) to accommodate a large ballroom but he also planned several new features in the form of a bay window, a flared-roof verandah marked by octagonal projections at both ends and an ornamental balcony on the second storey, which would have transformed the building into a sophisticated and slightly exotic Picturesque villa. He also modified the plan by shifting the main entrance onto the east end of the building thereby permitting a degree of privacy to the southern rooms, all of which had direct access to the gardens and verandah via the French windows. Although the ballroom and new entrance were completed, it is not clear whether Browne's other proposals were carried out. In 1860 Spencer Wood burned down. (Fig. 79, Archives nationales du Québec, Quebec, collection initiale; Fig. 80, Public Archives Canada, National Map Collection)

81. Piedmont in the Nineteenth Century, Mount Royal, Montreal, Quebec
Constructed ca. 1819; **Demolished** 1939; **Material** stone
Piedmont, built for Charles Louis Foucher, judge and solicitor-general of Lower Canada, was one of the earlier suburban residences to seek the elevated seclusion and broad vistas afforded by the wooded slopes of Mount Royal. Parts of this house may date before 1819 for in February of that year Montreal resident Augusta Sewell described Judge Foucher's house as a "common one-storey building." The second-storey was added perhaps later that year, since in August 1819 Foucher had hired a local plasterer to carry out considerable interior renovations. It is difficult to determine whether the verandah dates from this period. According to Miss Sewell, treillaged verandahs or, to use her terms, "Galleries ... with post and railings resembling in some measure chinese work" had appeared in Montreal by this time. (Musée du Château Ramezay, Montreal)

country mansions were being built, a less formal type of country villa appeared. The Maison Montmorency, known also as Haldimand House or Kent House (in reference to its one-time occupant, the Duke of Kent), was built in the early 1780s as a summer residence for the governor of Quebec, Sir Frederick Haldimand (Fig. 82). Spectacularly situated on a precipice overlooking Montmorency Falls, one of the colony's most famous natural attractions, this square two-storey, wood-frame building was vaguely Palladian in its general layout which featured two end pavilions linked to the main block by an open colonnade. Beyond this, however, there is little in the design reflecting the correct classicism of this style. The central building is fully encircled by verandahs on both levels sheltered by the broad overhanging eaves of the hipped roof. Like the early villas of Upper Canada such as Davenport (Fig. 30), this slightly exotic design was drawn from a colonial building type found throughout the British Empire.

To describe any of these buildings, with the exception of the Maison Montmorency, as expressive of Picturesque values is misleading. At this early stage these square compact, close-eaved buildings were still strongly rooted in an eighteenth century classical tradition. In fact, these buildings appear even less responsive to architectural forms associated with the Picturesque than those found in the rough, backwoods colony of Upper Canada. The pre-1830 villas of Upper Canada occasionally introduced French windows, projecting bays, or roughcast or stucco walls — features so characteristic of later designs. In these early villas of Lower Canada only the incorporation of the verandah, the effective use of natural setting, and the exploitation of vista, suggest later developments in the villa.

The *cottages ornés* built by English gentlemen in Quebec in the first three decades of the nineteenth century were a more interesting phenomenon. In many respects they resembled their Upper Canadian counterparts but they also displayed distinctive characteristics. Three early cottages found in the Quebec vicinity — Morton Lodge of ca. 1821, Thornhill of 1825 and Rosewood Cottage of ca. 1827 (Figs 83-85) — featured a square one-storey plan, hipped roof and a treillaged verandah, similar to Upper Canadian cottages.

Of these three buildings, however, only Thornhill fits well into the Upper Canadian pattern. Morton Lodge and Rosewood, designs more accurately foreshadowing later developments in the Quebec cottage, introduce new elements and characteristics in the form of a steeply sloped roof, short casement windows, massive central chimneys and dormer windows sitting low on the eave line.

In the contemporary architectural terminology of Quebec, these cottages are described as early examples of the Anglo-Norman cottage.[32] Although for the sake of continuity and clarity these structures will continue to be referred to as *cottages ornés,* in many respects this regional label, "Anglo-Norman," is quite appropriate; for the elements setting these Quebec *cottages ornés* apart from their Ontario counterparts were drawn from the traditional Quebec house of the seventeenth and eighteenth centuries. In the earliest given example, Morton Lodge, the Norman or French element is most evident. Its steep *pavillon* roof, casement windows, and dormers sitting low on the eave line mimic the traditional Quebec farm of the first half of the eighteenth century. The addition of the verandah adds a new and Anglo element to this traditional Norman cottage. Although covered *galeries* had been employed in French building before the conquest, they were usually found on the second storey of urban residences.[33] To the English, the wide verandah overgrown with climbing vines was an essential ingredient of the cottage, both as a place to enjoy the fresh air and as a means of accenting the Picturesque appearance of their "Canadian-inspired" country retreats.

At Morton Lodge the verandah was simply added to the facade in the manner typical of Upper Canadian cottages but at the later Rosewood Cottage, the verandah was incorporated into the main roofline which flared outwards at the bottom to allow for the broad overhanging eaves. A slight outward curve of the roof appeared on Quebec buildings throughout the eighteenth century,[34] but at Rosewood, the curve becomes exaggerated partly to accommodate the verandah and partly to create a more interesting roof silhouette. The design of Rosewood set the standard pattern for the *cottage orné* of Lower Canada that survived well into the nineteenth century.

82. Maison Montmorency (Kent House) in 1781, 2490 Avenue Royal, Courville, Quebec
Constructed 1781; **Material** wood; watercolour by James Peachy, 1781

Although still referred to as Kent House, little remains of the original house occupied by the Duke of Kent between 1791 and 1794. As constructed in 1781 for Governor Sir Frederick Haldimand the house was two and a half storeys, three bays wide with a hipped roof, dormers and a two-storey verandah which surrounded the building on three sides. Two open colonnades linked the main building with two one-storey pavilions with flat balustraded roofs. Although these two flanking wings suggest a Palladian villa plan their use in the context of a verandahed villa with open colonnades is without architectural precedent. These elements seemed to have been devised purely to provide sheltered yet open vantage points from which to enjoy the view of Montmorency Falls which in the minds of British travellers in the early nineteenth century vied with Niagara Falls. The setting can still be appreciated although the original house is barely recognizable beneath the numerous alterations and additions carried out throughout the nineteenth and early twentieth centuries. (Public Archives Canada, Picture Division)

83. Morton Lodge in 1865, Ste-Foy Road, Ste-Foy, Quebec
Constructed probably in 1821; **Demolished; Material** wood

Morton Lodge, with its steeply pitched roof, large central chimney and small dormers sitting directly on the eave line, retains a strong flavour of the traditional eighteenth century Quebec farmhouse. This blending of traditions was characteristic of the pre-1830 *cottages ornés* built by the wealthy English colonials on the suburban outskirts of Quebec City. Although it is impossible to firmly date this building, in 1865 James MacPherson Lemoine states that Morton Lodge was built approximately fifty years earlier for James Black, a Quebec merchant. In 1821 the same James Black drew up a building contract with Remy Reinfret, a Quebec mason, for the construction of foundations and chimneys for a house on Ste-Foy Road. This document probably refers to the house illustrated although perhaps with some modifications. The fact that the verandah was tacked onto the facade rather than incorporated into the roofline, which was the general practice for cottages in Quebec, may indicate that this feature was a later addition. If this is the case the original building would have been similar in design to a typical farmhouse of New France. The wing and conservatory to the right would also likely date to a later period. (James MacPherson Lemoine, *Maple Leaves: Canadian History and Quebec Scenery,* 3rd ser., Quebec: Hunter Rose, 1865, opp. p. 113)

84. Thornhill in 1901, Saint-Louis Road, Sillery, Quebec
Constructed 1825; **Demolished; Material** stone and stucco

The influence of French building is less evident in the design of Thornhill. Unlike Morton Lodge or Rosewood the hipped roof has a fairly gentle slope much more in keeping with the *cottage orné* of Ontario. Unlike the typical Quebec Picturesque cottage which generally featured a continuous roofline, the flared roof of the verandah has been attached to the front facade thereby creating a design that would be quite at home in the suburbs of York (Toronto). The projecting frontispiece with its Greek Revival architrave was probably a later addition dating perhaps from the mid-nineteenth century when this type of detail was fashionable. Thornhill, situated across Saint-Louis Road from Spencer Wood, was built for Alexander Simpson. In 1913 this small cottage was transformed into a large country house by a series of additions designed by the Quebec firm of Stavely and Stavely (son and grandson of Edward). Thornhill was demolished in this century. (Archives nationales du Québec, Quebec, Wurtele Collection)

85. Rosewood Cottage in 1865, Faubourg Saint-Louis, Quebec, Quebec
Constructed probably in 1827; **Demolished; Material** wood

According to James MacPherson Lemoine "this tiny unostentatious cottage buried amongst the trees" was built as the summer residence of James Gibbs. Lemoine does not suggest a date of construction for this building; however, in 1827 Joseph Rousseau, a local builder and carpenter, was hired by Gibbs to build a house to be situated in the Faubourg Saint-Louis, the area immediately west of the city walls of Quebec along the cliffs. This contrast describes a very small one-storey structure only fifteen by eighteen feet featuring two casement windows six panes high and a main doorway. There is no mention of a verandah although the height given for the windows implies they were of the French variety which, by association, suggests they may have opened up onto some sort of terrace or verandah. Although the documentation is far from conclusive, this description generally conforms to this photograph with the exception of the large addition to the right. Such an early date for this building is supported by the steep pitch of the roof. In later examples of the *cottage orné* the roof always adopted a much gentler slope. (James MacPherson Lemoine, *Maple Leaves: Canadian History and Quebec Scenery*, 3rd ser., Quebec: Hunter Rose, 1865, opp. p. 96)

The French element may be partially explained by the fact that native Quebec builders were often employed in the construction of these early *cottages ornés*. But the development of this distinctly Quebec cottage type probably owes more to the tastes of the client than to the lack of versatility on the part of the local craftsmen. Affecting certain native and rustic or exotic ways was part of the romantic experience of colonial life.

Although the buildings that housed the institutions of British culture such as the church or government appeared generally uncompromisingly British, in the design of a cottage retreat it was considered fashionable to suggest indigenous building types that appealed to English romantic sensibilities. It was a response similar to the discovery in England of the rustic medieval cottage with its associations with simple rural pleasures. Similarly in India, these sentiments were directed towards the native bungalow. In Lower Canada it was the Quebec farmhouse. As described by one observer,

> The houses, some of which are built after a very Picturesque order, display all the appearance of having descended from sire to son; and their snug gardens and orchards bending under their golden burdens denote a happy and domestic people, although perhaps wanting in ambition and dollar-making enterprise.[35]

Like the rustic English cottage, the traditional Quebec cottage was admired as a Picturesque embellishment to the landscape in harmony with its natural surroundings and as a romanticized symbol of simple rural tranquility which the English gentleman found so appealing.

In England a gentleman who wished to surround himself with the more agrestic pleasures built himself a rustic, thatched-roof cottage, but in Lower Canada the appropriate form was the native Canadian cottage. The response of Lady Aylmer, wife of the governor of Lower Canada for 1831 to 1835, to her summer residence at Sorel on the Richelieu River illustrates well the English romantic view of this native architecture (Figs 86, 87). Although much rebuilt by the Royal Engineers in 1823, the residence with its off-centre door, casement windows, steep roof and roughcast walls was very similar to the local vernacular architecture of the region.[36] The French character of the building thoroughly delighted Lady Aylmer who wrote to a friend, "I wish you could possess such a Cottage as the one I am now engaged in ornamenting... it consists of a low building with a long slanting roof which all the houses of the 'Habitants' of Lower Canada have..."[37] At first certain aspects of the cottage displeased her, namely the glaring white walls and the square, unshaded garden; in accordance with the Picturesque principles of congruity and harmony she painted the walls a more subdued colour, and the shutters and railing, a dark green. In the garden she allowed wild vines and Virginia creeper to entwine itself around

---

Strategically located at the mouth of the Richelieu River, the seigniory of Sorel was purchased by the colonial government in 1781 both to guard this important waterway from invasion from the south and to encourage settlement in the area by the United Empire Loyalists. Supposedly the Governor's Cottage, originally known as William Henry after the future William IV, was built in 1782 as a commandant's residence and later served as the summer abode of the governor in Quebec. Although apparently built by British military personnel, this one-and-a-half-storey building, with its steeply pitched roof, dormers and roughcast wall coating, was not British in design but draws from a distinctly *canadien* house type. The treillaged verandah and the French windows (not evident on the 1823 plan but described by Lady Aylmer in 1831) represent the imposition of British ideas of a Picturesque cottage on the traditional architecture of Quebec. (Fig. 86, Canadian Inventory of Historic Building; Fig. 87, Public Archives Canada, National Map Collection)

86. Governor's Cottage (Manoir de Sorel), 90 Saint Ours Road, Sorel, Quebec
Constructed ca. 1782; **Material** roughcast

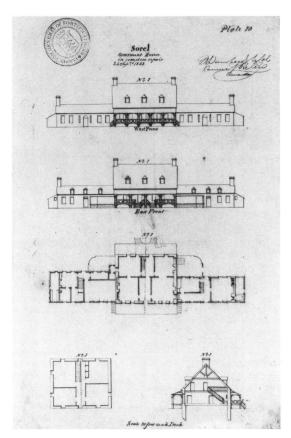

87. Architectural Drawing by E.W. Durnford, R.E., in 1823

the treillage. She planted trees, laid out flower gardens and walks for strolling and improved the "lovely drives through the natural Woods of Magnificent Firs, Cedars and Oak" so as to "provide all the necessary ingredients towards a pretty cottage pleasure ground...which in England is so perfectly understood."[38]

The English response to the indigenous architectural forms of New France provides a unique North American illustration of the process of architectural discovery which produced architecture of the Picturesque. To the newly arrived English colonials the local rural farmhouse was viewed as a quaint yet slightly exotic form which they borrowed and modified to conform to their concept of the cottage while retaining a certain native character. The Picturesque point of view, in opening the eyes to the landscape, uncovered a whole new range of building forms which earned a degree of architectural legitimacy as congruent elements of their particular natural environments, whether it be a Gothic abbey, an Italian villa, a Swiss chalet or a Canadian cottage.

Quebec: Post-1830

The 1830s and 1840s saw the introduction to Lower Canada of new architectural forms more expressive of Picturesque tastes. As in Upper Canada this transition was due largely to the arrival of the British-trained architect in the early 1830s. During this period an English gentleman in Quebec City no longer had to rely on local French builders untutored in English tastes in domestic architecture. Instead he could call on the services of an architect such as Frederick Hacker of Quebec who offered the impressive credentials of having been in the "employ of John Nash esquire, the late King's architect"[39] or on the newly arrived George Browne of Dublin who in 1834 could promise to supply on demand "Designs for Town and Country Houses, Plain and Ornamental Villas and Cottages, Cupolas, Spires, ..."[40] These architects imported a fresher and more sophisticated interpretation of Picturesque values in architecture to the suburban estates of Quebec and Montreal. The increased activity in villa and cottage building of this period was also encouraged by the presence of an expanding bourgeoisie. In Quebec the timber trade had brought new economic prosperity to the city and had created many new gentlemen of wealth who required homes suitable to their situation. Moreover, the retreat to the suburbs was also prompted by the cholera epidemic of the early 1830s — a phenomenon that plagued Upper Canadian cities as well — which gave crowded urban centres an unhealthy reputation.[41]

The major problem in examining this period and taste in domestic building in Lower Canada is the lack of supporting visual documentation. Research has uncovered little visual evidence of villas built between 1830 and 1845, the period in which Upper Canada witnessed the most adventurous architectural experiments in the Picturesque. An examination of the building contracts issued in Quebec indicates several important villas were constructed during this key period but most have unfortunately disappeared without a trace.[42] Only by assembling information from the often vague written descriptions and the few available visual documents can one formulate a hazy picture of the elegant villa designs produced by these immigrant architects.

One of the earliest buildings in Quebec to illustrate this changing character was a double house of 1833 designed by Frederick Hacker for James Hastings Kerr on the Ste-Foy Road (Fig. 88). Although closer in character to a town house than to a villa or cottage, it nevertheless incorporates architectural elements and design characteristics associated with Picturesque architecture not evident in the previous era of villa and cottage building. First, one observes that familiar combination of a flared-roof verandah, treillage and French window set against the smooth reflective surface of the roughcast walls, coloured in the drawing an appropriately subdued yellow. One can also detect the architect's indoctrination into the Picturesque design principle of simplicity with variety. No unnecessary detailing, beyond a plain stringcourse defining the interior floor divisions and a shallow architrave accenting the entrance, interrupts the simple balance between solid and void of the elevation. The slight projection in the wall plane and the decorative screen of the treillaged verandah create those shifting patterns of light and shadow essential to a Picturesque design.

88. Plan for a Double Cottage for James Hastings Kerr, Ste-Foy Road, Ste-Foy, Quebec
Constructed 1832-33; **Demolished; Architect** Frederick Hacker; **Material** brick and stucco
The use of an elevated verandah was probably suggested because of a location in a more confined town lot which bordered on the well-travelled Ste-Foy Road. Such an environment did not invite the use of French windows and verandah opening directly onto the garden. John Nash employed a similar arrangement in his series of Double Cottages at Park Village East in Regent's Park, London (Fig. 5), although in these examples the verandahs overlooked a canal which ran behind the cottages. In fact, Hacker could have been inspired directly by the buildings for he claimed that he had been employed in the office of John Nash before immigrating to Lower Canada. Unfortunately, little is known of Hacker's villa and cottage designs. He built several substantial country residences in the suburbs of Quebec in the 1830s and 1840s but most have disappeared. (Drawing based on plan held in the Archives nationales du Québec)

Frederick Hacker's reputation as a villa and cottage designer was apparently overshadowed by the Dublin architect George Browne who immigrated to Quebec City in 1830. More is known of his work, both as an architect and as a landscape designer, in Upper Canada, particularly Kingston, where several of his designs survive today, but during the 1830s and 1840s he received several commissions for major villas which, if they had survived, would have vied with a Dundurn or a Summerhill. As more research is carried out on this period of domestic architecture, Browne's importance as a leading exponent of the Picturesque in Quebec should be more firmly established.

One of Browne's earliest and most

grandiose villa schemes was designed in 1835 for the Quebec brewer Colin McCallum on the Beauport Road just east of the city. Known only through Browne's written specifications this large residence was defined by a central block forty-five feet square flanked by two wings twenty-two by eleven feet. It contained a drawing room, dining room and saloon. A picture gallery on the mezzanine level was lit from above by a lantern. Apparently the McCallum villa was also characterized by the same dual facade noted on the large villas of Upper Canada. One elevation was articulated by a large portico supported by two large piers and two inset columns (a feature seen on Rockwood in Kingston); the other facade was punctuated by a row of French windows on the ground floor which led onto a colonnade that linked the two wings. If the pattern established in Upper Canada can be maintained this plan would have been developed to allow for the separation of the formal street facade with its central portico probably facing north, and the private garden facade with its spacious colonnade and row of French windows facing south. The McCallum villa also featured a three-foot cantilevered eave and two projecting octagons, probably on the garden facade, both familiar features of villa architecture in Upper Canada.[43]

Around 1847 Browne designed on an equally grand scale a country villa probably for John Molson, Jr. for his Montreal estate on the north side of Mount Royal off Côte-des-Neiges Road (Fig. 89). Built of stone, it featured decorative recessed panelling on a flat street facade, and a large projecting bow window probably punctuated by French windows on what was no doubt intended as the garden facade. The use of a verandah was unusual for Browne who seemed to prefer the heavier, more robust forms of a columned terrace over the insubstantial forms of the treillaged verandah. Browne's general lack of affection for this form is indicated by their inconspicuous location on the side elevations so that they appear as extraneous appendages to the building rather than as integral parts of the design.

As in Upper Canada the eclectic approach inherent in Picturesque architecture was not readily accepted by Lower Canadians who preferred more familiar Regular styles. Nevertheless, a few examples of design in an alternative stylistic vocabulary appeared in the 1830s and early 1840s and again it was George Browne who led the way in these experiments. His design for Benmore, built ca. 1834 for Dominick Daly on his Sillery estate, represents a fairly timid foray into the medieval idiom (Fig. 90). Basically Regular in style, its drip labels around the second-storey windows and its Tudor-arch windows with diamond-shaped panes on the ground floor give the design a mild Gothic flavour. In 1844 Browne produced a more adventurous Gothic design for a cottage for the Molson family on Ile Ste-Marguerite downstream from Montreal (Fig. 91). Adhering to the purist's definition of the Picturesque cottage, it employed an asymmetrical, L-shaped plan and featured pointed-arch dormers, label mouldings and Browne's

---

89. Plan for a Villa; Architect George Browne; drawn ca. 1847 (?)

This plan with its proposed frontage of eighty feet represents Geroge Browne's most ambitious scheme for a country villa. The design itself was characteristic of Browne's style. It incorporated several elements, such as the inset entrance (likely placed on the north street facade) accented by two piers and two columns *in antis* and the shallow recessions in the wall surface, which were also found on Browne's 1841 design for Rockwood in Kingston (Fig. 60). The verandahs appear to have been inconspicuously placed on the east and west sides rather than on the southern garden facade. Unlike John Howard in Toronto, Browne did not have a great affection for the flimsy verandah of the period. He preferred the bold simplicity of the sweeping bowed front to vary and enliven the long southern facade. The plans are undated but they probably represent an early proposal for a villa that was constructed in 1847-48 for John Molson on Chemin de la Reine Marie in Montreal. The villa known as Terra Nova was only three bays wide and featured a verandah across the front facade. In the same mould as Rockwood and Benmore in Quebec (Fig. 90), the executed building was obviously the work of George Browne. (Public Archives Canada, National Map Collection, Molson Family Paper)

119

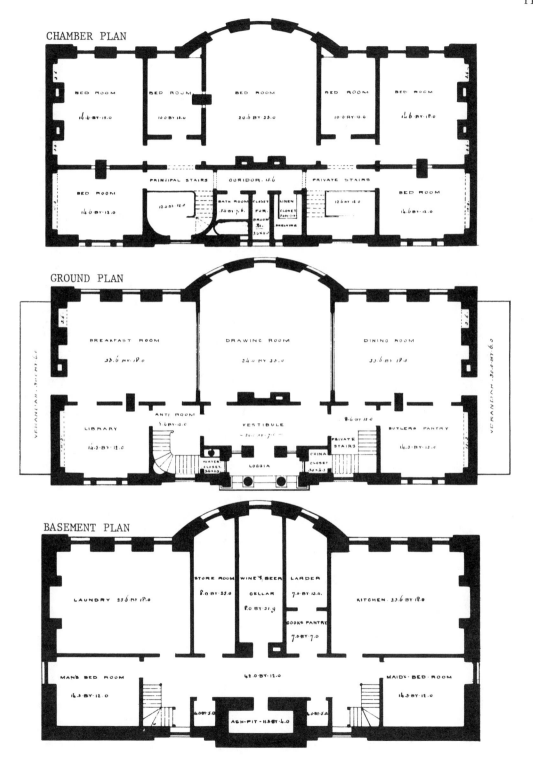

90. Benmore in 1865, 2071 Saint-Louis Road, Sillery, Quebec
Constructed 1834; **Architect** George Browne; **Material** stucco

Although George Browne referred to this building as a Gothic cottage it is described more accurately as designed in a Regular style to which a few Gothicisms had been applied in the form of pointed-arch windows with diamond-shaped panes and drip labels over the second-storey windows. The verandah, which was not mentioned in the original building contract, was probably a later addition. One of many spacious estates which lined the road between Quebec and Cap Rouge, Benmore was built for Sir Dominick Daly, an important colonial official who came to Quebec in 1827. In 1848 Daly left the colony to achieve greater fame as lieutenant-governor of Tobaga (1851), governor of Prince Edward Island (1854-57) and finally as governor of South Australia (1861-68). His Sillery property was sold to Colonel William Rhodes. Benmore is now owned by Les Soeurs Missionnaires Notre-Dame d'Afrique who have carried out extensive alterations including the addition of a mansard roof. (James MacPherson Lemoine, *Maple Leaves: Canadian History and Quebec Scenery*, 3rd ser., Quebec: Hunter Rose, 1865, opp. p. 85)

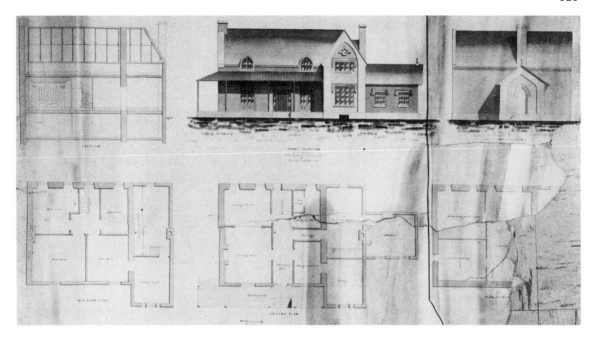

91. Plan for a Cottage for John Molson, Ile Ste-Marguerite, Quebec
Constructed 1844-45; **Architect** George Browne; **Material** stone, brick and stucco

One of several designs produced by George Browne for the Molson family of Montreal, this cottage situated on Ile Ste-Marguerite on the St. Lawrence River downstream from Montreal was not an entirely new structure but a rebuilding and enlargement of an older stone house badly damaged in a fire. The remnants of the original building are outlined in the thicker stone walls indicated on the plan and visible in the parapeted gable, a feature suggesting a typical vernacular cottage common to the upper St. Lawrence River. By adding French windows, a verandah, Gothic dormers, stucco sheathing, and two brick extensions detailed with a pointed, recessed arch and drip labels over the windows, Browne has transformed this traditional French building type into a Picturesquely irregular cottage in the Gothic style. (Archives nationales du Québec, Montreal, No. 1649)

usual recessed wall panels, in this case given a Gothic outline.

From this unfortunately sketchy documentation it appears some of the most interesting and sophisticated architectural expressions of the Picturesque in Lower Canada belonged to the period from 1830 to 1845 paralleling the Upper Canadian experience. From 1845 to 1860 patterns of villa building established in the 1830s survived mainly on a vernacular level in Upper Canada. In Lower Canada a second generation of architects emerged who

continued to produce villa designs based on earlier models. Names such as Edward Stavely,[44] John Cliff, Richard John Cooper, and a native Quebec architect, Charles Baillargé,[45] emerge in connection with some of the important villas of this period.

Quebec buildings such as Spencer Grange of ca. 1844 and Beauvoir designed by John Cliff in 1849 provide typical examples of a Lower Canadian suburban villa of this late Picturesque taste (Figs 92-94). Square and compact, the designers made no attempt to

122

modulate or vary the wall planes or silhouettes with the usual Picturesque devices of projecting bays, recessed panels or decorated, cantilevered eaves. Roughcast or stucco walls were rarely in evidence in these late villas. Wood or a buff-coloured brick were the common materials. All adopted the standard centre-hall plan regardless of their orientation on the lot.

The aesthetic link with Picturesque architecture was expressed primarily in terms of setting, which invariably featured spacious wooded parklands, gardens, and scenic walks and lookouts, and also in the use of the French window and verandah which served as the focus for these designs.[46] As if to compensate for the plainness of the underlying structure the architects concentrated all their decorative inventiveness on the verandah. Drawing on the well-established local woodworking skills, the Lower Canadian verandah was noted for its delicate patterns of treillage which set up a lace-like veil in front of the building. This fanciful appearance was occasionally accentuated by the addition of a scalloped fringe along the roof of the verandah.

Not all villas of this period displayed such ornate verandahs. Two villas near Quebec Cataraqui designed by Edward Stavely in 1850 and Charles Baillairgé's Ravenswood of 1849 — employed simple columns (Figs 95, 96). When adopting this plainer verandah, the architect's eye for varied visual effects realized that these widely spaced columns could not mask the flat wall behind. To compensate for this plainness the wall projects slightly in the centre to modulate the otherwise unbroken plane.

The Quebec *cottage orné* or Anglo-Norman cottage had a much more significant and longer lasting impact on Quebec building. Although first built for the English, it was adopted into the architectural repertoire of the Quebec builder. No doubt the French roots of this form enabled it to be comfortably absorbed into Quebec building patterns.

The Quebec *cottage orné* did not, however, experience equal popularity throughout the colony. The buildings of this type recorded by the Canadian Inventory of Historic Building show a fairly uneven geographic distribution. The greatest number was concentrated in those areas around the city of Quebec and to lesser extent, Montreal, where the *cottage orné* first emerged and radiated outwards to the neighbouring counties.

Situated on a forty-acre lot which comprised the southwest portion of the original Spencer Wood estate, Spencer Grange was built ca. 1844 as a rental property for Henry Atkinson who then resided at Spencer Wood. The basic design of this spacious wooden villa defined by its square, symmetrical plan, hipped roof, French windows (which overlooked the garden and river to the south) and flared-roof verandah supported by delicate treillage was recreated on several later villas built in the suburban communities of Sillery and Ste-Foy during the late 1840s and 1850s. Hamwood, another villa of similar design, was built for J.W. Leycraft in nearby Ste-Foy in the same year. This building, illustrated in Lemoine's *Maple Leaves* (3rd series, opp. p. 114), was designed by local architect Richard John Cooper. In 1852, when the government of the United Canadas purchased Spencer Wood for use as the new Government House, Henry Atkinson moved next door into Spencer Grange. An avid horticulturalist, Atkinson constructed several conservatories and graperies and, according to an 1865 description by Quebec historian James MacPherson Lemoine, improved the grounds in "the English landscape style" with shaded walks, ornamental flower gardens and even a rustic bower perched on the clifftop. Lemoine in fact bought the property from Atkinson in 1860 and it was Lemoine who carried out the extensive interior renovation in 1882 and who added a new northern street facade in an asymmetrical design with an off-centre tower. The southern facade was only slightly modified by the addition of three dormer windows and roof cresting. (Fig. 92, Canadian Inventory of Historic Building; Fig. 93, James MacPherson Lemoine, *Maple Leaves: Canadian History and Quebec Scenery*, 3rd ser., Quebec: Hunter Rose, 1865, opp. p. 79)

92. Spencer Grange, ca. 1972, 1321 Lemoine Avenue, Sillery, Quebec
Constructed ca. 1844; Material wood

93. Spencer Grange in 1865

94. Beauvoir in 1865, 2315 Saint-Louis Road, Sillery, Quebec
Constructed 1849; **Architect** John Cliff; **Material** yellow brick

Beauvoir was built in 1849 for Henry Lemesurier according to plans drawn up by John Cliff, a Quebec architect of whom little is known. Its symmetrical facade and rectangular centre-hall plan surmounted by a low, close-eaved hipped roof illustrates the fairly conservative character of the typical Quebec villa of this period, a contrast to its Ontario counterpart. The verandah with its wide treillage and scalloped fringe is, however, much more fanciful and picturesque in its treatment than the typical Ontario verandah. The raised ground storey was also a feature peculiar to Quebec architecture. In 1866 Beauvoir burned down, but the following year it was rebuilt according to the original plans and specifications of 1849. Although it has received several additions since then, the main part of the building has remained relatively unchanged. Since 1939 Beauvoir has been used as a boys' school run by the Maristes Fathers of Quebec. (James MacPherson Lemoine, *Maple Leaves: Canadian History and Quebec Scenery*, 3rd ser., Quebec: Hunter Rose, 1865, p. 89)

95. Cataraqui, 2141 Saint-Louis Road, Sillery, Quebec
Constructed 1850-51; **Architect** Edward Stavely; **Material** brick
Built for Quebec merchant Henry Burstall, Cataraqui is one of the few country villas in Quebec to have survived in any recognizable form. The design, however, retains only a few architectural elements associated with Picturesque architecture — the wide verandah, French windows and the subdued colour of the buff brick. The richer, more elaborate detailing — eared mouldings around the windows, the quoining at the corners and the heaviness of the verandah supports — is more in keeping with Victorian tastes, and contrasts with the lightness and simplicity of design which characterized the earlier villas and cottages, particularly those found in Ontario. When Spencer Wood burned down in 1860 Cataraqui was taken over as the governor-general's residence until 1863. The two flanking wings were probably added then. (Canadian Inventory of Historic Building)

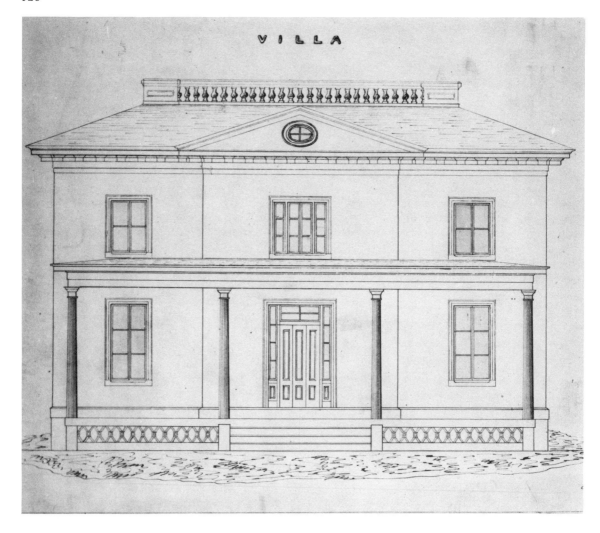

96. Plan of Ravenswood, Cap-Rouge Road, Sillery, Quebec
Constructed ca. 1849; **Demolished; Architect** Charles Baillairgé; **Material** brick

"Here was, for a man familiar with the park-like scenery of England, a store of materials to work into shape. That dense forest must be thinned; that indispensible adjunct of every Sillery home, a velvety lawn, must be had; a peep through the trees, on the surrounding country obtained...." This description of the landscape improvements at Ravenswood by Quebec historian James MacPherson Lemoine in 1865 could probably be applied to most of the country villas found in the vicinity of Quebec and illustrates well the continuation of Picturesque values and tastes in landscape design well into the nineteenth century. The house was designed in 1849 by native-born architect Charles Baillairgé for Samuel Wright and supposedly completed in that year although with some modifications and simplifications in the cornice and roof detail. (Archives de la ville de Québec, Charles Baillairgé Papers, file no. 1: Les maisons privées —pièce nº 9)

The typical *cottage orné* of the 1840s was a continuation of the pattern established in Rosewood cottage. Typified by Kirk Ella (Fig. 97), and the Henry cottage at 82 Grande Allée in Quebec (Fig. 98), it featured the same square symmetrical, one-storey plan with a hipped roof, usually bellcast, and a wide verandah to support the broad overhanging eaves. In this later period the incline of the roof became gentler assuming that low-lying profile similar to the Ontario *cottage orné*. French windows were also introduced into the facade and the large central chimney of pre-1830 cottages was replaced by two tall chimneys located on the outer side walls.

A second less common type of cottage dating to the 1830s employed a terrace, that is, an open deck without the usual, upright supports. One of the earliest examples the Manoir Campbell-Rankin of 1835 at Pointe-Sèche, Kamouraska (Fig. 99), was unusual for its decorative quoining and its entrance arrangement whereby the two main doors were placed on short facades accented by gables at each end. The open wooden terrace was not part of the cottage vocabulary of England but it had been employed in the architecture of New France, providing another illustration of the incorporation of local forms to reinforce the French and slightly exotic flavour of the rural cottage retreat in Quebec.

One of the most curious interpretations of this type was the Manoir Saint-Roch-des-Aulnaies designed by Charles Baillairgé (Fig. 100). Here Baillairgé demonstrates his ability to synthesize his own French building traditions with Picturesque forms to create a thoroughly unique design. The manoir's low flared roof, overhanging eaves, scalloped fringe and the uneven roofline conform to Picturesque tastes for varied line and plane and effects of light and shadow. The octagonal projections were a common motif in Picturesque architecture but this layout could also be interpreted as a reference to the U-shaped plan of the manoirs of New France. The raised cantilevered terrace was also a feature associated with the vernacular architecture of Quebec.

After 1850 the Quebec *cottage orné* experienced a rejuvenation. Previously a form associated with a predominantly English clientele, it became accepted into a wider Quebec building repertoire. The Maison Hamel in Sillery built between 1849 and 1855 provides a particularly fine example of this type (Fig. 101). It was very similar to Kirk Ella in its general silhouette, its wide treillaged verandah and its landscaped gardens, but unlike the classic Picturesque cottage it substituted the usual French window for the shorter casement type. Generally, however, the difference between the Picturesque cottage and these later generic descendants was much sharper. The cottage at Les Cèdres just south of Montreal represents a more typical version (Fig. 102). It retains the familiar cottage profile and encircling verandah in this case supported by simple posts instead of treillage, but the decorative treatment of the door and window surrounds constrasts with the general restraint in surface detail evident in the original *cottage orné*. The applied pilasters around the door and stylized window pediments reflect the strong influence of classical motifs on Quebec architecture. The most significant departure from Picturesque values is its setting. Pushed right up against the road the front verandah is completely unprotected from the noise and dust of the street and a bare agricultural landscape stretches out behind.

Another common variation of the Quebec cottage illustrated by a house in Lévis (Fig. 103), represents a continuation of the design theme established by the Manoir Campbell-Rankin. This type often featured a cantilevered terrace surrounded by a low railing unique to Quebec. The distinctive roofline of the Lévis cottage created by the curved lines of the bellcast roof and the concave soffit is found on several buildings in the province.

An unusual variation of the Quebec cottage, of which there are a few examples in the vicinity of Quebec, incorporated a second storey. Two now-demolished residences in Ste-Foy are two of the most elaborate examples of this type (Figs 104, 105). Bellevue, built in 1847, featured a two-storey columned gallery although generally verandahs were not employed on this enlarged cottage type. If external galleries were used, they were usually open decks or terraces as in Boisbrillant. Because of its scale, it should have been included perhaps in the villa category but its bellcast silhouette indicates the source of its design was the *cottage orné* simply expanded by one storey.

97. Kirk Ella in 1865, Saint-Louis Road, Sillery, Quebec
Constructed ca. 1850; **Demolished** 1879; **Material** brick

Kirk Ella was probably built around 1850 for Edward Burstall of Quebec. This date is substantiated by Kirk Ella's design which closely conforms to the standard cottage pattern of the period as defined by the mid-nineteenth century cottages of 82 Grande Allée and Maison Hamel (Figs 98, 101). Ten years after this photograph was taken, Kirk Ella was considerably enlarged according to the plans of Quebec architect Harry Stavely (the son of Edward Stavely). A second storey was added and the building was given a Victorian up-date by the addition of heavy scroll brackets under the eaves. Kirk Ella was demolished in 1879. (James MacPherson Lemoine, *Maple Leaves: Canadian History and Quebec Scenery*, 3rd ser., Quebec: Hunter Rose, 1865, opp. p. 86)

98. Henry Cottage, 82 Grande Allée West, Quebec City, Quebec
Constructed 1849-50 by Joseph Archer; **Material** brick

Situated on a small cottage lot but buffered from Grande Allée by a fence, lawn and a screen of trees and shrubbery, this cottage provides a well-preserved example of the so-called Anglo-Norman cottage, that distinctly Quebec version of the *cottage orné*. Built and likely designed by English-born builder Joseph Archer for Mrs. William Henry, its walls were composed of a subdued buff brick, a popular material for both villa and cottage architecture in Quebec. The use of plain post supports rather than the more common treillage gives the building a slightly more austere appearance although the presence of attached trellis-work indicates that climbing vines were intended to mask the simplicity of these forms. The off-centre glazing bars or mullions of the French windows observed on several villas and cottages in Ontario re-emerge on this Quebec building. (Canadian Inventory of Historic Building)

99. Manoir Campbell-Rankin, at Pointe-Sèche, Saint-Germain-de-Kamouraska, Quebec
Material stone and stucco

Built on the foundations of an earlier building, the Manoir Campbell-Rankin was constructed for John Saxton Campbell, a wealthy Quebec businessman. Although built by Quebec contractor Joseph Turcotte, a reference to both plans and a wooden model in the building specifications of 1835 suggests that it was not designed by him. The design represents an unusual expression of the *cottage orné* unique to Quebec. The low hipped profile, French windows, stucco walls and elevated landscaped setting overlooking the St. Lawrence River conform to the basic format of the typical *cottage orné*. The balustraded roof deck, corner quoins and location of the main door on the short facade provide novel variations to this type. The open terrace and bellcast roof, both features related to traditional French building, are generally found only on cottage design in Quebec. It is noteworthy that the building specifications describe the roof as "formed in the Chinese style" although it is unlikely that it was the intention of the architect to make any specific reference to Chinese architecture. Often the term "Chinese" was used to describe forms of a slightly exotic character not rooted in the classical or Gothic traditions native to Europe. (Canadian Inventory of Historic Building)

100. Manoir Saint-Roch-des-Aulnaies, Saint-Roch-des-Aulnaies, Quebec
Constructed 1852-53; **Architect** Charles Baillairgé; **Material** wood

The seignory of Saint-Roch-des-Aulnaies (or Grand Anse) is situated on the south shore of the lower St. Lawrence River downstream from Quebec. Ceded to Nicholas Juchereau in 1656 the property remained in that family until 1833 when it was purchased by Amable Dionne. The present *manoir* built for the Dionne family by Charles Baillairgé represents a striking and unique synthesis of several architectural traditions. The U-shaped plan and raised terrace recall the traditional architecture of New France while the bellcast roof, projecting pavilions which are accented in the roofline by decorative urns, the wide eaves and the scalloped eave fringe reinterpret this basic form in a thoroughly Picturesque manner. A third stylistic theme is introduced by the richly ornamented door and window trim which reflected the influence of the then-popular pattern books of American Greek-Revivalist architect Minard Lafever. In 1894 the property passed to the Miville-Deschenes family and in 1963 it was purchased by the province of Quebec which has undertaken its restoration. (Canadian Inventory of Historic Building)

101. Maison Hamel, 2068 Saint-Louis Road, Sillery, Quebec
Constructed 1849-55; **Material** wood

Maison Hamel is a finely detailed and well-proportioned example of the typical vernacular version of the Quebec *cottage orné*. This type of building which endured well into the late nineteenth century demonstrated a strong link with established French building traditions in its use of the shorter casement windows in preference to the French window so strongly associated with Picturesque architecture in Canada. It is noteworthy that its treillage design is almost identical to that of Kirk Ella (Fig. 97). Specific patterns of treillage often reappeared with only slight variations on several buildings within a given area. This borrowing often arose from the economical practice of specifying carpenter's work in terms of existing models in the neighbourhood rather than going to the expense of drawing up a new set of plans. (Canadian Inventory of Historic Building)

The cottage at Les Cèdres and the cottage at Lévis represent two variations of a vernacular Quebec house descended from the Picturesque *cottage orné*. This design type characterized by its low hipped or bellcast roof, wide overhanging eaves, tall chimneys and either a verandah or open terrace along three sides adopts the basic profile of the Quebec *cottage orné* defined by a cottage like Kirk Ella in Sillery (Fig. 97). Unlike Kirk Ella these buildings are set close to the road on bare, open lots unprotected from the noise and dust of the street. The Picturesque idea of the cottage as a gentleman's tranquil retreat set in the natural splendours of a romantic landscape has been lost. These vernacular buildings may represent Picturesque values in general appearance but not in spirit. (Figs 102, 103, Canadian Inventory of Historic Building)

102. House, 1274 River Road, Les Cèdres, Quebec; Material wood and stucco

103. Cottage, 118 Saint-Georges Street West, Lévis, Quebec; Material wood

104. Boisbrillant, Quatre Bourgeois Road, Ste-Foy, Quebec
Constructed ca. 1860; **Demolished** 1949; **Material** brick

Boisbrillant is believed to have been built around 1860 for Siméon LeSage. Its design is derived from the Quebec Picturesque cottage which featured an open terrace or deck as illustrated in the Manoir Campbell-Rankin (Fig. 99) but considerably expanded by the addition of an extra storey and two flanking wings. Although several of these enlarged versions of the Picturesque cottage were built in the vicinity of Quebec, none was as elaborate or as finely detailed as this building. A unique design in Quebec architecture, it was unfortunately demolished in 1949. (Ministère des Affaires culturelles, Inventaire des Biens culturels, Centre de documentation, Morisset Papers, Quebec, 14947 C-1)

105. Bellevue, 750 Ste-Foy Road, Ste-Foy, Quebec
Constructed 1847-48; **Demolished** 1970; **Material** stone

Bellevue could be described as a late descendent of the Maison Montmorency. Like the late eighteenth century villa belonging to Governor Haldimand, Bellevue features a two-storey gallery surrounding three sides of the building. The use of Doric columns instead of post or treillage supports lends a slightly more formal character to the design. Bellevue was built in 1847 for Julien Chouinard, a merchant of Quebec. Although no architect has been identified the construction contract cited Jean Paquet as the stone mason. In 1866 Bellevue was sold to D.W. Dunscomb who changed the name of his residence to Monument House in reference to the *Monument aux braves* which was situated on the edge of his property. Bellevue was demolished in 1970 to make way for apartment buildings. (Canadian Inventory of Historic Building)

136

The late phase of cottage building is not a direct product of the Picturesque Movement. These buildings have borrowed a basic form which grew out of this aesthetic but modified it to conform to indigenous tastes in building. This blending of architectural values created a fresh and original design type.

Atlantic Provinces

As Britain's oldest colonies in Canada and closest geographically, one might expect the influence of British tastes to be most prevalent in the Atlantic provinces; however, it was here that the Picturesque point of view in landscape and architecture had the least impact. Unlike Ontario and Quebec, no consistent patterns of villa and cottage design emerged in the Atlantic provinces during the early nineteenth century. The few examples that can be found scattered throughout the provinces of Nova Scotia, New Brunswick, Prince Edward Island and Newfoundland stand out as architectural oddities removed from the mainstream of popular building modes.

Newfoundland did not provide fertile ground for architecture of the Picturesque. The development of Newfoundland as a self-sufficient colony had been intentionally retarded by the British government which wanted to maintain the colony purely as a summer base for the Grand Banks fishing grounds to be controlled from English ports. Although permanent settlements can be dated back to the beginning of the seventeenth century, they were of a transient character, isolated from each other, and rising and falling in size according to the shifting fortunes of the fishing industry.[47]

By the end of the eighteenth century British policy towards Newfoundland was forced to acknowledge the presence of a permanent resident community but it was not until 1825 that Britain officially recognized Newfoundland as a colony.[48] Even with this new status the character of Newfoundland did not change drastically. Newfoundland's harsh climate and poor soil, which rendered it unsuitable for agricultural development, made it an unpopular destination for immigrants. Many poor Irish workers settled in

Newfoundland during the 1810s to work on the fishing boats or in related trades on shore but by the 1820s, a period in which Upper Canada witnessed the arrival of many middle-class English immigrants and with them contemporary tastes in domestic architecture, immigration from Britain slowed to a trickle.[49]

In the first half of the nineteenth century the character of Newfoundland architecture, with the exception of a few major government buildings, remained unpretentious. The typical Newfoundland house was a square wooden structure based on vernacular types found in Ireland and England and generally devoid of any ambitions to style.[50] Only in the design of a few cottages built for a small resident group of educated English gentlemen in the vicinity of St. John's can one identify a modest influence of the Picturesque taste.

A somewhat similar pattern of early development, although arising from slightly different causes, was experienced in Prince Edward Island. In 1758 the original Acadian population had been expelled and in 1769 the island received its own colonial government. At that point the entire island was subdivided into lots in anticipation of a large-scale settlement from Britain. Unfortunately, the land was purchased by investors in England who had no intention of settling in Prince Edward Island and had little interest in its development. Settlers were sent out from Britain to farm the land but they were generally poor tenant farmers — not the type of immigrant who built fashionable villas and cottages.[51] The middle-class immigrant of moderate fortune who, in Upper and Lower Canada, had promoted the Picturesque taste in architecture did not settle initially in Prince Edward Island. Even by the late 1820s this colony was described by one immigrant's guide as "wretchedly poor, nothing but heaps of rocks covered with fir trees."[52]

Again, one has to look to the colonial centre of Charlottetown to identify any influences of the Picturesque taste. But even here, although elegant houses were built during the first half of the nineteenth century, their designs tended to follow patterns of building found in the nearby colonies of New Brunswick and Nova Scotia which, as will be seen, were not directly derived from British tastes.

The development of Nova Scotia and New Brunswick was not stunted in the same way as Newfoundland or Prince Edward Island. By the turn of the nineteenth century they offered several large prosperous communities; yet, still the Picturesque point of view in landscape and architecture was not a prominent element in domestic building design. The explanation of the unpicturesque quality of the architecture in these provinces lies in the influence of a dominant American element in their early development.

From the early seventeenth century, New England, which regarded the Maritimes as its northeastern frontier, exerted a profound impact on its character and development.[53] Although many British and foreign immigrants made their way to the Maritimes before 1800, they were generally not the type to possess land or give leadership to the pioneer community. It was left to the pre-Loyalist settlers to transform the British military stronghold, centred around Halifax, into an organized resident community. The American element in the Maritime population was greatly strengthened after 1776 with the arrival of the United Empire Loyalists. Not surprisingly many of these Loyalists were drawn from the old colonial elite of the British American colonies. They were men of influence, education and good income and they naturally assumed prominent positions in their new home.[54]

These New England settlers saw themselves as loyal British subjects but culturally they had been Americanized; the architectural character of their dwellings survives as witness to their cultural roots. *Acadian Magazine* of 1827 described a typical Maritime house as "being built of wood, two storeys high with a pitch roof and covered with shingles."[55] A basic box-like form was punctuated by a symmetrical three- or five-bay facade with an interior plan featuring an even distribution of rooms around a centre hall. Their homes imparted a sense of Puritan austerity drawn from the American colonial building tradition.[56]

The American character of the communities in Nova Scotia and New Brunswick was often remarked upon by British visitors to the region. One traveller in New Brunswick in 1847 observed,

It is a common remark, that the customs and manners of the inhabitants of New Brunswick are more similar to those of the people of the United States than to those of any other British Province. This cannot be surprising, when it is considered that its early settlers emigrated from the revolted Colonies, and, from being situated along the frontier, the frequent intercourse with their American neighbours has had some effect upon the social state of the people;[57]

The patrons and the architects responsible for introducing and promoting the Picturesque taste in the Canadas were not as prominent an element in the Atlantic provinces. Those middle-class British immigrants who did settle here tended to become absorbed into the well-established cultural and architectural patterns. The British-trained architect who in the Canadas had been so important in providing sophisticated Picturesque models was not present in the eastern colonies.[58] The Royal Engineers were trained in Britain, but their building activities were concentrated on large public and military structures usually designed in a late-Palladian style; they were not occupied with the building of elegant villas and cottages for a private clientele. As a result, the problem of identifying the Picturesque influence on domestic building in the Atlantic provinces is reduced to extracting a few specific details or general qualities in design or landscape applied to buildings whose architectural roots lay elsewhere.

As in Upper and Lower Canada the first examples of the English taste in landscape and architecture were introduced by high-level colonial officials, in this case, by the Duke of Kent who was stationed in Halifax from 1794 to 1800. A short distance from Halifax on the Bedford Basin he purchased a large tract of land. He subsequently tranformed the property into a gentleman's suburban estate complete with long avenues which wound through a well-treed park dotted with grottoes, arbours covered with climbing vines, a music pavilion and even a Chinese pagoda (Figs 106-107).[59] Today, of the original buildings abandoned after the departure of the duke, only the music pavilion has survived (Fig. 106). Similar in spirit to Governor Simcoe's rustic temple, Castle Frank in Toronto, the music pavilion, characterized by

106. Music Pavilion, Bedford Basin, Halifax, Nova Scotia; Constructed 1794; Material wood

Originally owned by William Foy, this large estate was purchased in 1794 by the Duke of Kent who was responsible for all the construction on the site and for laying out and beautifying the grounds. This watercolour, despite its amateurish hand, captures well the natural yet carefully composed character of a late eighteenth century landscape. The simple classical geometry of the music pavilion (the only surviving structure on the estate) is contrasted with its surrounding frame of lush vegetation. Its setting on top of a rise of land overlooking the Bedford Basin establishes this form as the compositional focus for the wide panorama of undulating hills, sea and rugged coastline as viewed from the gallery of the main lodge. After the departure of the Duke of Kent in 1800 the estate remained vacant and by 1836, according to Thomas Chandler Haliburton's description, the wooden buildings were already in a dilapidated state. (Fig. 106, Provincial Archives of Nova Scotia; Fig. 107, Metropolitan Toronto Library Board)

107. Watercolour Depicting the Duke of Kent's Estate in the Nineteenth Century

its play of circular and spherical forms, reflects a restrained classical purism which had little of the informal, often astylistic quality associated with much of Picturesque architecture. A sense of the Picturesque is expressed solely in terms of creating romantic and painterly compositions through effective setting in the eighteenth century manner of Capability Brown (Fig. 107).

The wealthy establishment of Halifax soon followed the royal retreat into the suburbs and by the 1820s several large country estates had been established on the outskirts of Halifax. The most fashionable properties were located on the wooded banks of the Northwest Arm. An article which appeared in the *Nova Scotian* in 1825 describes the recent improvements in this area.

> In place of a few scattered cottages, there is now an assemblage of gentleman's residences. To the south there is the princely mansion lately erected by Hon. E. Collins; to the west Mr. Richardson's beautiful seat of Studley which is perhaps the best resemblance to a gentleman's country residence in England...that is to be found in the neighbourhood of the town.[60]

The description of these two buildings as reminiscent of an English country estate, however, probably refers more to the general scale of the building, the extent of the property and to the extensive facilities — stables, barns, dairies and ornamental gardens — than to the character of the design. Studley in particular (Fig. 108) was a square, two-storey, wood-shingled building, regularly punctuated by small, double-hung sash windows, which more closely resembles a New England manor house than a Regency gentleman's villa of the 1820s. Gorsebrook (Fig. 109), the name given to the Collins estate, does display some design traits associated with Picturesque architecture, namely the flared treillaged verandah and the bow windows (which first apeared in Nova Scotia on the Royal Engineer's design for Government House of 1800). Nevertheless, its square, five-bay, two-storey form sheathed in wood shingles and close-eaved hipped roof basically adheres to the standard American colonial type.

One outstanding contrast to this apparent conservatism is Girvan Bank, built at Annapolis Royal in 1817 and located far from the major colonial centres (Fig. 110). While it adopts the basic symmetrical form of Gorsebrook with its two-storey bow windows, its design breaks away from the usual Maritime taste for classical balance and order.

108. Studley (Early View), Coburg Road, Halifax, Nova Scotia; Demolished; Material wood

The history of Studley has never been accurately documented. It is known that a house was built on the site in 1803 for Sir Archibald Croke, an English lawyer, who had been sent to Halifax the previous year to serve as the judge of the vice-admiralty court in Halifax. In 1815 Croke returned to England and the estate was sold in 1816 to Matthew Richardson, a local merchant. Before the sale, however, the house was, according to a notice in the *Acadian Recorder* of 1816, "considerably added to and put into complete repair." Other undocumented sources have stated that the original Studley burned down and was replaced by this structure. Whether this fire took place around 1816 and resulted in the extensive rebuilding of Studley alluded to in the newspaper notice is unknown although the strong similarities between Studley and Gorsebrook, which was built around 1818, suggest near-contemporary construction dates. (Public Archives of Nova Scotia)

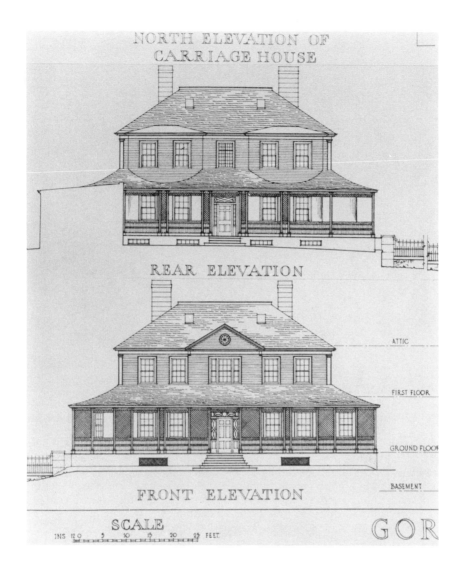

NORTH ELEVATION OF CARRIAGE HOUSE

REAR ELEVATION

ATTIC

FIRST FLOOR

GROUND FLOOR

BASEMENT

FRONT ELEVATION

SCALE

INS 12 O   5   10   15   20   25 FEET

GOR

109. Plan of Gorsebrook, Tower Road, Halifax, Nova Scotia
Constructed ca. 1818; **Demolished; Material** wood

If one removed the verandah and the bow windows, Gorsebrook, with its five-bay, two-and-a-half-storey frame punctuated with evenly proportioned windows, central pediment over the main entrance and decorative end-board pilasters, would fall neatly into the typical pattern of Maritime building rooted in the American vernacular tradition. The application of the full encircling verandah to this form was unusual and has led some historians to suspect it is a later addition. There is no documentation to support this supposition; moreover, this feature, with its flared roof and treillage supports, is in keeping with prevailing English taste in domestic architecture of the period. Gorsebrook was built for John Moody, a United Empire Loyalist and wealthy Halifax businessman, and later sold to Enos Collins, a gentleman of similar background and position. Unfortunately, this elegant country residence, complete with servant's wing, carriage house, stables and a fine interior decor in the Adamesque style, no longer stands. (Heritage Trust of Nova Scotia and the Nova Scotia Museum)

110. Girvan Bank, 478 Saint George Street, Annapolis Royal, Nova Scotia
Constructed 1817; **Material** wood

Built for the Reverend John Millidge, the Anglican rector of Annapolis, Girvan Bank stands out as an architectural oddity within the Maritime context. While the basic form of Girvan Bank with its two bow windows was probably influenced by two earlier Halifax buildings — Government House of 1800 and Gorsebrook of 1818 — the gentler sweep of the large bow windows, repeated in the overhanging eave line and finally merged into the slope of the gracefully flared roof, contrasts with the straighter, more formal lines of the Halifax examples. (Canadian Inventory of Historic Building)

The characteristic villa proportioning observed on the villas of Upper and Lower Canada, defined by the tall ground-floor windows and shorter windows above, emphasized the low-lying horizontality of the design. The familiar overhanging eaves, flared roof and large windows impart that sense of openness and astylistic informality the Picturesque point of view invited in architecture.

Of the smaller cottage variety there is little to compare to those snug, low-lying cottages built in Upper and Lower Canada during the 1810s and 1820s. Although the term "cottage" was often used to describe buildings, it generally referred to the small, one-and-a-half-storey wood-shingled house with gable ends found anywhere along the eastern seaboard. A few examples of this type, such as Morris House near Dartmouth built around 1803 (Fig. 111), incorporated the French window and verandah of the typical *cottage orné* but these elements appeared sporadically and were never absorbed into the vocabulary of Maritime building.

In St. John's the summer cottage of Sir Thomas Cochrane, Newfoundland's first colonial governor, which was built in the 1820s, was the best-known example of a

111. Morris House in the Nineteenth Century, Lake Loon, near Dartmouth, Nova Scotia
Constructed ca. 1803; **Demolished; Material** wood

Morris House, supposedly built in the first decade of the nineteenth century, is said to have been built for the son or grandson of Charles Morris, a land surveyor from New England sent to Halifax in 1749 to lay out lots for the future settlement of Nova Scotia. The North American roots of this family are evident in the design of his house. Except for the French window there is little in this building reflecting British architectural tastes of the nineteenth century. The square wooden frame sheathed in shingles, with the off-centre doorway, steep roof and bay dormers reflect the influence of the vernacular architecture of the old American colonies. Even the use of the verandah, which might be interpreted in terms of English tastes for the Picturesque, was more likely influenced by New England houses such as those found in the Hudson Valley which also featured front galleries. (Public Archives of Nova Scotia)

gentleman's cottage estate in the area. According to Sir Richard Henry Bonnycastle, in 1842 the property known as Virginia Water was situated,

> about three miles from St. John's, where a small picturesque lake flows almost around a projecting woodland, on which he [Sir Thomas Cochrane] built an ornamental cottage... A more elegant thought, carried more effectively into execution, could not have been devised, and it shews, what even the rugged neighbourhood of St. John's is capable of.[61]

The cottage itself, however, was a square wooden structure with a straight gable roof distinguished from the typical Newfoundland house only by the addition of a verandah and its Picturesque landscape setting which justified Bonnycastle's perception of this modest building as an ornamental cottage. Virginia Water, known only from a small nineteenth century photograph, was demolished in 1887.[62]

The conservatism of Maritime domestic building of the early nineteenth century did not differ remarkably from the contemporary villas and cottages found in Upper and Lower Canada which tended toward simple functional

144

designs. The difference between the cultural orientation of the Maritimes versus that of Ontario and the English colonials of Quebec becomes apparent after 1830. At a time when the British-trained architects of the Canadas were carrying out their most exotic experiments in the eclecticism of the Picturesque, Maritime architecture held fast to its traditions.

In Halifax's exclusive suburb of the Northwest Arm, several country residences were constructed in the 1830s but none of which we have visual record demonstrates any great sympathy for Picturesque tastes. For example, the Honourable Hugh Bell's suburban

estate of Bloomfield, a one-and-a-half-storey wood-frame building with a straight gable roof, small sash windows and flanking wings, illustrates well the unshakeable conservatism of the Maritime builder. The fact that Bloomfield was built in 1838, two years after John Howard's Colborne Lodge or seven years after John Henry Boulton's Holland House in Toronto, indicates the wide gulf between Maritime and Upper Canadian tastes.

Fairholm in Charlottetown, built around 1838 for Judge Thomas Haviland, is perhaps the closest approximation to a Picturesque villa in the Maritimes (Figs 112, 113). A continuation of the design theme set by

112. Fairholm in the Nineteenth Century, 230 Prince Street, Charlottetown, Prince Edward Island
Constructed 1837-40; **Material** brick

Fairholm, built for the English-born Thomas Heath Haviland, was the last in the series of double bow-fronted residences which were most common in Canada in the Maritimes. The lithograph inaccurately gives the building the appearance of being constructed of smoothly dressed stone. In reality it was red brick in contravention of Picturesque preferences in colour and materials. Fairholm has survived in good condition although a new front portico was built in the mid-nineteenth century and an enclosed sun porch was constructed over this in 1926. (Fig. 112, Public Archives of Nova Scotia; Fig. 113, Canadian Inventory of Historic Building)

113. Fairholm Today

Gorsebrook or Girvan Bank, Fairholm employed sweeping bow windows and slightly overhanging eaves. But the symmetrical centre-hall plan and the absence of typical villa amenities — the verandah and French window, and the use of red brick instead of roughcast or stone — links it firmly to local building patterns.

Similarly, in cottage building no clearly defined patterns of building reflecting Picturesque values in architecture were established in the Maritimes in the 1830s. John Townsend Coffin's country residence, Lonewater, built in 1832 and situated on the banks of the Nerepis River southwest of Saint John, New Brunswick, shows little development from the type illustrated by Morris House; moreover, its approach to landscape whereby a square parcel of land is carved out

of the natural landscape and laid out in a formal system of paths and vegetation was completely opposed to the Picturesque approach which strove to "cherish the accidental beauties of nature" (Fig. 114).

Hawthorne Cottage in Brigus, Newfoundland, built in the 1830s, features the verandah and low hipped roof reminiscent of the Ontario version of the *cottage orné* (Fig. 115). This modest expression of Picturesque architecture did not, however, establish any general pattern of building in this province.

A few examples of cottage estates set in Picturesque landscape settings did appear in Nova Scotia in the 1830s. One example was Clifton (Figs 116, 117) built in 1836 for Thomas Chandler Haliburton, a first-generation Maritimer of Loyalist stock, best remembered as the author of the Sam Slick

114. **Lonewater in the Nineteenth Century, Near Westfield, Kings County, New Brunswick**
Constructed pre-1832; **Demolished;** watercolour by George N. Smith in 1839

In 1765 General John Coffin of Boston, Massachusetts, purchased 600 acres of land near the mouth of the Nerepis River in Kings County, New Brunswick, and in 1783 he moved there permanently having fled the United States after the revolutionary war. Lonewater, one of several Coffin houses on this large estate, was occupied in 1832 by the general's son, Captain (later Admiral) John Townshend Coffin, who lived there only two years before moving to England. Like Morris House near Dartmouth (Fig. 111), Lonewater featured French windows and a verandah on three sides but otherwise there is little in this regular box-like design set into its square, symmetrical garden that demonstrates any consciousness of Picturesque effect in architectural design or in landscape composition. (Courtesy The New Brunswick Museum)

115. Hawthorne Cottage, Brigus, Newfoundland; Constructed ca. 1830; **Material** wood

Hawthorne Cottage is one of the few buildings in Newfoundland that conformed generally to the *cottage orné* as found in Ontario or Quebec. The bellcast verandah surrounding the building on three sides is unusual for its rough fretwork detailing. Built for R.J.C. Leamon, a Brigus merchant, Hawthorne Cottage was originally situated outside the town but in 1834 Mrs. Leamon, not wanting to live in the country, insisted the house be moved the six miles into Brigus where it now stands. The two-storey rear addition was built in 1890. (Canadian Inventory of Historic Building)

148

stories. Another was the cottage built for Anglican missionary John Burnyeats near Truro, Nova Scotia (Fig. 118). Both functioned as country retreats set in park settings thereby fulfilling basic requirements of the *cottage orné*. Clifton in particular was famous throughout Nova Scotia for its raised setting and fine prospect over the town of Windsor and the Avon River. Its landscaped grounds, laid out by Haliburton and his Irish wife, consisted of a long winding entrance drive, shaded with a variety of trees, footpaths and a pond around which quaint rustic seats and nooks were secreted among the shrubbery providing quiet retreats for the stroller.

The designs for these buildings, however, related only slightly to Picturesque architecture. Although these low, one-storey hipped-roof structures conformed generally to the Canadian cottage type, their square wooden frames marked at the corners by panelled end boards suggestive of pilasters, and Clifton's closed wooden porch, a protection against the damp Maritime winds, were typical of North American rather than British building conventions. The use of Gothic windows on the cottage was unprecedented in Maritime building but this medieval touch had little to do with the Picturesque taste for the traditional medieval cottage and is better described as a vernacular adaptation of a carpenter's Gothic church to identify the building as the residence of an Anglican minister.

One building, a tavern in Stanley, New Brunswick, seems completely inconsistent with the Maritime building preferences of the first half of the nineteenth century (Fig. 119). A tavern should fall outside the scope of this study, but its design is one of the few clear expressions of Picturesque values. Although clearly not surrounded by a landscaped pleasure ground it was set into the romantic environment of New Brunswick's inland forests. Built of logs sheathed in roughcast, the building was composed of two gabled wings attached to a raised central section with a massive chimney creating a varied composition of roof forms. Like a Regular style villa the eaves were wide but heavy concave brackets extended down the full face of the gabled ends, in a manner vaguely reminiscent of the similar motifs of the Swiss chalet popularized in the Picturesque pattern books.

The existence of such an exotic structure in Stanley, a backwoods settlement far removed from any settled areas, is not surprising when one examines the circumstances surrounding its construction. The Stanley Taven was built as part of the settlement programme promoted by the New Brunswick and Nova Scotia Land Company, a land investment company set up by a group of London businessmen who had purchased large tracts of wilderness property in New Brunswick and Nova Scotia during the 1830s. By establishing an initial agricultural

Clifton has changed ownership many times and undergone many alterations. As first built for Thomas Chandler Haliburton, Clifton was a small low-lying cottage featuring a projecting front section and punctuated by two large windows. An unusual feature of the design was the division of the flanking wings into two floors. To mask this split-level planning and to maintain an exterior symmetry two blind windows were applied to the front facade. When windows were later inserted the present odd distribution of windows resulted. The central pediment, lantern and several rear additions (not visible in the photograph) were all built after Haliburton's time. Despite these modifications the surrounding landscape has been beautifully maintained and in fact improved by the now mature growth of trees which shelter the building and capture the atmosphere of pastoral repose which Haliburton envisioned when he and his wife first laid out the grounds. (Fig. 116, Metropolitan Toronto Library Board; Fig. 117, Canadian Inventory of Historic Building)

116. Clifton in the Mid-Nineteenth Century

117. Clifton, 416 Clifton Street, Windsor, Nova Scotia; Constructed 1836; Material wood

118. Burnyeat Cottage in the Nineteenth Century, Truro, Nova Scotia
Constructed pre-1832; **Demolished; Material** wood

This cottage was built for John Burnyeat, the rector of Saint John's Anglican Church in Truro, and later bequeathed to his daughter, the wife of the Honourable Adams G. Archibald (lieutenant-governor of Nova Scotia, 1873-83) who used the house as a summer residence. This view of the garden facade illustrates the unusual treatment of the Gothic windows which, similar to church design, extend through two storeys so that the dividing interior floor is visible from the exterior. The flanking one-storey wings, a recurring element in Maritime domestic architecture, feature French windows which provided easy access to the cottage pleasure-grounds, noted in 1864 for their long elm-shaded avenue and stream complete with a small waterfall. (Public Archives of Nova Scotia)

119. Stanley Tavern in 1835, Stanley, New Brunswick; Constructed 1835; Demolished; Material log

Lithograph by S. Russell from a sketch by P. Harry, 1835. The tavern formed the centre-piece of the pioneer settlement of Stanley established by the Nova Scotia and New Brunswick Land Company in 1834. Probably constructed by the resident company carpenters, James Malone and Charles Robbins, this two-storey log structure, supposedly built in the form of a cross, consisted of fourteen rooms and was used to house the original settlers before the completion of their log farmhouses. Although the wide eaves and the slight Swiss chalet appearance of the large brackets extending down the facade of the structure were reminiscent of motifs found on villa and cottage design of the English pattern books, the composition and general outline of the building was unique and probably represents the designer's romantic perception of the type of architecture congruent to the backwoods landscape of New Brunswick. The town of Stanley, after several setbacks in the initial settlement programme, developed into an important agricultural community although none of its original buildings have survived. (Courtesy The New Brunswick Museum)

settlement composed primarily of displaced or impoverished farmers from northern England and Scotland, sections of their holdings would be improved. This would in turn increase the value of the surrounding areas to be sold off later at higher prices. Recruiting the necessary farmers for the initial settlement phase was their first concern. The major attraction was the offer of 100 acres of land (five acres cleared and a log house) to be paid off over fifty years. But they also recognized the need to assure these potential pioneers they would not be abandoning all pleasures of civilized society, which to these northern England and Scottish farmers meant, not a church or a school, but a local tavern which formed the core of the settlement.[63] Financed by these London entrepreneurs, the Stanley Tavern was planned entirely in England or by employees of the company who were sent from England to carry out the initial building projects. Because the community was so remote there could be no input from local builders. A direct transplant from England, Stanley Tavern was unmarked by indigenous building patterns.

CONCLUSION

The villas and cottages examined reflect a direct cultural transference of aesthetic values and tastes in landscape and architecture formulated in England during the late eighteenth and early nineteenth centuries. This relationship does not imply, however, that the architectural expressions of these values as developed in the British North American colonies are mere colonial replicas of their counterparts in Britain. The adaptation of Picturesque principles to the conditions and character of the colonial environment resulted in evident differences in architectural design.

During the first two and a half decades of the nineteenth century — a time when British architects were experimenting with an ever broadening range of stylistic solutions to the villa and the cottage — the British colonies of North America were just beginning to establish themselves, either amid the wilderness environment of Upper Canada or amid the distinct cultural milieu of the Maritime regions or Lower Canada. Although British immigrants attempted to recreate domestic environments based on English tastes, the pioneer conditions and the absence of builders and designers versed in the aesthetics of the Picturesque permitted only rough translations of Picturesque tastes to the Canadian landscape. During this early period (before 1830) villas and cottages drew on functional building types rooted in established vernacular traditions. Instead they relied on the character of the setting and on the application of a few specific details, such as the verandah, to impart a romantic sense of the Picturesque to their otherwise humble dwellings.

In the Maritimes and in much of Quebec, early Picturesque architecture did not evolve beyond this embryonic phase. Here, the villas and cottages generally retained a distinctive regional character quite apart from popular British tastes. Picturesque values generally acted as a modifying influence on these buildings creating new variants of traditional building types such as the Quebec version of the *cottage orné,* the so-called Anglo-Norman cottage.

Only in Upper Canada and in the English strongholds of post-1830 Quebec does one find villas and cottages providing close architectural equivalents of design types found in England. The growing sophistication was due largely to the rapid immigration from Britain. The presence of many new middle-class immigrants who demanded fashionable suburban and rural residences similar to those back home and the arrival of several British-trained architects capable of meeting these demands produced buildings such as Colborne Lodge, Dundurn, Saint Helen's or Holland House, villas and cottages equally at home in the English countryside.

But even on this more sophisticated level one cannot equate the British with the colonial architecture of the Picturesque. The Canadian patron of the Picturesque demanded his country estate imitate popular British fashion but he was also selective in his tastes. Picturesque architectural forms as developed in England went through a weeding-out process before arriving in Canada. The colonial patron initially rejected some of the more avant-garde expressions of the Picturesque such as the medieval thatched-roof cottage or the rambling Gothic abbeys. In general Canadian domestic architecture was dominated by the more conservative products of the Picturesque modest regular villas enriched with touches of classical, Gothic or Modern Fancy detail or small stone or pale stucco cottages dressed with the Picturesque paraphernalia of verandahs and French windows.

To fully examine the impact of the Picturesque point of view on Canadian architecture would lead one far beyond the boundaries of this study and into the realm of nineteenth and twentieth century design. The Picturesque point of view, by breaking down the supremacy of the classical model, by promoting an eclectic approach to architectural style, and by emphasizing visual qualities of design such as irregularity and variety of form, colour and texture, paved the way for later architectural developments which were to determine the future course of Canadian building. The American Gothic Revival of the mid-nineteenth century, popularized through the works of men like Andrew Jackson Downing and High and Late Victorian eclecticisms including the Second Empire style, the Renaissance Revival, the Jacobethan style and finally the Queen Anne Movement at the end of the century, all owe much to the aesthetic principles established by the Picturesque Movement of the late eighteenth century.

The villas and cottages examined both in England and in Canada represent the architects' initial interpretation of the Picturesque point of view. By later Victorian standards these buildings were fairly tame, modest-looking buildings. The early domestic Picturesque architecture, particularly as developed in Canada, still owed much to traditional building types of the eighteenth century in its symmetry, regularity and restraint in form, detail and colour. These buildings did, however, introduce revolutionary themes and approaches to design. On the most immediate level they established new patterns of building. The one-storey cottage or the two-storey stuccoed villa as well as specific architectural details, such as the verandah and the French window, became standard elements in the vocabulary of Canadian domestic building. On a more theoretical level the Picturesque aesthetic cultivated a taste for the naturalistic landscape setting and, more significantly, it promoted the view of architecture as an integral part of this landscape whose design should blend into and enrich the overall composition. It was this view that lay at the root of the revolution in architectural aesthetic which the Picturesque Movement brought about. Although in practice the relationship between the character of a setting and its architectural component was less direct than the theory implied, the acceptance of this principle of congruency had a liberating effect on design. No longer confined by classical dogma or its vocabulary, the architect of the Picturesque was free to draw upon the varied resources of past architectural styles and to freely manipulate these decorative forms, the massing, planes, plan and the colours of this architecture to achieve designs that satisfied the architect's eye for abstract Picturesque effect. These design standards laid the foundations for future developments in Canadian architecture.

154

APPENDIX. LIST OF ILLUSTRATIONS

156

ENDNOTES

Introduction

1 The discussion on the Picturesque and its influence on British domestic architecture will be brief and will emphasize those aspects most relevant to the Canadian interpretations of the Picturesque. For a more detailed and extensive examination of this taste in Britain refer to the following studies: Peter Collins, Changing Ideals in Modern Architecture, 1750-1950 (London: Faber and Faber, 1965), Chap. 1; Walter John Hipple, The Beautiful, The Sublime, and The Picturesque in Eighteenth Century British Aesthetic Theory (Carbondale: Southern Illinois University Press, 1957); Henry-Russell Hitchcock, Architecture: Nineteenth and Twentieth Centuries (Harmondsworth, Middlesex: Penguin Books, 1959) thereafter cited as Architecture), Chap. 6; Christopher Hussey, The Picturesque, Studies in a Point of View (London: G.P. Putnam, 1927); Michael McMordie, "Pre-Victorian Origins of Modern Architectural Theory" (Ph.D. thesis; University of Edinburgh, 1972) (hereafter cited as "Pre-Victorian Origins"); Carroll Meeks, "Picturesque Eclecticism," Art Bulletin, Vol. 32 (Sept. 1950), pp. 226-35; Donald Pilcher, The Regency Style, 1800 to 1830 (London: B.T. Batsford, 1947); John Summerson, Architecture in Britain, 1530-1830, 5th ed. (Harmondsworth, Middlesex: Penguin Books, 1970) (hereafter cited as Architecture in Britain), Chap. 28.

2 Several studies on Canadian architecture refer to domestic Picturesque architecture as being in the Regency style. This term is probably derived from the British practice of referring to Picturesque architecture as Regency architecture. In the British context, however, this label does not define a specific style but refers only to the general manner of building in the Regency period during which several architectural theories and tastes were expressed, the Picturesque aesthetic being just one. An early study of this period of building by Donald

Pilcher is misleadingly entitled The Regency Style, 1800 to 1830 for Pilcher himself writes, "strictly speaking there is no Regency 'style'." (London: B.T. Batsford, 1947, p. 57.)

Marion MacRae in The Ancestral Roof: Domestic Architecture of Upper Canada (Toronto: Clarke, Irwin, 1963) (hereafter cited as The Ancestral Roof), pp. 67-107 was probably not the first Canadian historian to use the term "Regency" in a stylistic sense but her analysis of the characteristics of this style is probably the most influential and the most clearly defined. According to MacRae the typical Regency cottage "would be located on a dramatic or romantic site; that it would be a storey and a half in height; that in plan it might be square, octagonal or rectangular with wings or bays; that is would have large windows and a relatively insignificant entrance door; that there would be an awning-roofed verandah with fanciful treillage and tall decorative chimneys." She also refers to the Regency preference for stucco over brick and the use of cylindrical forms particularly on the Regency villa. One cannot dispute these characteristics as typical of the domestic architecture of the Regency period in Canada but these characteristics are only the outward manifestations of the much broader and more comprehensive taste defined by the Picturesque. To do justice to Marion MacRae's work, she does recognize the underlying principles of the Picturesque — its delight in real nature and its cultivation in landscape, the importance of congruency between setting and architecture, the stylistic eclecticism — but because of her tendency to equate this taste with the specific architectural paraphernalia of the Picturesque, she often ignores some important buildings that expressed this point of view. Because buildings such as Bellevue, Rockwood or Saint Andrew's Manse draw on the Italianate and the classical styles, which has a Victorian afterlife, she lifts them out of their Picturesque context and treats them as part of separate stylistic idioms.

Part I The Picturesque in Britain

Origins of the Picturesque

1   Quotation from the writings of the Third Earl of Shaftesbury (1709) cited from John Summerson, Architecture in Britain, p. 345.

2   For a full examination of the development of the English landscape style see Julia S. Berrall, The Garden: An Illustrated History (Harmondsworth, Middlesex: Penguin Books, 1978), Chap. 10; Norman T. Newton, Design on the Land: The Development of Landscape Architecture (Cambridge, Mass.: Belknap Press, 1971), Chap. 15; Derek Clifford, A History of Garden Design, 2nd ed. (London: Faber and Faber, 1966), Chaps 6-7.

3   Oxford English Dictionary, 1971 ed., s.v. "picturesque."

4   For an examination of the theories of William Gilpin see Walter John Hipple, op. cit., pp. 192-201.

5   Edmund Burke, A Philosophical Enquiry into the Origins of Our Ideas of the Sublime and the Beautiful, ed. and intro. by J.T. Boulton (London: Routledge, Kegan and Paul, 1958), "on the Sublime," p. 57, "on the Beautiful," p. 117.

6   Michael McMordie, "Pre-Victorian Origins," p. 80.

7   For a general analysis of the development of the theory of the "Association of Ideas" see Michael McMordie, "Pre-Victorian Origins," pp. 70-90. The chapter on Archibald Alison in Walter John Hipple, op. cit., pp. 158-85 provides a good analysis of Alison's explanation of the philosophical and aesthetic significance of this theory.

8   The Palladian style and its influence on Canadian architecture is the subject of a study presently underway by Parks Canada. This study, being prepared by Nathalie Clerk, is entitled "L'influence du style palladien sur l'architecture au Canada" and will be published by Parks Canada.

9   Neoclassicism and its influence on Canadian architecture is the subject of a study presently being prepared by Leslie Maitland, an architectural historian at Parks Canada. It is entitled "Neoclassical Architecture in Canada" and will be published by Parks Canada.

10   In 1744 Sanderson Miller built a small cottage with "gothick" detailing but the best known example of mid-Georgian Gothic design was Horace Walpole's residence of Strawberry Hill which he transformed into a Gothic Fantasy between 1747 and 1776.

The Picturesque in Theory

1   The themes expressed in The Landscape: A Didactic Poem of Three Books Addressed to Uvedale Price, esq. (1795; reprint ed., Farnborough: Gregg International Publishers, 1972) (hereafter cited as The Landscape) were expanded upon in R.P. Knight's later publication entitled An Analytical Enquiry into the Principles of Taste (1808; reprint ed., Farnborough: Gregg International Publishers, 1972) (hereafter cited as An Analytical Enquiry).

2   Other later publications by Humphry Repton include Observations on the Theory and Practice of Landscape Gardening (1803) and Fragments on the Theory and Practice of Landscape Gardening (1816). All were reprinted in The Landscape Gardening and Landscape Architecture of the Late Humphry Repton, ed., J.C. Loudon (London: Longman; Edinburgh: A.C. Black, 1840).

3   Sir Uvedale Price, Sir Uvedale Price: On the Picturesque, ed. Sir Thomas Dick Lauder (1794; reprint ed., Edinburgh: Caldwell Lloyd; London: W.S. Orr, 1842), p. 70. Although Knight prefers to define the term "Picturesque" a little more broadly as anything in nature that "may be represented to advantage in painting," he nevertheless identifies scenes that demonstrate variety in colours, ruggedness, light and shadow and irregularity as providing the most suitable subjects for painting. R.P. Knight, An Analytical Enquiry, pp. 156-57.

4   R.P. Knight, An Analytical Enquiry, p. 160.
5   Uvedale Price, op. cit., p. 64; Knight expressed similar ideas regarding the importance of painting techniques to landscape design when he wrote, "By working on the same principles; by carefully collecting and cherishing the accidental beauties of nature; by judiciously arranging them and skillfully combining them with each other and the embellishment of art; I cannot but think that the landscape gardener might produce complete and faultless compositions in nature," R.P. Knight, The Landscape, p. 47.
6   R.P. Knight, ibid., pp. 217-20.
7   Uvedale Price, op. cit., p. 329.
8   According to Price "Architecture in towns may be said to be principal and independent — in the country it is in some degree subordinate and dependent on the surrounding objects"; ibid, p. 328.
9   John Summerson, Architecture in Britain, p. 473.
10 R.P. Knight, An Analytical Enquiry, p. 225. Price, however, believed that "gothic architecture is generally considered as more picturesque," Uvedale Price, op. cit., p. 83.
11 Humphry Repton, op. cit., pp. 56-57.
12 Ibid., p. 413.
13 Uvedale Price, op. cit., p. 189; R.P. Knight, An Analytical Enquiry, p. 221.
14 Uvedale Price, op. cit., p. 331; R.P. Knight, An Analytical Enquiry, p. 221.
15 Humphry Repton, op. cit., p. 262-63.
16 Uvedale Price, op. cit., p. 129.
17 Ibid., p. 352.
18 Humphry Repton, op. cit., p. 235.
19 Ibid., p. 213.
20 Ibid., p. 263.
21 Ibid., pp. 56-57.
22 Ibid., pp. 237-38.
23 Uvedale Price, op. cit., p. 368.

The Theory into Practice
1   Henry-Russell Hitchcock, Architecture, p. 3.
2   For a more complete examination of John Nash's career refer to Terence Davis, The Architecture of John Nash, intro. Sir John Summerson (London: Studio Books, 1960).
3   For a brief outline of Soane's career see Dorothy Stroud's The Architecture of John Soane, intro. Henry Russell Hitchcock (London: Studio Books, 1961).
4   According to Stroud the influence of the Picturesque on Soane's work becomes most evident between 1810 and 1819 when his designs become less explicitly classical. Picturesque design qualities such as broken silhouettes, shifting wall planes, and the juxtaposition of three-dimensional geometric forms and their resulting effects of light and shadow characterize Soane's work at this time. The blend of Neoclassical theory and the Picturesque which defined Soane's style is clearly outlined in a series of lectures Soane prepared as professor of architecture at the Royal Academy from 1809 to 1836 (Sir John Soane, Lectures on Architecture... as delivered to the students of the Royal Academy from 1809 to 1836, etc., ed. Arthur T. Bolton (London: Sir John Soane Museum, 1929) (hereafter cited as Lectures).
5   Two recent studies on the pattern book phenomenon of the late Georgian period are Michael McMordie's "Picturesque Pattern Books and Pre-Victorian Designers," Architectural History, Vol. 18 (1975), pp. 43-49, and Sandra Blutman's "Books of Designs for Country Houses, 1778-1815," Architectural History, Vol. 11 (1968), pp. 25-33.
6   Michael McMordie, ibid., p. 43.
7   The transition between late Georgian and Victorian architecture has been analysed by Henry-Russell Hitchcock in Early Victorian Architecture in Britain (New York: Da Capo Press, 1972), Vol. 1, Chap. 2.
8   The development of the "cottage idea" is traced in Michael McMordie's "Pre-Victorian Origins," pp. 95-117. A condensed version by the same author appeared in "The Cottage Idea," Revue d'art canadienne/Canadian Art Review, Vol. 6, No. 1 (1979), pp. 17-27.
9   William Fuller Pocock, Architectural Designs for Rustic Cottages, etc. (1807; reprint ed., Farnborough: Gregg International Publishers, 1972), p. 8.
10 The use of rough logs as supports was a

whimsical play on the Vitruvian theory of the origins of architectural forms which stated that columns were refined expressions of upright tree trunks used as roof supports in primitive buildings. The theory of the primitive hut was central to Neoclassical eighteenth century doctrine for it illustrated the inherent rationalism of architectural form overlooked in previous design. Although Neoclassical theorists undoubtedly disapproved of this literal translation of the theory, the architects of these cottages viewed these forms as enhancement of the rustic, primitive character appropriate to the cottage.

11   David Laing, Hints for Dwellings, etc. (1800; reprint ed., Farnborough: Gregg International Publishers, 1972), p. iv.

12   The growing importance of the villa in eighteenth century Britain is discussed in John Summerson, Architecture in Britain, Chap. 22. See also Peter Collins, op. cit., pp. 42, 52.

13   William Fuller Pocock, op. cit., p. 9.

14   John B. Papworth, Rural Residences, etc. (1818; reprint ed., Farnborough: Gregg International Publishers, 1971), p. 25.

15   Sir John Soane, Lectures, p. 114.

16   As expressed by William Fuller Pocock "How can these Edifices and Ornaments referring to Grecian architecture be suitable to the domestic buildings of the climate without essential and radical variations?" William Fuller Pocock, op. cit., p. 12.

17   Sir John Soane, Lectures, p. 114.

18   Robert Lugar, Architectural Sketches for Cottages, etc. (London: J. Taylor, 1805), p. 15.

19   David Laing, op. cit., p. iv.

20   Francis Goodwin, Domestic Architecture, etc., 3rd. ed., (London: Henry G. Bohn, 1850), p. 15.

21   Sir John Soane, Lectures, p. 114.

22   Ibid., p. 117.

23   John B. Papworth, op. cit., p. 57.

24   Ibid., p. 104.

25   William Fuller Pocock, op. cit., p. 9.

26   John B. Papworth, op. cit., p. 57.

27   James Malton, An Essay on British Cottage Architecture, etc., (1798; reprint ed., Farnborough: Gregg International Publishers, 1972), pp. 9 - 10.

Part II The Picturesque in Canada

Patrons of the Picturesque

1   Edwin C. Guillet, The Pioneer Farmer and Backwoodsman (Toronto: University of Toronto Press, 1963) (hereafter cited as The Pioneer Farmer), Vol. 1, pp. 218-19, Vol. 2, p. 343. See also G.P. de T. Glazebrook, Life in Ontario: A Social History (Toronto: University of Toronto Press, 1968), pp. 22-24, 31, 36.

2   Sir Richard Henry Bonnycastle, The Canadas in 1841 (1841; reprint ed., East Ardsley, Wakefield, Yorkshire: S.R. Publisher, 1968), Vol. 2, p. 121.

3   Catharine Parr Traill, The Backwoods of Canada: being the letters from the wife of an emigrant officer, etc. (London: Charles Knight, 1836), p. 86.

4   Anna Brownell Jameson, Winter Studies and Summer Rambles in Canada (1838; reprint ed., Toronto: McClelland and Stewart, 1923), p. 49.

5   Mary Sophia O'Brien, The Journals of Mary O'Brien, 1828-38, ed. Audrey Saunders Miller (Toronto: Macmillan, 1968), p. 193.

6   Catharine Parr Traill, op. cit., p. 199.

7   Ibid., p. 142.

8   The conflict between the romantic ideal and the reality of the wilderness has been examined in the light of the writings of four settlers in Edward H. Dahl, "Mid Forests Wild ": A Study of the Concept of the Wilderness in the Writings of Susanna Moodie, J.W.D. Moodie, Catharine Parr Traill and Samuel Strickland, c. 1830-1855. (Ottawa: National Museum of Man, 1973). Mercury Series, Paper No. 3.

9   The closing paragraphs of Roughing It In the Bush are a warning to gentlefolk like herself planning on settling in the backwoods: "If these sketches should prove the means of deterring one family from sinking their property, and shipwrecking their hopes, by going to reside in the backwoods of Canada, I shall .... feel that I have not toiled in vain." Susanna Moodie, Roughing it in the Bush; or Life

in Canada, 2nd ed. (New York: George P. Putnam, 1852), Vol. 2, p. 221.

10   Susanna Moodie abandoned her wilderness farm in 1840 and moved to Belleville, Ontario, where her husband had obtained the post of sheriff.

11   Susanna Moodie, Life in the Clearings, ed. and intro. Robert L. MacDougall (Toronto: Macmillan, 1959). This is an account of Susanna Moodie's life in Belleville and her observations on colonial society in the 1840s and 1850s.

12   John Ireland, "Andrew Drew and the Founding of Woodstock," Ontario History, Vol. 60, No. 4 (Dec. 1968), pp. 229-45.

13   Edwin C. Guillet, The Pioneer Farmer, Vol. 1, p. 279.

14   Sir Richard Henry Bonnycastle, Canada and the Canadians in 1846 (London: Henry Colburn, 1849), Vol. 2, pp. 75-76.

15   John Beverley Robinson's remarks on Cobourg and Woodstock appeared in Canada and the Canada Bill: Being an Examination of the Proposed Measure for the Future Government of Canada; with an Introductory Chapter, Containing Some General Views Respecting the British Provinces in North America (London: 1840). Cited from Terry Cook, "John Beverley Robinson and the Conservative Blueprint for the Upper Canadian Community," in Historical Essays on Upper Canada, ed., J.K. Johnson (Toronto: McClelland and Stewart, 1971), p. 353.

16   G.P. de T. Glazebrook, The Story of Toronto (Toronto: University of Toronto Press, 1971), p. 22.

17   Frederick Marryat, A Diary in America, with Remarks on its Institutions (Philadelphia: Carey and Hart, 1839), Vol. 1, p. 108.

18   For an examination of the villa and cottage in the vicinity of Quebec in the eighteenth and nineteenth centuries see France Gagnon-Pratte, L'architecture et la nature à Québec au dix-neuvième siècle: Les villas (Quebec: Ministère des Affaires culturelles, 1980).

19   James Silk Buckingham, Canada, Nova Scotia, New Brunswick, and other British Provinces of North America; with a Plan of National Colonization (London: Fisher, 1843), p. 106.

Regional Studies in the Picturesque

1   Gerald M. Craig, Upper Canada: The Formative Years, 1784-1841 (Toronto: McClelland and Stewart, 1963) (hereafter cited as Upper Canada), p. 87. Canadian Centenary Series, Vol. 7.

2   Ibid., pp. 124-25.

3   Martin Doyle (William Hickey), Hints on Emigration to Upper Canada; Especially Addressed to the Middle and Lower Classes in Great Britain and Ireland (Dublin: William Curry, 1831), p. 11.

4   John Ross Robertson, Robertson's Landmarks of Toronto; a Collection of Historical Sketches of the Old Town of York from 1762 until 1837, and of Toronto from 1834 to 1914. (Toronto: J.R. Robertson, 1894-1914) (hereafter cited as Robertson's Landmarks), Pt. 1, p. 3.

5   J.F. Fitzgerald de Ros, Personal Narrative of Travels in the United States and Canada in 1826, 3rd ed. (London: W.H. Ainsworth, 1827), p. 181.

6   Anna Brownell Jameson, op. cit., p. 100.

7   Sir James Edward Alexander, Transatlantic Sketches, comprising visits to the most interesting scenes in North and South America, and the West Indies. With Notes on Negro Slavery and Canadian Emigration (London: Richard Bentley, 1833) (hereafter cited as Transatlantic Sketches) Vol. 2, p. 179.

8   John Ross Robertson, Robertson's Landmarks, Pt. 4, p. 303.

9   A general survey of the various possible origins of the verandah has been prepared by Sandy Easterbrook in, "The Evolution of the Verandah in Canadian Architecture of the Pre-Confederation Period." Manuscript on file, National Historic Parks and Sites Branch, Parks Canada, Ottawa, 1978.

10   R. Greenhill, K. Macpherson and D. Richardson, Ontario Towns (Ottawa: Oberon, 1974), n.p.

11   Anonymous, "A Traveller's Impressions in 1792-93," quoted in G.M. Craig, ed., Early Travellers in the Canadas, 1791-1867 (Toronto: Macmillan, 1955), p. 7.

12   Basil Hall, Travels in North America in the Years 1827 and 1828, 2nd ed. (London: Simpkin and Marshall; Edinburgh: Cadell, 1830), Vol. 1, p. 264.

13 Catherine Parr Traill, op. cit., p. 142.

14 Anna Brownell Jameson, op. cit., p. 135.

15 Basil Hall, op. cit., p. 264.

16 Mary Sophia O'Brien, op. cit., p. 216.

17 Sir James E. Alexander, L'Acadie; or Seven Years' Exploration in British America (London: Henry Colburn, 1849), Vol. 1, p. 230.

18 Basil Hall, op. cit., pp. 205-7.

19 Anna Brownell Jameson, op. cit., p. 100.

20 Within three years, from 1830 to 1833, the population of Upper Canada increased by nearly fifty percent. After that the influx fell off somewhat but continued at a substantial rate until 1837. Gerald M. Craig, Upper Canada, p. 228.

21 See Figure 33 for biographical information on John Howard.

22 A comprehensive study of the background and character of MacNab and the history of Dundurn has been written by Marion MacRae, MacNab of Dundurn (Toronto: Clarke, Irwin, 1971).

23 Journal Express (Hamilton), 26 Feb. 1841.

24 Marion MacRae, MacNab of Dundurn (Toronto: Clarke, Irwin, 1971), pp. 50, 55, 64.

25 Canada. Department of Public Works, Annual Report for the Year 1866, "Additions and Improvements to Rideau Hall," dated 13 June 1865 (Ottawa: Maclean, 1866), App. 14; see also, Canada. Public Archives, RG 11, Vol. 425, pp. 909-11. Description of Rideau Hall by F.P. Rubidge, dated 4 April 1964.

26 J. Douglas Stewart and Mary Stewart, "John Solomon Cartwright: Upper Canadian Gentleman and a Regency Man of Taste," Historic Kingston, Vol. 27 (Jan. 1979), pp. 64-68.

27 Bellevue and the Howard villa were the immediate descendants of Nash's Cronkhill but they were not strictly speaking their only descendants. The Italianate or Tuscan villa became popular in Canada during the 1850s and 1860s but these later examples reflected more the influence of Victorian and American interpretations of this mode. Generally these later buildings featured heavier more ornate details and often incorporated several materials to give the designs the polychromatic treatment characteristic of Victorian design.

28 L. Noppen, C. Paulette and M. Tremblay, Québec: Trois siècles d'architecture (Quebec: Libre Expression, 1979), p. 41.

29 Quebec. Archives du séminaire de Québec, Seigneuries, 48 No. 7F. Deed of sale for Powell Place (Spencer Wood), Henry Percival to Henry Atkinson, 18 May 1825.

30 James Silk Buckingham, op. cit., p. 273.

31 James Pattison Cockburn, Quebec and its Environs; a Picturesque Guide to the Stranger (Quebec: Thomas Cary, 1831), p. 11.

32 The term "Anglo-Norman" seems to have been popularized by architectural historian Gérard Morisset in the 1940s. Although he dates its emergence in Quebec to the 1840s he viewed this type, which he defined as a low one-storey building, with a hipped roof and verandah on four sides, as a blend of French and English influences. Gérard Morisset, L'Architecture en Nouvelle-France (Quebec: Collection Champlain, 1949), p. 35.

33 Michel Lessard and Gilles Vilandré, La Maison traditionelle du Québec (Montreal, Bruxelles: Les éditions de l'homme, 1974), p. 156.

34 Ibid., p. 207.

35 David Wilkie, Sketches of a Summer Trip to New York and the Canadas (Edinburgh: J. Anderson; London: Sherwood and Piper, 1837), p. 243.

36 Raymonde Gauthier, Les manoirs du Québec (Quebec: Fides, 1976), p. 62.

37 Lady L.A. Aylmer, "Recollections of Canada, 1831," in Rapport de l'archiviste de la Province de Québec, (Quebec: Rédempti Paradis, 1935), Vol. 15 (1934-1935), pp. 313-14.

38 Ibid., pp. 305, 314.

39 Quebec. Ministère des Affaires culturelles, Centre de documentation. File on Frederick Hacker, No. 2H118.5 F852.5/5. Frederick Hacker to John George Earl of Durham, Governor-in-Chief, and Captain General over the Province of British North America, n.d. Hacker claims to have arrived in Lower Canada in 1822 although his first building contract in Quebec did

not appear until the year 1833.

40 A.J.H. Richardson, "Guide to the Architecturally and Historically most Significant Buildings of the Old City of Quebec, etc. "Bulletin of the Association for Preservation Technology, Vol. 2 Nos. 3-4 (1970), p. 76.

41 France Gagnon-Pratte, L'architecture et la nature à Québec au dix-neuvième siècle: Les villas (Quebec: Ministère des Affaires culturelles, 1980), p. 50. France Gagnon-Pratte describes the period 1830-40 as the golden age of villa building although she too was unable to find visual documentation for many villas of this period. Most of the villas illustrating this period of domestic building date from 1845 to 1860.

42 For an inventory of the building contracts issued in Quebec before 1870 see G.G. Bastien, D.D. Dubé, C. Southam, "Inventaire des marchés de construction des archives civiles de Québec, 1800-1870," Histoire et Archéologie, 1 (1975).

43 Quebec. Archives nationales du Québec (Quebec) (hereafter cited as ANQQ), Greffe, Josiah Hunt, contract between Collin McCallum and Germain Ste Pierre, carpenter, 10 Nov. 1835; contract between Colin McCallum and Joseph Brown and Joseph Lapin, Carpenters and Joiners, 19 Dec. 1835; contract between Colin McCallum and Michel Beaumont, carpenter and joiner, 21 Dec. 1835; contract between Colin McCallum and J.B. Lavoi, joiner, 22 Dec. 1835. Each contract contains specifications prepared by George Browne.

44 Edward Stavely began his architectural career in Quebec in partnership with Frederick Hacker and on Hacker's death in 1846 Stavely took over the firm. He was later succeeded in practice by his son Harry and his grandson Edward B. who remained active in Quebec until 1950. A.J.H. Richardson, op. cit., p. 93.

45 Ibid., pp. 71-72. Charles Baillairgé (1826-1906) was trained in Quebec under his cousin Thomas Baillairgé, an important Quebec architect and sculptor of the first half of the nineteenth century. Charles began his architectural career in 1846 and he soon established himself as a leading architect of the province.

46 For detailed descriptions of several of these large villa estates in the vicinity of Quebec see Sir James MacPherson Lemoine, Maple Leaves: Canadian History and Quebec Scenery, 3rd ser. (Quebec: Hunter and Rose, 1865) (hereafter cited as Maple Leaves).

47 Keith Matthews, Lectures on the History of Newfoundland, 1500 to 1830 (St. John's: Memorial University, 1973), pp. 9-16.

48 Paul O'Neill, The Oldest City: The Story of St. John's Newfoundland (Erin, Ont.: Porcepic Press, 1975), pp. 52-55.

49 Keith Matthews, op. cit., p. 234.

50 Newfoundland Historic Trust, A Gift of Heritage (St. John's: Newfoundland Historic Trust, 1975), Vol. 1, pp. 4-5.

51 Andrew Hill Clark, Three Centuries and the Island: A Historical Geography of Settlement and Agriculture in Prince Edward Island (Toronto: University of Toronto Press, 1959), Chap. 4.

52 William Cobbett, The Emigrant's Guide (London: 1829-30), p. 40.

53 G.A. Rawlyk, ed., Historical Essays on the Atlantic Provinces (Toronto: McClelland and Stewart, 1967), pp. 1-2.

54 Ibid., D.C. Harvey, "The Intellectual Awakening of Nova Scotia," pp. 103-4.

55 "Western Scenes," Acadian Magazine, Vol. 1, No. 7, Jan. 1827.

56 Michael Hugo-Brunt, The Origin of Colonial Settlement in the Maritimes (n.p., 1959), p. 106. Copy held in the Public Archives Canada Library.

57 Abraham Gesner, New Brunswick; with Notes for Emigrants (London: Simmonds and Ward, 1847), p. 330.

58 The only British architect practising in the Maritimes known to be well-versed in Picturesque architectural values was John Plaw (1746-1820), discussed previously as the author of one of the earliest Picturesque pattern books published in England (Fig. 9). Plaw immigrated to Prince Edward Island in 1807 and remained there until his death in 1820. Unfortunately, Charlottetown at this time offered few opportunities for Plaw to demonstrate his skills. Although he produced several designs for public buildings in that city (all of which have disappeared), not a single residential

building is known to have been designed by him. What prompted Plaw, who seemed to have established a fairly reputable practice in England, to bury himself in such a remote, underdeveloped colony as Prince Edward Island is still a mystery. A paper about John Plaw's career in Charlottetown was delivered by Irene Rogers at the conference of the Society for the Study of Architecture in Canada held in London, Ontario, in 1978.

59 Thomas Chandler Haliburton, Sam Slick, ed. Ray Palmer Baker (New York: George H. Doran, 1923), pp. 120-22.

60 "On the Scenery of Nova Scotia," Nova Scotian, 10 Aug. 1825, p. 159.

61 Sir Richard Henry Bonnycastle, Newfoundland in 1842 (London: Henry Colburn, 1842), Vol. 2, p. 156.

62 The photograph of Virginia Water is located in the British Museum in London. A reproduction appeared in R.G. Moyle's Complaints is many and various but the odd divil likes it (Toronto: Peter Martin, 1975), p. 75.

63 Ivan J. Saunders, "New Brunswick and Nova Scotia Land Company and the Settlement of Stanley, New Brunswick" (M.A. thesis, University of New Brunswick, 1969), pp. 194-97.

LEGEND SOURCES

1 Michael Kitson, "Claude Lorrain," in The Encyclopedia of Art (New York, Toronto, London: McGraw-Hill, 1958), pp. 340-42.

2 Humphry Repton, The Landscape Gardening and Landscape Architecture of the Late Humphry Repton, ed. J.C. Loudon (London: Longman; Edinburgh: A.C. Black, 1840), pp. 142-43, 164; Dorothy Stroud, Humphry Repton (London: Country Life, 1962), p. 53-54.

3 Nikolaus Pevsner, "Richard Payne Knight," Art Bulletin, Vol. 3, No. 4 (Dec. 1949), pp. 293-96; Alistair Rowan, "Downton Castle, Herefordshire," in The Country Seat: Studies in the History of the British Country House, etc., ed. Howard Colvin and John Harris (London: Allen Lane, 1970), pp. 170-73; John Summerson, Architecture in Britain, p. 475.

4 Terence Davis, John Nash: The Prince Regent's Architect (London: Country Life, 1966), p. 42; John Summerson, Architecture in Britain, p. 477.

5 J. Mordaunt Crook, "The Villas of Regent's Park," Country Life, Vol. 144 (4 July 1968), pp. 22-25; Terence Davis, The Architecture of John Nash (London: Studio Books, 1960), p. 70; Terence Davis, John Nash: The Prince Regent's Architect (London: Country Life, 1966), pp. 63-82.

6 Dorothy Stroud, The Architecture of Sir John Soane, intro. Henry-Russell Hitchcock (London: Studio Books, 1961), pp. 14, 31; Sir John Soane, Lectures, p. 114.

7 Dorothy Stroud, The Architecture of Sir John Soane, intro. Henry-Russell Hitchcock (London: Studio Books, 1961), pp. 16, 111-12.

8 Howard Colvin, A Biographical Dictionary of British Architects 1600-1840 (London: John Murray, 1978), pp. 526-27; Robert Lugar, The Country Gentleman's Architect; etc. (1807; reprint ed., Farnborough: Gregg International Publishers, 1971), p. 4.

9 Howard Colvin, op. cit., p. 642; John Plaw, Ferme Ornée; or Rural Improvements. A Series of Domestic or Ornamental Designs suited to Parks, Plantations, etc. (1795; reprint ed., Farnborough: Gregg International Publishers, 1972), Pl. 17, p. 7; The Living Webster: Encyclopedic Dictionary of the English Language, s.v. "piazza." According to Irene Rogers, Charlottetown, Prince Edward Island, Plaw submitted a plan for a house on 3rd Street in Philadelphia to the Society of Artists and the Free Society in London in 1790.

164

10 Howard M. Colvin, op. cit., pp. 436-43; John B. Papworth, Rural Residences, etc. (1818; reprint ed., Farnborough: Gregg International Publishers, 1971), pp. 25, 53-54, pl. 13.

11 Howard Colvin, op. cit., p. 374; Edward Gyfford, Designs for elegant cottages and small villas, etc. (1806; reprint ed., Farnborough: Gregg International Publishers, 1972), p. 5, pls. 7-9.

12 H.M. Colvin, op. cit., p. 242; Francis Goodwin, Domestic Architecture, etc., 3rd ed. (London: Henry G. Bohn, 1850), Vol. 2, pl. 24.

13 Howard Colvin, op. cit., p. 649; William Fuller Pocock, op. cit., pp. v, 11-12, 32.

14 Robert Lugar, Architectural Sketches for Cottages, Rural Dwellings, and Villas, etc. (London: J. Taylor, 1805), pp. 15-17; Robert Lugar, Villa Architecture... Buildings Executed in England, Scotland, etc. (London: 1828), pl. 13.

15 Laning Roper, "The Gardens of Fairfield House," Country Life, Vol. 165 (17 May 1979), pp. 1510-12.

16 Stanley C. Ramsay, Small Houses of the Late Georgian Period, 1750-1820 (New York: W. Helburn; London: Technical Journals, 1919), pp. 2, 4.

17 Canada. Public Archives (hereafter cited as PAC), National Map Collection, V1/440-Kingston-1865. Map of the City of Kingston, Canada West, 1865. Surveyed by John Innes. Published by John Creighton, New York. The villa phenomenon in Kingston has been examined in Dana Johnson and C.J. Taylor, "Nothing in the Least Interesting or Remarkable," in Reports on Selected Buildings in Kingston, Ontario, Manuscript Report Series No. 261, Vol. 1 (Ottawa: Parks Canada, 1976-77), pp. 17-30.

18 PAC, National Map Collection, Atlas of the City and County of Quebec, surveyed by H.W. Hopkins (Quebec: Provincial Surveying and Publishing, 1879), pl. 35.

19 Eric Ross Arthur, Toronto: No Mean City (Toronto: University of Toronto Press, 1964), p. 15; Lucy Booth Martyn, Toronto: 100 Years of Grandeur (Toronto, Pagurian Press, 1978), pp. 19-24; John Ross Robertson, ed., Robertson's Landmarks, Pt. 1, pp. 3-4.

20 R. Greenhill, K. Macpherson and D. Richardson, op. cit., pl. 8; Florence B. LeDoux, Sketches of Niagara (St Catharines: Peninsula Press, 1955), p. 17; John Ross Robertson, Landmarks of Canada, etc. (Toronto: Toronto Public Library, 1917-21) hereafter cited as Landmarks of Canada, Vol. 1, p. 204.

21 Susan Algie, "Roselands," in Reports on Selected Buildings in Ontario, Manuscript Report Series No. 390 (Ottawa: Parks Canada, 1979), pp. 167-71; John Ridout, "A Biographical Sketch of Samuel Ridout," Proceedings of the Ontario Land Surveyors Association (1887), p. 129; John Ross Robertson, Landmarks of Canada, Vol. 1, p. 548; Henry Scadding, Toronto of Old, etc. (1873; reprint ed., Toronto: Oxford University Press, 1966), p. 376.

22 PAC, RG11, Vol. 612, Insurance Policy for House on Lot 8, York, 14 Mar. 1828; John Ross Robertson, Robertson's Landmarks, Pt. 4, p 303.

23, 24 James E. Alexander, L'Acadie; or Seven Years' Exploration in British America (London: Henry Colburn, 1849), Vol. 1, p. 230; Susan Algie, "Drumsnab," op. cit., pp. 109-20; Eric Ross Arthur, Toronto: No Mean City (Toronto: University of Toronto Press, 1964), p. 50; Elmes Henderson, "Bloor Street, Toronto, and the Village of Yorkville in 1849," Papers and Records of the Ontario Historical Society, Vol. 26 (1930), p. 445; Lucy Booth Martyn, op. cit., pp. 83-87; Henry Scadding, op. cit., p. 175.

25 PAC, MG13, WO44, Vol. 15, reel B217, p. 377. Lt. Pooley to Col. Ellicombe, 7 Feb. 1835. In this letter Pooley states that By's cottage was built during the winter of 1826 at By's own expense. I thank Robert Passfield, Parks Canada, for identifying this document; Sir James Edward Alexander, Transatlantic Sketches, Vol. 2, pp. 179-80; Joseph Bouchette, The British Dominions in North America, etc. (London: Longman, Rees, Orme, Browne, Green and Longman, 1832), Vol. 1, p. 81; A.H.D. Ross, Ottawa, Past and Present (Ottawa: Thornburn and Abbot, 1927), pp. 91-92.

26 Margaret Angus, Old Stones of Kingston; Its Buildings Before 1867 (Toronto: Uni-

versity of Toronto Press, 1966), p. 42; Marion MacRae, The Ancestral Roof, p. 238.

27   Robert J. Burns "Inverarden: Retirement Home of Fur Trader John McDonald of Garth," History and Archaeology/Histoire et archéologie, 25 (1979); Peter J. Stokes, "Inverarden." Manuscript on file, Historic Sites and Monuments Board of Canada, Ottawa, Agenda Paper 1968-7, June 1968, pp. 83-103.

28   PAC, RG11, Vol. 612, Insurance Policy covering a "Cottage at Stamford" dated 7 April 1828; John F. Fitzgerald de Ros, Personal Narrative of Travels in the United States and Canada in 1826, 3rd ed. (London: W.H. Ainsworth, 1827), pp. 181-82; Anna Brownell Jameson, op. cit., p. 100; James C. Morden, Historic Niagara Falls (Niagara Falls: Lundy's Lane Historical Society, 1932), p. 41.

29   PAC, RG7, G1, Vol. 58, p. 105, Dispatch from Lord Bathurst (Colonial Secretary) to Lt.-Gov. Gore approving sum of £2060.11.6 for repair of Elmsley House, 3 Oct. 1816; PAC, RG11, Vol. 612, Insurance Policy on Government House, 2 Aug. 1827; Insurance Policy on Government House, 4 Sept. 1839; PAC, National Map Collection, V2/440-Toronto-1827, Plan of Town of York by J.G. Chewett, 1827; John George Howard, Incidents in the Life of John G. Howard, Esq. (Toronto: Copp Clark, 1885), p. 20; John Ross Robertson, Landmarks of Canada, Vol. 1, pp. 47, 49; Upper Canada. House of Assembly. Journals of the House of Assembly, 1836 (Toronto: M. Reynolds, 1836), p. 269. Account of repairs to Government House.

30   Eric Ross Arthur, Toronto: No Mean City (Toronto: University of Toronto Press, 1964), p. 43; PAC, Upper Canada Land Book, J, 1816-1819, p. 94. Land petition from Lt.-Col. Joseph Wells for 1200 acres of land, 26 Feb. 1817; PAC, Land Petitions, W14/15, 1823-26. Petition from Joseph Wells for land grant accepted, 7 Dec. 1825; Lucy Booth Martyn, op. cit., p. 38-43; John Ross Robertson, Landmarks of Canada, Vol. 1, p. 138.

31   Cobourg. Local Architectural Conservation Advisory Committee (LACAC), unpublished research notes; R. Greenhill,

K. Macpherson and D. Richardson, Ontario Towns (Ottawa: Oberon, 1974), pl. 6.

32   Kingston. Royal Military College, Massey Library, Naval Dockyard Point Frederick, July 1815, watercolour by Emeric Essex Vidal.

33, 34, 35 Eric Ross Arthur, Toronto: No Mean City (Toronto: University of Toronto Press, 1964), p. 58. Wendy Fletcher, "John Howard and the Picturesque Villa" (M.A. thesis, University of Toronto, 1979), pp. 34-36. The various construction stages of Colborne Lodge have been documented in this paper. Lucy Booth Martyn, op. cit., pp. 89-96; Toronto. Metropolitan Toronto Public Library, Howard Collection, L25. Letter from J.G. Howard to Sydney Mountcastle, 12 Oct. 1833.

36, 37 John G. Howard, op. cit., p. 18; Toronto. Metropolitan Toronto Public Library, Howard Collection, Unidentified plan for a Gothic cottage, Plan No. 48; Plan for Ridout Cottage of 1836, Plan Nos 45-47; Plan for three unidentified cottages, Plan No. 555; John Ross Robertson, Robertson's Landmarks, Vol. 1, p. 27.

38, 39 I thank Olive Newcombe of the Dundas Historical Society for supplying the historical background on this building. PAC, National Map Collection, H3/420-Wentworth-1859. Map of the County of Wentworth Canada West, comp. Robert Surtees (Hamilton: Hardy Gregory, 1859).

40   John Ireland, "Andrew Drew and the Founding of Woodstock," Ontario History, Vol. 60, No. 4 (Dec. 1968), pp. 229-45; Marion MacRae, The Ancestral Roof, p. 87.

41   H. Beldon, Illustrated Historical Atlas of the County of Huron, Ontario (Toronto: H. Beldon, 1879), p. 31; Marion MacRae, The Ancestral Roof, p. 87; James Scott, Huron County in Pioneer Times (Seaforth: Huron County Historical Society, 1954), p. 46.

42   Alan Gowans, Building Canada: An Architectural History of Canadian Life (Toronto: Oxford University Press, 1966), p. 101; R. Greenhill, K. Macpherson and D. Richardson, op. cit., pl. 28; Marion

MacRae, The Ancestral Roof, pp. 87-89.

43 PAC, National Map Collection, V1/420-Lincoln and Welland-1862, Tremaine's Map of the Counties of Lincoln and Welland, Canada West (Toronto: Geo. R. and G.M. Tremaine, 1862); Lundy's Lane Historical Society, Our Old Buildings (Niagara Falls: Lundy's Lane Historical Society, 1970), p. 6.

44 Toronto. Metropolitan Toronto Library Board, Howard Collection, L27, No. 39, "Plan elevation fo Mr. Place," 1 April 1835; John G. Howard, op. cit., p. 19.

45 PAC, National Map Collection, V1/420-Renfrew and Lanark-1863, Map of the Counties of Lanark and Renfrew, Canada West, from surveys by H.F. Walling, 1863; "George Rochester Lived in Bytown as a Boy," Citizen (Ottawa), 25 Oct. 1908. I wish to thank Mr. Lloyd B. Rochester of Ottawa, Mr. Harry Hinchley of Renfrew and Mrs. Carrie Fortneath of Burnstown for providing information on the Cottage in Burnstown.

46 PAC, National Map Collection, H3/440-Brockville-1853, Map of Brockville, Canada West, published by Wall and Forest, New York, 1853; Thad W.H. Leavitt, History of Leeds and Grenville Ontario, from 1749 to 1879 (Brockville: Recorder Press, 1879), pp. 190-91.

47 I thank the Norfolk Historical Society, Simcoe, Ontario, for establishing the construction date for this building.

48 Cobourg. Local Architectural Conservation Advisory Committee, unpublished research on 250 Mathew Street. The Cobourg LACAC has identified at least six other buildings with a roofline similar to the cottage on Mathew Street. Marion MacRae, The Ancestral Roof, p. 241; Toronto. Metropolitan Toronto Library Board, Toronto and Early Canada Collection, No. 292. Photograph of Sir Francis Hincks Cottage, Spadina Avenue Toronto, ca. 1885.

49 City of Kingston. Land Registry Division, Copybook. Instrument No. Q300. Bargain and Sale, Smith Bartlett to James Hutton, 15 April 1844; Instrument No. R338, James Hutton to John Counter, 24 April 1846. City of Kingston, Buildings of Historic and Architectural Significance (Kingston: City of Kingston, 1971), Vol. 1, pp. 77-78. Kingston Chronicle and Gazette, 28 July 1841, col. 4, p. 4. Janet Wright, "Sunnyside and Otterburn." Unpublished research paper prepared for the Department of Art, Queen's University, Kingston, 1982.

50 Advertisement for Tenders, Chronicle and Gazette (Kingston), 5 May 1841. Reference taken from J. Douglas Stewart, "Architecture for a Boom Town: The Primitive and Neo-Baroque in George Browne's Kingston Buildings." In To Preserve and Defend: Eassays on Kingston in the Nineteenth Century, ed. Gerald Tulchinsky (Montreal, London: McGill-Queen's, 1976); p. 348; Kingston, City of Buildings of Historic and Architectural Significance (Kingston: City of Kingston, 1971), Vol. 1, pp. 88, 90; Marion MacRae, The Ancestral Roof; pp. 151-53.

51 Marion MacRae, The Ancestral Roof, p. 90.

52 The property at 1 Sainte Anne Place was purchased in 1850 by John Farrin and the house was probably built soon after. I thank Mr. Don Cousins of St. Thomas, Ontario, for supplying this information.

53 John Lutman, Reports on Selected Buildings in London, Ontario, Manuscript Report Series No. 266 (Ottawa: Parks Canada, 1976-77), pp. 161-65.

54, 55, 56 Anthony Adamson, "Architecture in British Canada: The Georgian Influence, 1745-1845," Canadian Collector, Vol. 9, No. 1 (Jan./Feb. 1974), p. 30; Architectural Conservancy of Ontario, Victorian Architecture in Hamilton (Hamilton: Architectural Conservancy of Ontario, 1966), pp. 2-4; T. Melville Bailey, "Dundurn and Sir Allan MacNab," Ontario Historical Society, Vol. 36 (1944), pp. 94-104; "Dundurn Castle Restoration: Documentary Research Committee File." Manuscript on file, Canadian Inventory of Historic Building, Parks Canada, Ottawa, 1964-67; Marion MacRae, MacNab of Dundurn (Toronto: Clarke, Irwin, 1971), pp. 50-65.

57 Margaret Angus, Old Stones of Kingston; Its Buildings Before 1867 (Toronto: University of Toronto Press, 1966), p. 78; Margaret Angus "Summerhill in the

Nineteenth Century: Its Use and Users," Historic Kingston, Vol. 29 (Jan. 1981), pp. 123-136; A.H. Young "The Rev'd George O'Kill Stuart, Second Rector of York and of Kingston," Ontario Historical Society, Vol. 24 (1927), pp. 512-15.

58, 59 PAC, RG11, Vol. 425, pp. 909-11. Description of the Residence situated on the MacKay Estate adjoining the City of Ottawa, known as Rideau Hall, prepared by F.P. Rubidge, 5 April 1864; PAC, National Map Collection, V1/440-Ottawa-1864, Topographical Map of MacKay Estate, drawn by Thomas Keefer; R.H. Hubbard, Rideau Hall: An Illustrated History of Government House (Ottawa: Queen's Printer, 1967), pp. 9-15; Marion MacRae, The Ancestral Roof, pp. 102-6; C.J. Taylor and Janet Wright, "Rideau Hall," Agenda Paper, Historic Sites and Monuments Board of Canada, Parks Canada, Ottawa, Nov. 1977, pp. 233-61.

60, 61 Kingston, City of, op. cit., Vol. 1, pp. 100-104; Dana Johnson and C.J. Taylor, Reports on Selected Buildings in Kingston, Ontario, Manuscript Report Series No. 261 (Ottawa: Parks Canada, 1976-77), Vol. 1, pp. 407-25; Marion MacRae, The Ancestral Roof, pp. 116-18; J. Douglas Stewart, op. cit., pp. 46-52; J. Douglas Stewart and Mary Stewart, "John Solomon Cartwright: Upper Canadian Gentleman and Regency Man of Taste," Historic Kingston, Vol. 27 (Jan. 1979), pp. 61-77.

62 Susan Algie, "Castlefield," op. cit., pp. 99-107; Scadding, op. cit., p. 317.

63 Eric Ross Arthur, Toronto: No Mean City (Toronto: University of Toronto Press, 1964), p. 40; William Dendy, Lost Toronto (Toronto: Oxford University Press, 1978), pp. 13-14; Marion MacRae, The Ancestral Roof, pp. 96-98; Lucy Booth Martyn, op. cit., pp. 77-82; John Ross Robertson, Robertson's Landmarks, Pt. 1, p. 7. Henry Scadding, op. cit., pp. 25-26.

64 Wendy Fletcher, op. cit., footnote p. 25; J.K. Johnson, ed., The Canadian Directory of Parliament, 1867-1967 (Ottawa: Public Archives Canada, 1968), p. 66, "John Young Bown."

65, 66 Margaret Angus, "Bellevue, Kingston,"

Research report prepared for Canadian Inventory of Historic Building, Parks Canada, Ottawa, 1964. Kingston, City of, op. cit., Vol. 1, pp. 85-87; Dana Johnson and C.J. Taylor, op. cit., Vol. 1, pp. 303-7; Marion MacRae, The Ancestral Roof, pp. 149-51; John J. Stewart, op. cit., pp. 7-9. In the past Bellevue has been dated ca. 1838 even though Charles Hales did not purchase the lot until Feb. 1841. The earlier date was based on the fact the Hales paid the large sum of £1217 for the property which was considered too high a price for a vacant lot. For this reason it was believed that the house must have been built before 1841. According to Jennifer McKendry of Kingston this sum would have been quite in keeping with the inflated prices for undeveloped land of the period.

67 William Dendy, op. cit., p. 15. John Ross Robertson, Robertson's Landmarks, Vol. 3, p. 226; Toronto. Metropolitan Toronto Library Board, Howard Collection, "Sketch shewing two methods of making an addition to the Villa of James M. Strachan, Toronto, 4 Dec. 1854;" "Design for a Cottage Villa for T.M. Jones, esq. York, U.C., 28 June 1833."

68 Susan Algie. "Mashquoteh," op. cit., pp. 141-47; "Mashquoteh: the Home of W.A. Baldwin was a Deer Park Beauty Spot," Telegram (Toronto), 9 Sept. 1927.

69 Susan Algie, "Elmsley Villa," op. cit., pp. 121-29; PAC, National Map Collection, V2/440-Toronto-1842. Plan of the City of Toronto in 1842, James Cane, surveyor; John Ross Robertson, Landmarks of Canada, Vol. 1, p. 288; Rowsell's City of Toronto and County of York Directory for 1850-51, ed. J. Armstrong (Toronto: Henry Rowsell, 1850), p. 61.

70 Margaret Angus, "John Counter," Historic Kingston, Vol. 27. (Jan 1979), pp. 16-25. Kingston, City of, Land Registry Division, Copy Book, Instrument No. 0140. Bargain and Sale, Smith Bartlett to John Counter, 4 Nov. 1840. Kingston, City of, op. cit., Vol. 2, pp. 149-51. Mary Fraser, "William Coverdale, Kingston Architect, 1801?-1865," Historic Kingston, Vol. 26 (March 1978), pp. 71-80. Janet Wright, "Sunnyside and

168

Otterburn," Unpublished research paper, Department of Art, Queen's University, Kingston, 1982. I thank Professor Pierre du Prey, Queen's University, for pointing out the similarities between these buildings and for suggesting the possibility of a common architect.

71 Margaret Angus, Old Stones of Kingston: Its Buildings Before 1867 (Toronto: University of Toronto Press, 1966), p. 90; Kingston, City of, op. cit., Vol. 1, pp. 91-94, Dana H. Johnson and C.J. Taylor, op. cit., Vol. 2, pp. 271-77; Janet Wright, "St. Helen's." Research paper prepared for Department of Art History, Queen's University, Kingston, 1977.

72 Kingston, City of, op. cit., Vol. 1, pp. 70-73; J. Douglas Stewart, op. cit., pp. 44-46; J. Douglas Stewart and Ian E. Wilson, Heritage Kingston (Kingston: Agnes Etherington Art Centre, Queen's University, 1973), pp. 115-16.

73 Margaret Angus, Old Stones of Kingston: Its Buildings Before 1867 (Toronto: University of Toronto Press, 1966), p. 64; Kingston, City of, op. cit., pp. 64-65; Mary Fraser, op. cit., pp. 71-80; Dana H. Johnson and C.J. Taylor, op. cit., Vol. 2, pp. 485-92.

74, 75 Wendy Fletcher, op. cit., pp. 47, 71; Norah Story, "Canada Company," The Oxford Companion to Canadian History and Literature (Toronto, London, New York: Oxford University Press, 1967), p. 145.

76 Guelph, City of, Unpublished research notes on 59 Green Street. Research carried out by Gordon Couling Architectural Historian, Guelph.

77 I thank Mrs. Thora Harvey and the Local Architectural Conservation Advisory Committee (LACAC) of Woodstock, Ontario, for supplying the documentation on this building.

78 I thank Mrs. Bobi Grant and the Barrie LACAC for supplying the documentation on this building.

79, 80 James Silk Buckingham, op. cit., p. 273; PAC, National Map Collection, H3/350-Quebec-1852. Plan of renovations to Spencer Wood, drawn by George Browne, notarized 30 April 1852; Lt.-Col. James Pattison Cockburn, Quebec and its Environs; a Picturesque Guide to the Stranger (Quebec: Thomas Cary, 1831), p. 11; James MacPherson Lemoine, Maple Leaves, pp. 76-78; ANQQ, greffe Joseph Petitclerc, Building contract, John Pye, John Young — Queen Victoria, 4 March 1852, No. 6525; Building contract, Michael Mernaugh — Queen Victoria, 30 April 1852, No. 6647; Building contract, Samuel Corneil — Queen Victoria, 3 June 1852, No. 6707; Building contract, T. Murphy, J. O'Leary -Queen Victoria, 16 June 1852; Quebec. Archives du séminaire de Québec, Seigneuries, Sale of Powell Place to H. Atkinson by H. Percival, 18 May 1825; Quebec. Ministère des Affaires culturelles, Centre de documentation, Report on Spencer Wood, 1978.

81 Edward Andrew Collins, "An Estate on Mount Royal," Gazette (Montreal), 15 April 1978; Luc d'Iberville-Moreau, Lost Montreal (Toronto: Oxford University Press, 1975), p. 76; Quebec. Archives nationales du Québec (Montreal) (hereafter cited as ANQM), greffe Nicolas Benjamin Doucett, contract for plasterwork between Jeebediah Spaulding and Hon. Louis Charles Foucher, 5 Aug. 1819, No. 6493; Montreal. McCord Museum, Archives, letter written by Augusta Sewell (later wife of Captain Durnford, R.E.), 6 Feb. 1819, Montreal).

82 André Giroux and Christina Cameron, "Maison Montmorency (Kent House)," Screening Paper, Historic Sites and Monuments Board of Canada, Ottawa, June 1977, pp. 293-318; Maurice LaPierre, "Dossier Préliminaire: La maison Montmorency (Kent House)." Manuscript on file, Ministère des Affaires culturelles, Quebec, 1974; James MacPherson Lemoine, Maple Leaves, p. 64; Pierre Georges Roy, Old Manors, Old Houses (Quebec: Historic Monuments Commission of the Province of Quebec, 1927), p. 271.

83 France Gagnon-Pratte, op. cit., pp. 283-84.

84 James MacPherson Lemoine, Maple Leaves, p. 113; ANQQ, greffe Louis Panet, building contract between James Black and Remy Reinfret dit Malouin, 9 Feb. 1821, No. 178.

85 France Gagnon-Pratte, op. cit., pp. 297-

98; James MacPherson Lemoine, Maple Leaves, p. 97; ANQQ, greffe Charles Ainslie, building contract between James Gibbs and Joseph Rousseau, 12 Feb. 1827, No. 40.

86, 87 Lady L.A. Aylmer, op. cit., pp. 305, 313-14; PAC, National Map Collection, H3/350-Sorel-1823. Plan of public buildings at the post of William Henry, 24 Sept. 1823, drawn by E.W. Durnford, R.E.; J. Frederick Fitzgerald de Ros, op. cit., p. 142; Raymonde Gauthier, op. cit., p. 62.

88 Gazette de Québec, advertisement for Frederick Hacker, architect, 11 June 1832; ANQQ, greffe Pierre LaForce, contract between Charles Smith and Frederick Hacker for James Hastings Kerr, 26 July 1832 (architectural plans included), No. 2689; greffe Denis Charles Planté, building contract between Joseph Brown and Frederick Hacker, 12 Feb. 1833, No. 1168; Quebec. Ministère des Affaires culturelles, Centre de documentation. Architects and Artisans, 2H118.5 F852.5/1. Transcript of Memorial sent to Governor Lord Durham from Frederick Hacker, n.d.

89 Canadian Centre for Architecture, "Eight Villas on Mount Royal," ARQ: Architecture/Quebec (Oct. 1983), n.p. PAC, National Map Collection, Molson Collection, Nos. 151-53. Floor plans for a villa signed Browne, n.d.; ANQM, greffe W. Easton, Building contract, Gibeau and Son — John Molson Jr., for the foundations of a villa according to plans and specifications of George Browne, 18 Feb. 1848, No. 2851.

90 André Bernier, Le Vieux-Sillery (Quebec: Ministère des Affaires culturelles, Direction générale du Patrimoine, 1977), p. 87. Les cahiers du Patrimoine No. 7; Dictionary of National Biography (London: Oxford, 1949-50), Vol. 5, s.v. "Dominick Daly"; James MacPherson Lemoine, Maple Leaves p. 85-86; ANQQ, greffe E.G. Cannon, building contract between Dominick Daly and Charles Macquire, 8 Oct. 1834, No. 16; 13 Dec. 1834, No. 21; A.J.H. Richardson, op. cit., p. 76.

91 ANQM, greffe Henry Griffin, contract between John Molson and Henry

Macaulay, 5 Oct. 1844, No. 20,832; Section de la Cartographie, Plan for a Cottage for John Molson by George Browne, approved 16 Oct. 1844, Plan No. 1646; La Minerve (Montreal), Notice to builders, 22 Sept, 1845, p. 3.

92, 93 A.G. Doughty, Quebec Under Two Flags (Quebec; Quebec News, 1905), pp. 402-3; France Gagnon-Pratte, op. cit., pp. 246-49 (Hamwood), pp. 308-10 (Spencer Grange); Gazette de Québec, "For sale or rent — New Dwellings at Spencer Wood Farm having 13 apartments," 28 Feb. 1845; James MacPherson Lemoine, Maple Leaves, pp. 79-81; ANQQ, greffe Joseph Petitclerc, contract of sale, Henry Atkinson to James MacPherson Lemoine 3 Feb. 1860; France Gagnon-Pratte, pp. 190-94.

94 James MacPherson Lemoine, Maple Leaves, pp. 89-90.

95 Christina Cameron, "Cataraqui." Manuscript on file, Canadian Inventory of Historic Building, Parks Canada, Ottawa, n.d.; James MacPherson Lemoine, Maple Leaves, p. 88; ANQQ, greffe Joseph Petitclerc, building contract between Simon Peters and Henry Burstall (owner), 6 Dec. 1850, No. 5974; greffe Joseph Petitclerc, building contract between George Blaiklock and Henry Burstall (owner), 6 Dec. 1850, No. 5975; ANQQ, Section de la Cartographie, Stavely Papers, Plan of Cataraqui, Nos 12-13, Oct. 1850; Maurice Lapierre, "Le domaine de Cataraqui, Sillery." Manuscript on file, Ministère des Affaires culturelles, Quebec, 1976, No. 20-1616.11.52 C357.

96 Quebec. Archives de la ville de Québec, Charles Baillairgé Papers.

97 James MacPherson Lemoine, Maple Leaves, p. 86; ANQQ, Section de la Cartographie, Stavely Papers, plans of alterations to Kirk Ella, signed Harry Stavely, dated 24 Oct. 1874.

98 ANQQ, greffe Olivier-Felix Campeau, Discharge with Subrogation in favour of Archibald Campbell by Joseph Archer, 2 May 1850, No. 590 (building specifications included with this document); A.J.H. Richardson, op. cit., p. 71.

99 Raymonde Gauthier, op. cit., p. 152; Mrs. Daniel MacPherson, Old Memories: Amusing and Historical (Montreal:

Mrs. Daniel MacPherson, 1890), p. 66; ANQQ, greffe Archibald Campbell, building contract Charles Touchette — John Saxton Campbell, 4 June 1835.

100 Raymonde Gauthier, op. cit., p. 162. "Manoir Juchereau," Screening Paper 1972-G, Historic Sites and Monuments Board of Canada, Ottawa, 1972; Pierre Georges Roy, op. cit., pp. 219-21.

101 Line Chabot, Comptes rendus de certains bâtiments dans la ville de Québec (P.Q.) et dans les municipalités avoisinantes, Travail inédit No. 298, (Ottawa: Parks Canada, 1978), pp. 85-91; Annette Viel and Francine Guay, "Maison Hamel: Dossier d'analyse architecturale." Manuscript on file, Ministère des Affaires culturelles, Quebec, 1979.

102, 103 For an examination of the Anglo-Norman cottage of Quebec see Gérard Morisset, op. cit., p. 35; Michel Lessard and Huguette Marquis, Encyclopédie de la maison Québecoise: Trois siècles d'habitations (Montreal: Les éditions de l'homme, 1978), pp. 340-48; and Ramsay Traquair, The Old Architecture of Quebec, etc. (Toronto: Macmillan, 1947), pp. 60, 67-68.

104 France Gagnon-Pratte, op. cit., pp. 206 and 207.

105 France Gagnon-Pratte, op. cit., p. 195.

106, 107 Thomas Chandler Haliburton, op. cit., pp. 119-23; Heritage Trust of Nova Scotia, Founded Upon a Rock; Historic Buildings of Halifax and Vicinity Standing in 1967 (Halifax: Heritage Trust of Nova Scotia, 1967), p. 110; John Ross Robertson, Landmarks of Canada, Vol. 1, p. 549.

108 Acadian Recorder (Halifax), 9 Nov. 1816. p. 3; Adams G. Archibald, "Sir Alexander Croke," Report and Collections of the Nova Scotia Historical Society, Vol. 2 (1879-80), pp. 112, 127; J.W. Regan, Sketches and Traditions of Northwest Arm Halifax, 2nd ed. (Halifax: MacAlpine Publishing, 1909), pp. 153-54.

109 Alan Gowans, op. cit., p. 79, pl. 92; "Gorsebrook," Halifax Mail and Star, 18 June 1959, p. 3; Arthur W. Wallace, "Gorsebrook," Royal Architectural Institute of Canada, Journal, Vol. 8, No. 11 (Nov. 1931), pp. 392-400.

110 Heritage Trust of Nova Scotia, Seasoned Timbers: A Sampling of Historic Buildings Unique to Western Nova Scotia (Halifax: Petheric Press, 1972) (hereafter cited as Seasoned Timbers), n.p.; Charlotte Isabella Perkins, The Oldest Buildings Along Saint George Street, Annapolis Royal, Nova Scotia (Saint John, N.B.: Barnes and Co., 1925), pp. 28-29.

111 Ethel Crathorne, "The Morris Family, Surveyors-General," Nova Scotia Historical Quarterly, Vol. 6, No 2 (1976), pp. 207-15.

112, 113 Irene L. Rogers, Reports on Selected Buildings in Charlottetown, P.E.I., Manuscript Report Series, No. 269 (Ottawa: Parks Canada, 1974, 1976), pp. 35-39.

114 New Brunswick Museum, Archives, Webster Manuscript Collection, Packet No. 199, "The Coffin Manor," pp. 2-7; New Brunswick Museum. John Clarence Webster Canadiana Collection (Pictorial Section), Catalogue, comp. J. C. Webster (Saint John, N.B.: New Brunswick Museum, 1939-49), Catalogue No. 1, Nos 412-15.

115 Mary Devine, "Hawthorne Cottage," Canadian Collector, Vol. 10, No. 2 (March/April 1975), pp. 70-72; "Hawthorne Cottage," Agenda Paper 1970-43, Historic Sites and Monuments Board of Canada, Ottawa, Nov. 1970.

116, 117 Heritage Trust of Nova Scotia, Seasoned Timbers, pp. 24-25; George P. Jones, Windsor: Its History, Points of Interest, and Representative Businessmen (Windsor, Nova Scotia: J.J. Anslow, 1893), pp. 19-20; Barbara B. Shaw, "Clifton," Heritage Canada (Summer 1974), pp. 21-22. The author would like to thank Yvonne Pigott of Halifax, Nova Scotia, for identifying the alterations to Clifton.

118 Elizabeth Frame, Descriptive Sketches of Nova Scotia (Halifax: A. and W. Mackinlay, 1864), p. 91; Nova Scotia. Public Archives, File on Lieutenant-Governor Adams G. Archibald Residence, D-Acc 33.74.

119 Ivan J. Saunders, "New Brunswick and Nova Scotia Land Company and the Settlement of Stanley, New Brunswick." (M.A. thesis, University of New Bruns-

wick, 1969), pp. 194-97, 212; Elizabeth P.G. Simcoe, Sketches of New Brunswick, Taken Principally with the Intention of Shewing the Nature and Description of the Land in a Tract Purchased by the New Brunswick and Nova Scotia Land Company in the Year 1835 (London: Ackerman and Co., 1836), pl. 7.

BIBLIOGRAPHY

Acadian Magazine (Halifax)
"Western Scenes." Vol. 1, No. 7 (Jan. 1827).

Acadian Recorder (Halifax)
Notice of Sale for Studley, 9 Nov. 1816, p. 3.

Adamson, Anthony
"Architecture in British Canada: The Georgian Influence, 1745-1845." Canadian Collector, Vol. 9, No. 1 (Jan./Feb. 1974), pp. 30-33. Toronto.

Alexander, Sir James Edward
L'Acadie; or Seven Years' Exploration in British America. Henry Colburn, London, 1849. 2 Vols.
---. Transatlantic Sketches, comprising visits to the most interesting scenes in North and South America, and the West Indies. With notes on Negro Slavery and Canadian Emigration. Richard Bentley, London, 1833. 2 Vols.

Algie, Susan
Reports on Selected Buildings in Ontario. Manuscript Report Series No. 390. Parks Canada, Ottawa, 1979.

Alison, Archibald
Essays on the Nature and Principles of Taste, with corrections and improvements by Abraham Mills. Harper & Bros., N.Y., 1856.

Allentuck, Marcia
"Sir Uvedale Price and the Picturesque Garden." In The Picturesque Garden and Its Influence Outside the British Isles. Ed. Sir Nikolaus Pevsner. Dumbarton Oaks, Trustees for Harvard University, Washington, 1974.

Allodi, Mary
Canadian Watercolours and Drawings in the Royal Ontario Museum. Royal Ontario Museum, Toronto, 1974. 2 vols.

Angus, Margaret
"Architects and Builders of Early Kingston." Historic Kingston, No. 11 (1963), pp. 25-27. Kingston.
---. "Bellevue, Kingston." Unpublished research report prepared for Canadian Inventory of Historic Building, Parks Canada, Ottawa, 1964.
---. "John Counter." Historic Kingston, Vol. 27 (Jan. 1979), pp. 16-25. Kingston.
---. Old Stones of Kingston; Its Buildings Before 1867. University of Toronto Press, Toronto, 1966.
---. "Summerhill in the Nineteenth Century. Its Use and Users. "Historic Kingston," Vol. 29 (Jan 1981), pp. 123-136. Kingston.

Archibald, Adams G.
"Sir Alexander Croke." Report and Collections of the Nova Scotia Historic Society, Vol. 2 (1879-80), pp. 110-28. Halifax.

Architectural Conservancy of Ontario
Victorian Architecture in Hamilton. Architectural Conservancy of Ontario, Hamilton, 1966.

Arthur, Eric Ross
Small Houses of the Late 18th and Early 19th Centuries in Ontario. University of Toronto, Toronto, 1926.
---. Toronto: No Mean City. University of Toronto Press, Toronto, 1964.

Atkinson, William
Views of Picturesque Cottages, with Plans; Selected from a collection of drawings taken in different parts of England, and intended as hints for the improvement of village scenery.

Reprint of 1805 ed. Gregg International Publishers, Farnborough, 1971.

Aylmer, Lady L.A.
"Recollections of Canada, 1831." Rapport de l'archiviste de la Province de Québec, Vol. 15 (1934-1935), pp. 281-318. Rédemti Paradis, Quebec.

Bailey, T. Melville
"Dundurn and Sir Allan MacNab." Ontario Historical Society. Vol. 36 (1944), pp. 94-104. Toronto.

Bastien, G.G., D.D. Dubé and C. Southam
"Inventaire des marchés de construction des archives civiles de Québec, 1800-1870." Histoire et archéologie, 1 (1975). 3 vols.

Belden, H. & Co.
Illustrated Historical Atlas of the County of Huron, Ontario. H. Belden, Toronto, 1879.

Bell, Reverend William
Hints to Emigrants; in a Series of Letters from Upper Canada. Waugh and Innes, Edinburgh, 1824.

Bernier, André
Le Vieux-Sillery. Ministère des Affaires culturelles, Direction générale du Patrimoine, Quebec, 1977. Les cahiers du Patrimoine No. 7.

Berrall, Julia S.
The Garden: An Illustrated History. Penguin Books, Harmondsworth, Middlesex, 1978.

Blake, Verschoyle B. and Ralph Greenhill
Rural Ontario. University of Toronto Press, Toronto, 1969.

Blutman, Sandra
"Books of Designs for Country Houses, 1778-1815." Architectural History, Vol. 9 (1968), pp. 25-33. London.

Bonnycastle, Sir Richard Henry
Canada and the Canadians in 1846. Henry Colburn, London, 1849. 2 vols.

---. The Canadas in 1841. Reprint of 1841 ed. S.R. Publisher East Ardsley, Wakefield, 1968. 2 vols.

---. Newfoundland in 1842. Henry Colburn, London, 1942. 2 vols.

Bouchette, Joseph
The British Dominions in North America; or a Topographical and Statistical Description of the Provinces of Lower and Upper Canada, New Brunswick, Nova Scotia, the Islands of Newfoundland, Prince Edward and Cape Breton. Longman, Rees, Orme, Brown, Green and Longman, London, 1832. 2 vols.

Buckingham, James Silk
Canada, Nova Scotia, New Brunswick, and the Other British Provinces of North America; with a Plan of National Colonization. Fisher, London, 1843.

Burke, Edmund
A Philosophical Enquiry into the Origin of Our Ideas of the Sublime and the Beautiful. Ed. and intro. J.T. Boulton. Routledge, Kegan and Paul, London, 1958.

Burns, Robert J.
"Inverarden: Retirement Home of Fur Trader John McDonald of Garth." History and Archaeology/Histoire et archéologie, 25 (1979), pp. 154-238.

Cameron, Christina
"Cataraqui." Manuscript on file, Canadian Inventory of Historic Building, Parks Canada, Ottawa, n.d.

Cameron, Christina and Jean Trudel
Québec au Temps de James Patterson Cockburn. Éditions Garneau, Quebec, 1976.

Canada. Department of Public Works.
"Additions and Improvements to Rideau Hall," Annual Report for the Year 1866. Maclean, Ottawa, 1866. App. 14.

Canada. Public Archives.
MG13, WO44, Vol. 15, p. 377
RG7, G1, Vol. 58, p. 105
RG11, Vol. 425, pp. 909-11
RG11, Vol. 612
Upper Canada Land Book, J, 1816-19
Upper Canada Land Petitions, W14/15, 1823-26

Canada. Public Archives. National Map Collection.
H3/350-Quebec-1852. Plan of renovations to Spencerwood, drawn by George Browne, 1852.
H3/350-Sorel-1823. Plan of public buildings at the post of William Henry, 24 Sept. 1823. Drwan by E.W. Durnford, R.E.
H3/420-Wentworth-1859. Map of the County of Wentworth Canada West. Compiled by Robert Surtees. Hardy Gregory, Hamilton, 1859.
H3/440-Brockville-1853. Map of Brockville, Canada West. Wall and Forest, New York, 1853.
V1/420-Lincoln and Welland-1862. Map of the Counties of Lincoln and Welland, Canada West. Geo. R. and G.M. Tremaine, Toronto, 1862.
V1/420-Renfrew and Lanark-1863. Map of the Counties of Lanark and Renfrew, Canada West. From Surveys by H.F. Walling, 1863.
V1/440-Kingston-1865. Map of the City of Kingston, Canada West, 1865. Surveyed by John Innes. Published by John Creighton, New York, 1865.
V1/440-Ottawa-1864. Topographical Map of MacKay Estate, Ottawa. Drawn by Thomas C. Keefer, 1864.
V2/440-Toronto-1827. Plan of Town of York by J.G. Chewett, 1827.
V2/440-Toronto-1842. Plan of City of Toronto in 1842. James Cane, Surveyor, 1842.
Atlas of the City and County of Quebec. Surveyed by H.W. Hopkins, Provincial Surveying and Publishing, 1879.
Molson Collection, Nos 151-53, floor plans for a villa signed Browne. n.d.

Chabot, Line
Comptes rendus de certains bâtiments dans la ville de Québec (P.Q.) et dans les municipalités avoisinantes. Travail inédit no. 298. Parks Canada, Ottawa, 1978

Chronicle and Gazette (Kingston)
5 May 1841.

Citizen (Ottawa)
"George Rochester lived in Bytown," 25 Oct. 1908.

Clark, Andrew Hill
Three Centuries and the Island: A Historical Geography of Settlement and Agriculture in

Prince Edward Island, Canada. University of Toronto Press, Toronto, 1959.

Clerk, Nathalie
"Le style palladien dans l'architecture au Canada." Forthcoming publication, Studies in Archaeology, Architecture and History, Parks Canada, Ottawa.

Clifford, Derek
A History of Garden Design. 2nd ed. Faber and Faber, London, 1966.

Cobbett, William
The Emigrant's Guide. London, 1829-30.

Cobourg. Local Architectural Conservation Adivsory Committee (LACAC)
Unpublished research notes.

Cockburn, Lt.-Col. James Pattison
Quebec and its Environs; a Picturesque Guide to the Stranger. Thomas Cary, Quebec, 1831.

Coke, Edward Thomas
A Subaltern's Furlough: Descriptive of Scenes in Various Parts of the United States, Upper and Lower Canada, New Brunswick and Nova Scotia, During the Summer and Autumn of 1832. Saunders and Otley, London, 1833.

Collins, Edward Andrew
"An estate on Mount Royal," Gazette (Montreal), 15 April 1978.

Collins, Peter
Changing Ideals in Modern Architecture 1750-1950. Faber and Faber, London, 1965.

Colvin, Howard
A Biographical Dictionary of British Architects 1600-1840. John Murray, London, 1978.

Colvin, Howard and John Harris, eds.
The County Seat: Studies in History of the British Country house presented to Sir John Summerson on his sixty-fifth birthday together with a selected bibliography of his published writings. Allen Lane, London, 1970.

Cook, Terry
"John Beverley Robinson and the Conservative Blueprint for the Upper Canadian Community." In Historic Essays on Upper Canada.

Ed. J.K. Johnson. McClelland Stewart, Toronto, 1971.

Cooper Union for the Advancement of Science and Art. Museum for the Arts of Decoration.
The Prince Regent's Style: Decorative Arts in England, 1800-1830. Exhibition Catalogue, New York, 1953.

Craig, Gerald Marquis, ed.
Early Travellers in the Canadas, 1791-1867. Macmillan, Toronto, 1955.
---. Upper Canada: The Formative Years, 1784-1841. McClelland and Stewart, Toronto, 1963. Canadian Centenary Series, Vol. 7.

Crathorne, Ethel
"The Morris Family, Surveyors-General." Nova Scotia Historical Quarterly, Vol. 6, No. 2 (1976) pp. 207-15. Halifax.

Crook, J. Mordaunt
The Greek Revival: Neo-classical Attitudes in British Architecture. John Murray, London, 1972.
---. "The Villas of Regent's Park." Country Life, Vol. 144 (4 July 1968), pp. 22-25; Vol. 144 (11 July 1968), pp. 84-87. London.

Dahl, Edward H.
"Mid Forests Wild": A Study of the Concept of the Wilderness in the Writings of Susanna Moodie, J.W.D. Moodie, Catherine Parr Traill and Samuel Strickland, c. 1830-1855. National Museum of Man, Ottawa, 1973. Mercury Series, History Division Paper, No. 3.

Davis, Terence
The Architecture of John Nash. Intro. Sir John Summerson. Studio Books, London, 1960.

---. John Nash: The Prince Regent's Architect. Country Life, London, 1966.

Dearn, Thomas Downes Wilmont
Designs for Lodges and Entrances to Parks and Pleasure Grounds, in the Gothic Cottage, and Fancy Styles; with Characteristic Scenery and Descriptive Letterpress. J. Taylor, London, 1823.

---. Sketches in Architecture, consisting of Original Designs for Public and Private Buildings. William Baynes, London, 1814.

Dendy, William
Lost Toronto. Oxford University Press, Toronto, 1978.

de Ros, John Frederick Fitzgerald
Personal Narrative of Travels in the United States and Canada in 1826. 3rd ed. W.H. Ainsworth, London, 1827.

Devine, Mary
"Hawthorne Cottage." Canadian Collector, Vol. 10, No. 2 (March/April 1975), pp. 70-72. Toronto.

D'Iberville-Moreau, Luc
Lost Montreal. Oxford University Press, Toronto, 1975.

Dictionary of National Biography
Oxford, London, 1949-50. 22 vols.

Doughty, A.G.
Quebec Under Two Flags. Quebec News, Quebec, 1905.

"Dundurn Castle Restoration: Documentary Research Committee File"
Manuscript on file, Canadian Inventory of Historic Building, Parks Canada, Ottawa, 1964-67.

Early, James
Romanticism and American Architecture. A.S. Barnes, New York, 1965.

Easterbrook, Sandy
"The Evolution of the Verandah in Canadian Architecture of the Pre-confederation Period." Manuscript on file, Canadian Inventory of Historic Building, Parks Canada, Ottawa, 1978.

Elsam, Richard
Hints for Improving the Condition of the Peasantry in all Parts of the United Kingdom by promoting comfort in their habitations. Reprint of 1816 ed. Gregg International Publishers, Farnborough, 1971.

Fletcher, Wendy
"John Howard and the Picturesque Villa." M.A. thesis, University of Toronto, 1979.

Flynn, Thomas
Directory of the City of Kingston, 1857-58.
Kingston, 1858.

Fort, Michael
"Francis Goodwin (1785-1835): An Architect of
the 1820s." Architectural History, Vol. 1
(1958), pp. 60-72. London.

Frame, Elizabeth
Descriptive Sketches of Nova Scotia. A. and
W. Mackinlay, 1864.

Fraser, Mary
"William Coverdale. Kingston Architect,
1801?-1865." Historic Kingston, Vol. 26
(March 1978), pp. 71-80. Kingston.

Gagnon-Pratte, France
L'architecture et la nature à Québec au dix-
neuvième siècle: Les villas. Ministère des
Affaires culturelles, Quebec, 1980. Exhibition
presented at Le Musée du Québec.

Gandy, Joseph M.
Designs for Cottages, Cottage Frams and
other Rural Buildings; including Entrance
Gates and Lodges. Reprint of 1805 ed. Gregg
International Publishers, Farnborough, 1971.
---. The Rural Architect: consisting of various
designs for country buildings, accompanied
with Ground Plans, Estimates, and Descriptions. Reprint of 1805 ed. Gregg International Publishers, Farnborough, 1971.

Gauthier, Raymonde
Les manoirs du Québec. Fides, Quebec, 1976.

Gazette de Québec
Advertisement for Frederick Hacker, 11 June
1832. "For Sale or Rent - New Dwelling at
Spencer Wood Farm." 29 Feb. 1845.

Gesner, Abraham
New Brunswick; with Notes for Emigrants.
Simmonds and Ward, London, 1847.

Giroux, André and Christina Cameron
"Maison Montmorency (Kent House)."
Screening Paper, Historic Sites and Monuments Board of Canada, Parks Canada, Ottawa, June 1977, pp. 193-218.

Glazebrook, George Parkin de Twenebroker
Life in Ontario: A Social History. University
of Toronto Press, Toronto, 1968.
---. The Story of Toronto. University of
Toronto Press, Toronto, 1971.

Gloag, John
Mr. Loudon's England: The Life and Work of
John Claudius Loudon, and his influence on
Architecture and Furniture Design. Oriel
Press, Newcastle-upon-Tyne, 1970.

Goodwin, Francis
Domestic Architecture, being a Series of De-
signs for Mansions, Villas, Rectory Houses,
Parsonage Houses, Bailiff's Lodge, Gardener's
Lodge, Game-Keeper's Lodge, Park Gate
Lodges, etc. in the Grecian, Italian and Old
English styles of Architecture. With Observa-
tions on the Appropriate Choice of Site. 3rd
ed. Henry G. Bohn, London, 1850. 2 vols.

Gowans, Alan
Building Canada: An Architectural History of
Canadian Life. Oxford University Press,
Toronto, 1966.

**Greenhill, R., K. Macpherson and D.
Richardson**
Ontario Towns. Oberon, Ottawa, 1974.

Guelph, City of
Unpublished research notes by Gordon Couling,
Architectural Historian, Guelph.

Guillet, Edwin Clarence
Cobourg, 1798-1948. Produced by the Business
and Professional Women's Club of Cobourg,
Goodfellow Printing, Oshawa, 1948.

---. The Pioneer Farmer and Backwoodsman.
University of Toronto Press, Toronto, 1963. 2
vols.

Gyfford, Edward
Designs for elegant cottages and small villas:
Calculated for the comfort and convenience of
persons of moderate and ample future. Re-
print of 1806 ed. Gregg International
Publishers, Farnborough, 1972.

Haliburton, Thomas Chandler
Sam Slick. Ed. Ray Palmer Baker. George H.
Doran, New York, 1923.

Halifax Mail and Star
"Gorsebrook," 18 June 1959, p. 3.

Hall, Basil
Travels in North America in the Years 1827 and 1828. 2nd ed. Simpkin and Marshall, London; Cadell, Edinburgh, 1830. 3 vols.

"Hawthorne Cottage"
Agenda paper 1970-43, Historic Sites and Monuments Board of Canada, Parks Canada, Ottawa, Nov. 1970.

Henderson, Elmes
"Bloor Street, Toronto, and the Village of Yorkville in 1849." Papers and Records of the Ontario Historical Society, Vol. 26 (1930), pp. 445-56. Toronto.

Heritage Trust of Nova Scotia
Founded Upon a Rock; Historic Buildings of Halifax and Vicinity Standing in 1967. Heritage Trust of Nova Scotia, Halifax, 1967.
---. Seasoned Timbers: A Sampling of Historic Buildings Unique to Western Nova Scotia. Petheric Press, Halifax, 1972.

Heward, S.A. and W.S. Wallace
"An American Lady in Old Toronto: The Letter of Julia Lambert, 1821-54." Royal Society of Canada. Transactions and Proceedings, 3rd Series, 40 (1946), pp. 101-42. Ottawa, Montreal.

Hickey, William [Martin Doyle]
Hints on Emigration to Upper Canada; Especially Addressed to the Middle and Lower Classes in Great Britain and Ireland. William Curry, Dublin, 1832.

Hipple, Walter John
The Beautiful, The Sublime and The Picturesque in Eighteenth-Century British Aesthetic Theory. Southern Illinois University Press, Carbondale, 1957.

Hitchcock, Henry-Russell
Architecture: Nineteenth and Twentieth Centuries. Penguin Books, Harmondsworth, Middlesex, 1958.

---. Early Victorian Architecture in Britain. Da Capo Press, New York, 1972. 2 vols. Architecture and Decorative Art Series.

Howard, John George
Incidents in the Life of John G. Howard, Esq. Copp Clark, Toronto, 1885.

Hubbard, Robert Hamilton
Rideau Hall: An Illustrated History of Government House, Ottawa. Queen's Printer, Ottawa, 1967.

Hugo-Brunt, Michael
"Downing and the English Landscape Tradition." In A.J. Downing's Cottage Residences. Library of Victorian Culture, Watkins Glen, N.Y., 1967.
---. The Origin of Colonial Settlement in the Maritimes. N.p., 1959. (This article is the revised text of a paper given to the Annual Metting of the Town Planning Institute of Canada, Fredericton, June 1959.) A copy is held in the Public Archives Canada Library.

Hunt, T.F.
Architectura Campestre: displayed in Lodges, Gardener's Houses, and Other Buildings, composed of simple and economical form in the modern or Italian style, introducing a picturesque mode of roofing. Henry G. Bohn, London, 1844.

Hussey, Christopher
English Country Houses: Mid Georgian, 1760-1800. Rev. ed. Country Life, London, 1963.

---. English Country Houses: Late Georgian, 1800-1840. Country Life, London, 1958.

---. The Picturesque; Studies in a Point of View. G.P. Putnam's Sons, London, New York, 1927.

Ireland, John
"Andrew Drew and the Founding of Woodstock." Ontario History, Vol. 60, No. 4 (Dec. 1968), pp. 229-45. Toronto.

Jameson, Anna Brownell
Winter Studies and Summer Rambles in Canada. Reprint of 1838 ed. McClelland and Stewart, Toronto, 1923.

Johnson, Dana and C.J. Taylor
Reports on Selected Buildings in Kingston, Ontario. Manuscript Report Series No. 261. Parks Canada, Ottawa, 1976-77. 2 vols.

Johnson, James Keith, ed.
The Canadian Directory of Parliament, 1867-1967. Public Archives Canada, Ottawa, 1968.

Jones, George P.
Windsor: Its History, Points of Interest and Representative Business Men. J.J. Anslow, Windsor, N.S., 1893.

Journal Express (Hamilton)
Advertisement of D.C. Wetherell, architect, 26 Feb. 1841, n.p.

Kingston, City of. Committee of Architectural Review
Buildings of Historic and Architectural Significance. City of Kingston, Kingston, 1971, 1973, 1975. 3 vols.

Kitson, Michael
"Claude Lorrain." In The Encyclopedia of Art. McGraw-Hill, New York, Toronto, London, 1958, pp. 340-42.

Knight, Sir Richard Payne
An Analytical Enquiry into the Principles of Taste. Reprint of 1808 ed. Gregg International Publishers, Farnborough, 1972.

---. The Landscape, A Didactic Poem of Three Books addressed to Uvedale Price, esq. Reprint of 1795 ed. Gregg International Publishers, Farnborough, 1972.

Laing, David
Hints for Dwellings: Consisting of Original Designs for Cottages, Farm-Houses, Villas, etc. Reprint of 1800 ed. Gregg International Publishers, Farnborough, 1972.

La Minerve (Montreal)
"Notice to Builders," 22 Sept. 1845, p. 3.

Lang, S.
"Richard Payne Knight and the Idea of Modernity." In Concerning Architecture: Essays on Architectural Writers. Presented to Nikolaus Pevsner, ed. John Summerson. Allen Lane, London, 1968, pp. 85-97.

Langton, Anne
A Gentlewoman in Upper Canada: The Journals of Anne Langton. Ed. H.H. Langton. Clarke, Irwin, Toronto, 1950.

LaPierre, Maurice
"Dossier Préliminaire: La maison Montmorency (Kent House)." Manuscript on file, Ministère des Affaires culturelles, Quebec, June 1976.
---. "Le domaine de Cataraqui, Sillery." Manuscript on file, Ministère des Affaires culturelles, 1976. No. 320-1616.11.52 C357.

Leavitt, Thad W.H.
History of Leeds and Grenville, Ontario, from 1749 to 1879. Recorder Press, Brockville, 1879.

LeDoux, Florence B.
Sketches of Niagara. Peninsula Press, St. Catharines, Ontario, 1955.

Lemoine, Sir James MacPherson
Maple Leaves: Canadian History and Quebec Scenery, 3rd ser. Hunter and Rose, Quebec, 1865.

Lessard, Michel and Huguette Marquis
L'encyclopédie de la maison québécoise; Trois siècles d'habitation. Éditions de l'homme, Montreal, 1978.

Lessard, Michel and Gilles Vilandré
La Maison traditionelle du Québec. Éditions de l'homme, Montreal, Bruxelles, 1974.

Loudon, John Claudius
An Encyclopaedia of Cottage, Farm, and Villa Architecture and Furniture; containing numerous designs for dwellings, from the villa to the cottage and the farm. New ed., ed. Mrs. Loudon. Longman, Green, Brown, and Longmans, 1846.

Lower, Arthur Reginald Marsden
Canadians in the Making; a social history of Canada. Longmans, Green, Toronto, 1958.

Lugar, Robert
Architectural Sketches for Cottages, Rural Dwellings, and Villas in Grecian, Gothic and Fancy Styles with Plans; Suitable to Persons of Genteel Life and Moderate Fortune. Preceeded by some observations on Scenery and Character proper to Picturesque Buildings. J. Taylor, London, 1805.
---. The Country Gentlemen's Architect; Containing a Variety of Designs for Farm Houses

and Farm Yards of Different Magnitudes, arranged on the Most Approved Principles. Reprint of 1807 ed. Gregg International Publishers, Farnborough, 1971.
---. Villa Architecture... Buildings Executed in England, Scotland, etc. London, 1828.

Lundy's Lane Historical Society
Our Old Buildings. Lundy's Lane Historical Society, Niagara Falls, 1970.

Lutman, John
Reports on Selected Buildings in London, Ontario. Manuscript Report Series No. 266. Parks Canada, Ottawa, 1976-77.

Lyall, Donald Sutherland
"Minor Domestic Architecture in England, and Pattern Books, 1790-1840." Ph.D thesis, University of London, 1974.

MacGregor, John
British America. William Blackwood, Edinburgh, 1832. 2 vols.
---. Historical and Descriptive Sketches of the Maritime Colonies of British America. Reprint of 1828 ed. S.R. Publishers, East Ardsley, Wakefield, Yorkshire, 1968.

MacPherson, Mrs. Daniel
Old Memories: Amusing and Historical. Printed by the author, Montreal, 1890.

MacRae, Marion
The Ancestral Roof: Domestic Architecture of Upper Canada. Clarke Irwin, Toronto, 1963.

---. McNab of Dundurn. Clarke, Irwin, Toronto, 1971.

Magrath, Thomas William
Authentic Letters from Upper Canada; with an account of Canadian Field Sports. William Curry, Dublin, 1833.

Maitland, Leslie
"Neoclassical Architecture in Canada." Forthcoming publication, Studies in Archaeology, Architecure and History, Parks Canada, Ottawa.

Malton, James
An Essay on British Cottage Architecture: being an attempt to perpetuate on principle,

the peculiar mode of building which was originally the effect of charm. Reprint of 1798 ed. Gregg International Publishers, Farnborough, 1972.

Manoir Juchereau (St. Roch des Aulnaies)
Screening Paper, 1972-76, Historic Sites and Monuments Board of Canada, Parks Canada, Ottawa, 1972.

Marryat, Frederick
A Diary in America, with Remarks on its Institutions. Carey and Hart, Philadelphia, 1839. 2 vols.

Martyn, Lucy Booth
Toronto: 100 years of Grandeur. Pagurian Press, Toronto, 1978.

Matthews, Keith
Lectures on the History of Newfoundland, 1500 to 1830. Memorial University, St. John's, 1973.

McMordie, Michael
"The Cottage Idea." Revue d'art canadienne/Canadian Art Review, Vol. 6, No. 1 (1979), pp. 17-27. Quebec.
---. "Picturesque Pattern Books and Pre-Victorian Designers." Architectural History, Vol. 18 (1975), pp. 43-59. London.
---. Pre-Victorian Origins of Modern Architectural Theory. Ph.D. thesis, Edinburgh University, 1972.

Meeks, Carroll
"Picturesque Eclecticism." The Art Bulletin, Vol. 32 (Sept. 1950), pp. 226-35. London.

Middleton, Charles
Picturesque and Architectural Views for Cottages, Farm Houses, and Country Villas. Reprint of 1793 ed. Gregg International Publishers, Farnborough, 1972.

Montreal. McCord Museum. Archives.
Letter written by Augusta Sewell, 6 Feb. 1819, Montreal.

Moodie, Susanna
Life in the Clearings. Reprint of 1853 ed. Ed. and intro. Robert L. MacDougall. Macmillan, Toronto, 1959.
---. Roughing It in the Bush; or, Life in

Canada. 2nd ed. George P. Putnam, New York, 1852. 2 vols.

Morden, James C.
Historic Niagara Falls. Lundy's Lane Historical Society, Niagara Falls, 1932.

Morisset, Gérard
L'architecture en Nouvelle-France. Collection Champlain, Quebec, 1949.

Morton, William Lewis
The Kingdom of Canada; a general history from earliest times. 2nd ed. McClelland and Stewart, Toronto, 1969.

Moyles, R.G.
Complaints is many and various, but the odd divil likes it. Peter Martin, Toronto, 1975.

New Brunswick Museum
John Clarence Webster Canadiana Collection (Pictorial Section), Catalogue. Comp. J.C. Webster. Saint John, N.B., 1939-49. 3 vols.

New Brunswick Museum. Archives
Webster Manuscript Collection, Packet No. 199, "The Coffin Manor."

Newfoundland Historic Trust
A Gift of Heritage. Newfoundland Historic Trust, St. John's, 1975. Newfoundland Historic Trust Publication, Vol. 1.

Newton, Norman T.
Design of the Land; The Development of Landscape Architecture. Belknap Press, Cambridge, Mass., 1971.

Noppen, L., C. Paulette and M. Tremblay
Québec: Trois siècles d'architecture. Libre Expression, Quebec, 1979.

Nova Scotia. Public Archives.
File on Lieutenant-Governor Adams G. Archibald Residence, D-Acc 33.74.

Nova Scotian (Halifax)
"On the Scenery of Nova Scotia," 10 Aug. 1825, p. 159.

O'Brien, Mary Sophia
The Journals of Mary O'Brien, 1828-1838. Ed.

Audrey Saunders Miller. MacMillan, Toronto, 1968.

O'Neill, Paul
The Oldest City: The Story of St. John's Newfoundland. Porcepic Press, Erin, Ont., 1975. 2 vols.

Papworth, John Buonarotti
Rural Residences: Consisting of a Series of Designs for Cottages, Decorated Cottages, Small Villas and Other Ornamental Buildings accompanied by hints on Situation, Conservation, Arrangement and Decoration in the Theory and Practice of Rural Architecture. Reprint of 1818 ed. Gregg International Publishers, Farnborough, 1971.

Perkins, Charlotte Isabella
The Oldest Buildings Along Saint George Street, Annapolis Royal, Nova Scotia. Barnes and Co., Saint John, N.B., 1925.

Pevsner, Sir Nikolaus
"The Genesis of the Picturesque." Architectural Review, Vol. 96, No. 575 (1944), pp. 139-43. London.
---. "Richard Payne Knight." Art Bulletin, Vol. 3, No. 4 (Dec. 1949), pp. 293-96. London.

Pierson, William H., Jr.
American Building and their Architects/Technology and the Picturesque: The Corporate and Early Gothic Styles. Doubleday, Garden City, N.Y., 1978. 2 vols.

Pilcher, Donald
The Regency Style, 1800 to 1830. B.T. Batsford, London, 1947.

Plaw, John
Ferme Ornée; or, Rural Improvements: A Series of Domestic or Ornamental Designs suited to Parks, Plantations, Rides, Walks, Rivers, Farms, etc. Reprint of 1795 ed. Gregg International Publishers, Farnborough, 1972.

---. Rural Architecture; or Designs, from the Simple Cottage to the Decorated Villa, Including Some which have been executed by John Plaw, architect and surveyor. Reprint of 1802 ed. Gregg International Publishers, Farnborough, 1971.

---. Sketches for Country Houses, Villas and Rural Dwellings; calculated for persons of moderate income and for comfortable retirement. Also some designs for cottages, which may be constructed of the simplest materials; with plans and general estimates. Reprint of 1800 ed. Gregg International Publishers, Farnborough, 1972.

Pocock, William Fuller
Architectural Designs for Rustic Cottages, Picturesque Dwellings, Villas, etc. with appropriate scenery, plans, and descriptions. To which are prefixed some critical observations on their style and character, and also Castles Abbies, and ancient English Houses, concluding with some practical remarks on building and the causes of the dry rot. Reprint of 1807 ed. Gregg International Publishers, Farnborough, 1972.

Price, Sir Uvedale
Sir Uvedale Price: On the Picturesque. Ed. Sir Thomas Dick Lauder. Reprint of 1794 ed. Caldwell Lloyd, Edinburgh; W.S. Orr, London, 1842.

Québec. Archives de la ville de Québec.
Charles Baillairgé Papers.
C. Baillargé: Dessins architecturaux, Ministère des Affaires culturelles, Québec, 1979.

Québec. Archives du séminaire de Québec.
Seigneuries, Sale of Powell Place to H. Atkinson by H. Percival, 18 May 1825.

Québec. Archives nationales du Québec (Montreal).
Greffe, Nicolas Benjamin Doucett. Marché de construction, 5 Aug. 1819, No. 6493.
Greffe, Henry Griffin. Marché de construction, 5 Oct. 1844, No. 20,832.
Greffe, W. Easton, Marché de construction, 18 Feb. 1848, No. 2851.

Québec. Archives nationales du Québec (Montreal). Section de la Cartographie.
Plan for a Cottage for John Molson, Boucherville, 16 Oct. 1844. Plan No. 1646.

Québec. Archives nationales du Québec (Quebec).
Greffe, Charles Ainslie. Marché de construction, 12 Feb. 1827, No. 40.

Greffe, Noel Hill Bowen. Marché de construction, 19 May 1857, No. 1121; 20 May 1857, No. 1122.
Greffe, Olivier-Felix Campeau. Discharge with Subrogation, 2 May 1850, No. 590.
Greffe, Archibald Campbell. Marché de construction, 4 June 1835, No. 6813.
Greffe, E.G. Cannon, Marché de construction, 8 Oct. 1834, No. 16; 13 Dec. 1834, No. 21.
Greffe, Josiah Hunt. Marché de construction, 10 Nov. 1835; 19 Dec. 1835; 21 Dec. 1835; 22 Dec. 1835.
Greffe, Pierre Laforce. Marché de construction, 12 Feb. 1833, No. 1168; 26 July 1832, No. 2689.
Greffe, Louis Panet. Marché de construction, 2 Feb. 1821, No. 178.
Greffe, Joseph Petitclerc. Marché de construction, 6 Dec. 1850, No. 5974; 6 Dec. 1850, No. 5975; 4 March 1852, No. 6525; 30 April 1852, No. 6647; 3 June 1852, No. 6707; Contract of Sale, 3 Feb. 1860.
Greffe, Denis Charles Planté. Marché de construction, 12 Feb. 1833, No. 1168.

Québec. Archives nationales du Québec (Quebec). Section de la Cartographie.
Stavely Papers.

Québec. Ministère des Affaires culturelles, Centre de documentation.
Architects and Artisans, 2H118.5 F852.5/1.
Transcript of Memorial sent to Governor Lord Durham from Frederick Hacker, n.d.
File on Frederick Hacker, No. 2H118.5 F852.5/5.
Report on Spencer Wood, 1978.

Ramsay, Stanley Churchill
Small Houses of the Late Georgian Period, 1750-1820. W. Helburn, New York; Technical Journals, London, 1919.

Rawlyk, G.A., ed.
Historical Essays on the Atlantic Provinces. McClelland and Stewart, Toronto, 1967.

Regan, John William
Sketches and Traditions of Northwest Arm Halifax. 2nd ed. McAlpine Publishing, Halifax, 1909.

Reilly, Paul
Introduction to Regency Architecture. Pelle-

grini and Cudahy, New York, 1948.

Repton, Humphry
The Landscape Gardening and Landscape Architecture of the Late Humphry Repton. Ed. J.C. Loudon. Longman, London; A.C. Black, Edinburgh, 1840.

Richardson, A.J.H.
"Guide to the Architecturally and Historically most Significant Buildings of the Old City of Québec with a Biographical Dictionary of Architects and Builders." Bulletin of the Association for Preservation Technology, Vol. 2, Nos. 3-4 (1970). Ottawa.

Ridout, John
"A Biographical Sketch of Samuel Ridout." Proceedings of the Ontario Land Surveyors Association (1887), p. 129. Toronto.

Robertson, John Ross
Landmarks of Canada. What Art Has done for Canadian History; a guide to the J. Ross Robertson Historical Collection in the Public Reference Library, Toronto, Canada. Presented to the Trustees of the Public Library by J. Ross Robertson, Toronto, 1917- 21 . 2 vols.
---. Robertson's Landmarks of Toronto; a Collection of Historical Sketches of the Old Town of York from 1762 until 1837, and of Toronto from 1834 to 1914. Republished from the Toronto Evening Telegram. J.R. Robertson, Toronto, 1894-1914. 6 vols.

Rogers, Irene L.
"John Plaw." Unpublished paper presented to the Society for the Study of Architecture in Canada, London, Ont., 1978.
---. Reports on Selected Buildings in Charlottetown, P.E.I. Manuscript Report Series No. 269. Parks Canada, Ottawa, 1974, 1976.

Roper, Laning
"The Gardens of Fairfield House." Country Life, Vol. 165 (17 May 1979), pp. 1510-12. London.

Ross, A.H.D.
Ottawa, Past and Present. Thornburn and Abbot, Ottawa, 1927.
---. Rowsell's City of Toronto and County of York Directory for 1850-51. Ed. J. Armstrong. Henry Rowsell, Toronto, 1850.

Rowan, Alistair
"Downton Castle, Herefordshire," in The Country Seat: Studies in the History of the British Country House, etc., ed. Howard Colvin and John Harris. Allen Lane, London, 1970.

Roy, Pierre Georges
Old Manors, Old Houses. Historic Monuments Commission of the Province of Québec, Quebec, 1927.

Saunders, Ivan J.
"New Brunswick and Nova Scotia Land Company and the Settlement of Stanley, New Brunswick." M.A. thesis, University of New Brunswick, 1969.

Scadding, Henry
Toronto of Old; Collections and Recollections Illustrative of the Early Settlement and Social Life of the Capital of Ontario. Ed. F.H. Armstrong. Reprint of 1873 ed. Oxford University Press, Toronto, 1966.

Scott, James
Huron County in Pioneer Times. Huron County Historical Society, Seaforth, 1954.

Shaw, Barbara B.
"Clifton." Heritage Canada (Summer 1974), pp. 21-22. Ottawa.

Simcoe, Elizabeth P.G.
The Diary of Mrs. John Graves Simcoe, wife of the first Lieutenant-Governor of Upper Canada, 1792-96. Ed. John Ross Robertson. W. Briggs, Toronto, 1911.
---. Sketches of New Brunswick, Taken Principally with the Intention of Shewing the Nature and Description of the Land in a Tract Purchased by the New Brunswick and Nova Scotia Land Company in the Year 1835. Ackerman and Co., London, 1836.

Soane, Sir John
Lectures on Architecture, by Sir John Soane....as delivered to the students of the Royal Academy from 1809 to 1836 in two courses of six lectures each. Ed. Arthur T. Bolton. Sir John Soane Museum, London, 1929.
---. Plans, Elevations and Sections of Buildings. Executed in the Counties of Norfolk, Sulfolk, Yorkshire, Staffordshire,

182

Warwickshire etc.. Reprint of 1788 ed. Gregg
International Publishers, Farnborough, 1971.

---. Sketches in Architecture, containing
Plans and Elevations of Cottages and Villas
and other Useful Buildings with Characteristics Scenery. Reprint of 1793 ed. Gregg
International Publishers, Farnborough, 1971.

Stewart, J. Douglas
"Architecture for a Boom Town: The Primitive
and Neo-Baroque in George Browne's Kingston
Buildings." In To Preserve and Defend: Essays
on Kingston in the Nineteenth Century. Ed.
Gerald Tulchinsky, McGill-Queen's, Montreal,
London, 1976, pp. 37-62.

Stewart, J. Douglas and Mary Stewart
"John Solomon Cartwright: Upper Canadian
Gentleman and a Regency Man of Taste."
Historic Kingston, Vol. 27 (Jan. 1979), pp. 61-
77. Kingston.

Stewart, J. Douglas and Ian E. Wilson
Heritage Kingston. Agnes Etherington Art
Centre, Queen's University, Kingston, 1973.

Stewart, John J.
"The Grounds of John A.'s Bellevue House."
Conservation Canada, Vol. 4, No. 2 (1978),
pp. 7-8. Ottawa.

Stokes, Peter John
"Inverarden." Agenda Paper 1968-7, Historic
Sites and Monuments Board of Canada, Parks
Canada, Ottawa (1968), pp. 83-103.

Story, Norah
The Oxford Companion to Canadian History
and Literature. Oxford University Press,
Toronto, London, New York, 1967.

Stroud, Dorothy
The Architecture of Sir John Soane. Intro.
Henry-Russell Hitchcock. Studio Books,
London, 1961.

---. Humphry Repton. Country Life, London,
1962.

Stuart, Charles
The Emigrant's Guide to Upper Canada; or
Sketches of the present state of that Province,
collected from a residence therein during the

years 1817, 1818, 1819. Longman, Hurst,
Rees, Orme, and Brown, London, 1820.

Summerson, Sir John
Architecture in Britain, 1630-1830. 5th ed.
paperback. Penguin Books, Harmondsworth,
Middlesex, 1970.
---. "Blaise Hamlet, an early nineteenth-
century essay in the revival of the Picturesque
cottage." Country Life, Vol. 86 (14 Oct.
1939), pp. 396-97. London.
---. John Nash: Architect to George IV. 2nd
ed. George Allen and Unwin, 1935.
---. "Soane: The Case History of a Personal
Style." Royal Institute of British Architects,
Journal, Vol. 58 (Jan. 1951), pp. 83-91.
London.

Taylor, C.J. and Janet Wright
"Rideau Hall." Agenda Paper, Historic Sites
and Monuments Board of Canada, Parks Canada, Ottawa, Nov. 1977, pp. 233-61.

Telegram (Toronto)
"Mashquoteh: The Home of W.A. Baldwin was
a Deer Park Beauty Spot," 9 Sept. 1927.

Temple, Nigel
"In Search of the Picturesque." Architectural
Review, Vol. 160, No. 954 (Aug. 1979), pp. 96-
100. London.

Tobey, George B.
A History of Landscape Architecture: The
Relationship of People of Environment.
American Elsevier, New York, 1973.

Toronto. Metropolitan Toronto Library Board
John George Howard Collection.

Traill, Catharine Parr
The Backwoods of Canada: being letters from
the wife of an emigrant officer, illustrative of
the Domestic economy of British America.
Charles Knight, London, 1836.

Traquair, Ramsay
The Cottages of Québec. McGill University,
Montreal, 1926.
---. The Old Architecture of Québec; A study
of the buildings erected in New France from
the earliest explorers to the middle of the
nineteenth century. Macmillan, Toronto,
1947.

Turnor, Reginald
The Smaller English House. B.T. Batsford, London, 1952.

Upper Canada. House of Assembly.
Journals of the House of Assembly, 1836. M. Reynolds, Toronto, 1836.

Viel, Annette and Francine Guay
"Maison Hamel: Dossier d'analyse architecturale." Manuscript on file. Ministère des Affaires culturelles, Québec, 1979.

Wallace, Arthur W.
An Album of Drawings of Early Buildings in Nova Scotia. Heritage Trust of Nova Scotia and the Nova Scotia Museum, Halifax, 1976.
---. "Gorsebrook." Royal Architectural Institute of Canada, Journal, Vol. 8, No. 11 (Nov. 1931), pp. 392-400. Toronto.

Webster's Third New International Dictionary
G. & C. Merriam Company, Springfield, Mass., 1966.

Wilkie, David
Sketches of a Summer Trip to New York and the Canadas. J. Anderson, Edinburgh; Sherwood and Piper, London, 1837.

Wood, John
A series of Plans for Cottages or Habitations of the Labourer, either in Husbandry or the Mechanic Arts, Adopted as well to town as to the country. Reprint of 1806 ed. Gregg International Publishers, Farnborough, 1972.

Woodeforde, John
Georgian Houses for All. Routledge and Kegan Paul, London, 1978.

Wright, Janet
"Saint Helen's." Unpublished research paper prepared for Department of Art, Queen's University, 1977.
---. "Sunnyside and Otterburn." Unpublished paper prepared for Department of Art, Queen's University, 1982.

Young, A.H.
"The Rev'd George O'Kill Stuart, Second Rector of York and of Kingston." Ontario Historical Society, Vol. 24 (1927), pp. 512-34. Toronto.